D1362866

Rules and Guidance for Pharmaceutical Manufacturers and Distributors 2002

Incorporating:

- EC Guides to Good Manufacturing Practice and Good Distribution Practice

- EC Directives on Manufacture, Wholesale Distribution and Good Manufacturing Practice

- Code of Practice for Qualified Persons and Guidance for Responsible Persons

- Standard Provisions for Manufacturer's Licences

- Standard Provisions for Wholesale dealer's Licences

- Guidance on Reporting Defective Medicines

- Voluntary Inspections for Good (Research) Clinical Practice and Manufacture of Active Pharmaceutical Ingredients

London: TSO

First published as the *Guide to Good Pharmaceutical Manufacturing Practice* in 1971, second edition 1977, third edition 1983, fourth edition as the *Rules and Guidance for Pharmaceutical Manufacturers* in 1993, fifth edition as *Rules and Guidance for Pharmaceutical Manufacturers and Distributors 1997*.

Sixth edition 2002
Fourth impression 2003

ISBN 011 322559 8

Contact for information on these guidance notes:

Inspection and Enforcement Division
Medicines Control Agency
Department of Health
Market Towers
1 Nine Elms Lane
London
SW8 5NQ

Telephone: 020 7273 0000
Fax: 020 7273 0353
e-mail: info@mca.gov.uk
website: www.mca.gov.uk

Published in the United Kingdom for the Stationery Office
Id 157957   C40   11/03   19585   901075

CONTENTS

PREFACE TO THE 2002 EDITION

Since the 1997 edition of *Rules and Guidance* (often known as the *Orange Guide*) there have been many changes and additions to the detailed European Community guidelines on Good Manufacturing Practice (Guide to GMP), although the statutory requirements on manufacturers and wholesale distributors in the UK have not changed. The additional guidance comes in new annexes to the EC Guide to GMP:

Annex 15 on qualification and validation,

Annex 16 giving detailed European guidance for the first time on the duties of a Qualified Person,

Annex 17 on parametric release of batches,

Annex 18 providing significant new guidance on the manufacture of active pharmaceutical ingredients (APIs) produced by the Q7A group of the International Committee on Harmonisation (ICH). For the moment this is only advisory; a requirement for the manufacture of APIs to comply with GMP is proposed by the European Commission and is currently the subject of consultation.

There have been revisions to annex 1 (paragraph 42) on the manufacture of sterile products, annex 6 on medicinal gases and annex 14 on products derived from human blood or plasma. All these changes are included in this edition. Annex 13 on the manufacture of investigational medicinal products to be used in clinical trials is under revision as this book goes to press.

Many of the European Directives on medicinal products issued over the last thirty five years were consolidated into two Directives during 2001, one for products used in humans and one for veterinary products. This makes the requirements more accessible. Although it is UK legislation, implementing the Directives, that bears directly on activities in the UK it is often helpful for manufacturers and wholesalers to be aware of the original EC obligations. This is particularly so when trading across boundaries of member states. So the 'Titles' or sections of the new Directive 2001/83/EC dealing with manufacture and wholesale distribution of products for human use are included in this edition. Directive 2001/82/EC dealing with veterinary products is virtually identical.

A fully detailed index to the EC Guide to GMP is provided and the several glossaries of terms used in the Guide and its annexes have been consolidated into a single glossary.

The UK's Code of Practice for Qualified Persons has been updated by the professional bodies in consultation with the MCA; this is included.

Recommendations on meeting the important requirement to ensure the 'proper conservation and distribution' of medicines requiring storage below ambient temperature ('cold-chain distribution') have been developed between representatives of wholesalers and the MCA. These were published originally in the Pharmaceutical Journal[1], were summarised in MAIL[2], and are reproduced here.

Finally, there is a new section on the activities and services of the Inspection and Enforcement Division of the MCA which will be of interest to manufacturers and wholesalers.

Much of the text in this book is available in its original form in other places, including various websites. However we are pleased that the *Orange Guide* continues to satisfy a demand for information in one authoritative and convenient place. We hope that this new edition will continue to be useful.

John Turner
Group Manager, Policy and Standards, Inspection and Enforcement Division

April 2002

---

(1) Taylor J, Recommendations on the control and monitoring of storage and transortation temperature of medicinal products. The Pharmaceutical Journal, 28 July 2001, Volume 267, pages 128–131.

(2) MCA Newsletter *MAIL*, Issue 131, May/June 2002.

INTRODUCTION

This publication brings together the main pharmaceutical regulations, directives and guidance which manufacturers and wholesalers are expected to follow when making and distributing medicinal products in the European Union and European Economic Area. It is of particular relevance to all holders of manufacturer's licences and wholesale dealer's licences and to their Qualified Persons (QPs) and Responsible Persons (RPs), who have a responsibility for ensuring compliance with many of these requirements.

The obligation on governments of all Member States of the European Union to ensure that pharmaceutical manufacturers are authorised is stated in Title IV of Directive 2001/83/EC (products for human use) and of Directive 2001/82/EC (veterinary products). These Titles, or sections, are also the source of requirements for compliance with Good Manufacturing Practice (GMP), employment of QPs and repeated inspections by the regulatory authorities. Title VII of the same Directives requires all wholesale distributors to be authorised, to have available RPs and comply with the guidelines on Good Distribution Practice (GDP).

The principles and guidelines of GMP are stated in the two almost identical Directives, 91/356/EEC for medicinal products for human use and 91/412/EEC for veterinary medicinal products. In the United Kingdom the provisions for manufacturers and wholesale dealers have been implemented by Standard Provisions and undertakings incorporated in regulations made under the Medicines Act 1968. Compliance with the principles and guidelines of GMP is a statutory requirement. The European Community Guide to GMP[1] including its annexes provides detailed guidance which interprets and expands on the statutory principles and guidelines. Changes in technical knowledge and in regulations are reflected by additional and revised annexes. GMP includes elements of the International Standard for Quality Management Systems ISO 9001:2000 with additional requirements specific to medicines.

The UK first produced a national guide to GMP (known affectionately as the *Orange Guide* from the colour of its cover) in 1971. Guidance on good pharmaceutical wholesaling practice was added in the 1977 edition and a further edition was produced in 1983. The EC guidance, first issued for GMP in 1989 and for GDP in 1993, supersedes this and all other national guides of Member States, although much that was familiar in the old UK Guide can still be recognised in the EC guidance. The Pharmaceutical Inspection Co-operation Scheme has adopted the text of the EC Guide to GMP ensuring harmonisation of guidelines by its member inspectorates throughout the world. Mutual Recognition Agreements between the EC and several third countries have recognised the equivalence of GMP requirements of the parties concerned.

Manufacturers are required to name a QP on their manufacturer's licence. No batch of medicinal product may be released to the market within the EU unless a nominated QP has certified that it has been manufactured and checked in compliance with the laws in force. Guidance to QPs in fulfilling their responsibilities is given in the EC Guide to GMP and in the Code of Practice for Qualified Persons[2] which they are expected to follow. In similar spirit, wholesalers are required to appoint a RP who has the knowledge and responsibility to ensure that correct procedures are followed during distribution. Notes on the qualifications and duties of RPs are given to assist this.

The aim of GMP and GDP is to assure the quality of the medicinal product for the safety, well-being and protection of the patient. In achieving this aim it is impossible to over emphasise the importance of people, at all levels, in the assurance of the quality of medicinal products. This is emphasised in the first principle in the EC Guide to GMP. The great majority of reported defective medicinal products has resulted from human error or carelessness, not from failures in technology. All the people involved with the production, Quality Control or distribution of medicinal products, whether key personnel, production or control or warehouse staff, inspectors of a regulatory authority or others involved in the many activities which lead to a patient taking a medicine, should bear this constantly in mind when performing their duties.

---

(1) COMMISSION OF THE EUROPEAN COMMUNITIES. The rules governing medicinal products in the European Community. Vol IV. Good Manufacturing Practice for medicinal products. Luxembourg: Office for Official Publications of the EC, 1998. ISBN 92-826-3180-X.

(2) THE INSTITUTE OF BIOLOGY, THE ROYAL PHARMACEUTICAL SOCIETY OF GREAT BRITAIN, THE ROYAL SOCIETY OF CHEMISTRY. Code of Practice for Qualified Persons. In: Register of Qualified Persons. London: Institute of Biology, Royal Pharmaceutical Society of Great Britain, Royal Society of Chemistry, 2001.

ACKNOWLEDGEMENTS

To the European Commission for permission to reproduce the text of the Directives, the EC Guide to GMP and the guidelines on Good Distribution Practice.

To the Institute of Biology, the Royal Pharmaceutical Society of Great Britain and the Royal Society of Chemistry for permission to reproduce the text of the Code of Practice for Qualified Persons.

Part I

Manufacture

UK LEGISLATION ON MANUFACTURE

Standard provisions for manufacturer's licences

Extracts from:

The Medicines (Standard Provisions for Licences and Certificates) Regulations 1971 (SI 1971 No 972) as amended by Amendment Regulations 1972 (SI 1972 No 1226), 1977 (SI 1977 No 1053), 1983 (SI 1983 No 1730), 1992 (SI 1992 No 2846), 1993 (SI 1993/833), 1999 (SI 1999 No 4) and 2002 (SI 2002 No 236).

Editor's note

These extracts from the Regulations are presented for the reader's convenience and incorporate amendments up to July 2002. For any definitive information reference must be made to the original Regulations.

Interpretation

The following definitions of terms used in the Standard Provisions for Manufacturer's Licences are inserted by SI 1992 No 2846 and SI 2002 No 236 to Regulations 2.1 of the Principal Regulations:

- *expiry date*, in relation to a medicinal product, means the date after which the product should not be used;

- *good manufacturing practice* means the part of quality assurance which ensures that medicinal products are consistently produced and controlled to the quality standards appropriate to their intended use, the principles and guidelines of which are specified in Chapter II of Commission Directive 91/356/EEC;

- *relevant period* means the period of five years from the date of certification of the relevant batch referred to in paragraph 16(3)(b) of Schedule 2 to these Regulations or the period of one year from the expiry date of the relevant batch, whichever expires later;

- *the 2001 Directive* means Directive 2001/83/EC of the European Parliament and of the Council on the Community code relating to medicines for human use.

Schedule 2 of the Regulations

1   The licence holder shall provide and maintain such staff, premises and plant as are necessary for carrying out in accordance with his licence and the relevant product licences of such stages of the manufacture and assembly of the medicinal products as are undertaken by him, and he shall not carry out any such manufacture or assembly except at the premises specified in his manufacturer's licence.

2   The licence holder shall provide and maintain such staff, premises, equipment and facilities for the handling, storage and distribution of the medicinal products which he handles, stores or distributes under his licence as are necessary to avoid deterioration of the medicinal products and he shall not use for such purposes premises other than those specified in the licence or which may be approved from time to time by the licensing authority.

3   The licence holder shall conduct all manufacture and assembly operations in such a way as to ensure that the medicinal products conform with the standards of strength, quality and purity applicable to them under the relevant product licences and, in relation to medicinal products for human use, shall conduct all such operations in accordance with the principles and guidelines of good manufacturing practice.

3A   The licence holder shall, in relation to medicinal products for human use, establish and implement an effective pharmaceutical quality assurance system involving the active participation of the management and personnel of the different services involved.

4   The licence holder, where animals are used in the production of any medicinal products and the relevant product licences contain provisions relating to them, shall arrange for the animals to be housed in premises of such a nature and to be managed in such a way as will facilitate compliance with such provisions.

5   The licence holder shall, in relation to medicinal products, other than for human use, either:

   (a)   provide and maintain such staff, premises and plant as are necessary for carrying out in accordance with the relevant product licences any tests of the strength, quality and purity of the medicinal products that he manufactures under his manufacturer's licence as required by those product licences, and when animals are used for such tests they shall be suitably housed and managed; or

   (b)   make arrangements with a person approved by the licensing authority for such tests to be carried out in accordance with the relevant product licences on his behalf by that person.

5A   (1)   The licence holder shall, in relation to medicinal products for human use:

       (a)   provide and maintain a designated quality control department having authority in relation to quality control and being independent from all other departments in the exercise of that authority; and

       (b)   place the quality control department under the authority of the person notified to the licensing authority in accordance with paragraph 7(2) of Schedule 1 to the Medicines (Applications for Manufacturer's and Wholesale Dealer's Licences) Regulations 1971 (SI 1971 No 974) as being responsible for quality control.

   (2)   Subject to paragraph 5B of this Schedule, the licence holder shall, in order to support the quality control department, provide and maintain such staff, premises and plant as are necessary for carrying out:

       (a)   such tests of the strength, quality and purity of the medicinal products which he manufactures for human use under the manufacturer's licence as are required by the relevant product licences; and

       (b)   any tests or controls which relate to the conditions of production and in-process controls.

   (3)   Any animals used for the tests referred to in sub-paragraph (2) of this paragraph shall be suitably housed and managed.

   (4)   The licence holder shall ensure that the quality control department, in determining whether finished medicinal products for human use are to be released for sale or distribution, takes into account, in addition to analytical results:

       (a)   the conditions of production;

       (b)   the result of in-process controls;

       (c)   the examination of manufacturing documents, and

       (d)   the conformity of products to the specification in the relevant product licence.

5B   A licence holder need not himself provide and maintain such staff, premises and plant as are necessary for carrying out such tests as are specified in paragraph 5A(2) of this Schedule provided that he makes arrangements with a person approved by the Licensing Authority to carry out such tests on his behalf in accordance with paragraph 5A(2) and (3) of this Schedule.

6   The licence holder shall provide such information as may be requested by the licensing authority for the purposes of the Act,

about the products currently being manufactured or assembled under his licence and of the operations being carried out in relation to such manufacture or assembly.

7   The licence holder shall inform the licensing authority before making any material alteration in the premises or plant used under his licence, or in the operations for which they are used, and he shall inform the licensing authority of any change that he proposes to make in any personnel named in his licence as respectively:

(a)   responsible for supervising the production operations, or

(b)   responsible for quality control of the medicinal products being manufactured or assembled, including the person named as the qualified person for the purposes of paragraph 16 or 17, as the case may be, of this Part of this Schedule, or

(c)   in charge of the animals from which are derived any substances used in the production of the medicinal products being manufactured or assembled, or

(d)   responsible for the culture of any living tissues used in the manufacture of the medicinal products being manufactured or assembled.

8   The licence holder shall keep readily available for inspection by a person authorised by the licensing authority durable records of the details of manufacture and assembly of each batch of every medicinal product being manufactured or assembled under his licence and of the tests carried out thereon, including any register or other record referred to in paragraph 16(3)(b), or 17(3)(b), as the case may be, in such a form that the records will be easily identifiable from the number of the batch as shown on each container in which the medicinal product is sold, supplied or exported, and he shall permit the person authorised to take copies or make extracts from such records. Such records shall not be destroyed without the consent of the licensing authority:

(a)   in relation to a medicinal product for human use, for the relevant period;

(b)   in any other case, for a period of five years from the date when the manufacture or assembly of the relevant batch occurred.

8A   The licence holder shall keep readily available for examination by a person authorised by the Licensing Authority samples of each batch of finished medicinal products for human use manufactured or assembled under his licence for at least a period of one year from their expiry date and shall retain samples of starting materials (other than solvents, gases or water) for at least a period of two years from the date of the release of the relevant batch of which the relevant starting materials formed part, except where the licence holder is authorised by the Licensing Authority to destroy any such samples earlier.

8B   The licence holder shall make suitable arrangements to ensure that any record or sample referred to in paragraphs 8 or 8A above relating to a medicinal product for human use is retained for the relevant period.

9   The licence holder shall, in relation to medicinal products other than for human use, keep such documents as will facilitate the withdrawal or recall from sale, supply or exportation of any such medicinal products to which the licence relates.

9A   (1)   The licence holder shall implement a system for recording and reviewing complaints in relation to medicinal products for human use manufactured or assembled under his licence, together with an effective system for recalling promptly and at any time such medicinal products in the distribution network.

     (2)   The licence holder shall record and investigate all complaints described in sub paragraph (1) of this paragraph and shall immediately inform the licensing authority of any defect which could result in recall from sale, supply or exportation or in an abnormal restriction on such sale, supply or exportation.

10   Where the licence holder has been informed by the licensing authority that any batch of any medicinal product to which his licence relates has been found not to conform as regards strength, quality or purity with the specification of the relevant product or with the provisions of the Act or of any regulations under the Act that are applicable to the medicinal product, he shall, if so directed, withhold such batch from sale, supply or exportation, so far as may be reasonably practicable, for such a period not exceeding six weeks as may be specified by the licensing authority.

11   The licence holder shall ensure that any tests for determining conformity with the standards and specifications applying to any particular product used in the manufacture shall, except so far as the conditions of the relevant product licence may otherwise provide, be applied to samples taken from the medicinal product after all manufacturing processes have been completed, or at such earlier stage in the manufacture as may be approved by the licensing authority.

12   (1)   The licence holder who is not the holder of a product licence in respect of the medicinal product to which the manufacturer's licence relates, shall comply with any provisions of such a product licence that relates to the sale of that medicinal product and shall, by means of a label or otherwise, communicate the particulars of such provisions as relate to mode of sale, or restriction as to sale, to any person to whom the licence holder sells or supplies that medicinal product.

(2)   Where the manufacturer's licence relates to the assembly of a medicinal product, and the licence holder sells or supplies that medicinal product at such a stage of assembly that does not fully comply with the provisions of the relevant product licence that relates to labelling, that licence holder shall communicate the particulars of those provisions to the person to whom that medicinal product has been so sold or supplied.

13   Where in his application for a manufacturer's licence the licence holder had specified a general classification of medicinal products in respect of which that licence was required or had given particulars of manufacturing operations and of substances or articles in accordance with paragraph 6 of Schedule 1 to the Medicines (Applications for Manufacturer's and Wholesale Dealer's Licences) Regulations 1971 (SI 1971 No 974) and there has been, or it is proposed that there shall be, a change in such general classification or such particulars, the licence holder shall forthwith notify the licensing authority in writing of such change or proposed change.

14   Where the manufacturer's licence relates to the assembly of a medicinal product and that medicinal product is not manufactured by the licence holder, and where particulars as to the name and address of the manufacturer of, or of the person who imports, that medicinal product had been given by the licence holder to the licensing authority, the licence holder shall forthwith notify the licensing authority in writing of any changes in such particulars.

15   The licence holder, for the purpose of enabling the licensing authority to ascertain whether there are any grounds for suspending, revoking or varying any licence or certificate granted or issued under Part II of the Act, shall permit, and provide all necessary facilities to enable, any person duly authorised in writing by the licensing authority, on production if required of his credentials, to carry out such inspection or to take such samples or copies, in relation to things belonging to, or any business carried on by, the licence holder, as such person would have the right to carry out or take under the Act for the purpose of verifying any statement contained in an application for a licence or certificate.

16   (1)   Subject to sub-paragraph (5) below, the licence holder shall at all times have at his disposal the services of a person who as respects qualifications and experience satisfies the provisions of Articles 49 and 50 of the 2001 Directive, to carry out the functions specified in sub-paragraph (3) below ('qualified person'). For the purposes of this paragraph, but without prejudice to sub-paragraph (4) below, the licence holder may regard a person as satisfying the provisions of the said Article 50 as respects formal qualifications if he produces evidence that he is a member of the Royal Pharmaceutical Society of Great

Britain or of the Royal Society of Chemistry or of such other body as may appear to the Licensing Authority to be an appropriate body for the purpose, and that he is regarded by the body of which he is a member as so satisfying those provisions.

(2) The licence holder shall at all times provide and maintain such staff, premises, equipment and facilities as will enable the qualified person who is at his disposal to carry out the said functions.

(3) The functions to be carried out by the qualified person shall be as follows:

(a) To ensure that each batch of the medicinal product to which the licence relates has been manufactured or assembled and checked in compliance with the provisions of the Act and Regulations made thereunder, the provisions of the licence and the provisions of the product licence which relates to the product.

(b) To certify in a register, or other record appropriate for the purpose, whether each production batch of the medicinal product to which the licence relates satisfies the requirements set out in (a) above and to ensure that such register or other record is regularly maintained, in particular that the appropriate entries in such register or other record are made as soon as practicable after each such batch has been manufactured.

(4) Where, after giving the licence holder and the person acting as a qualified person the opportunity of making representations to them (orally or in writing), the licensing authority are of the opinion that the person so acting does not satisfy the provision of the said Articles 49 and 50 of the 2001 Directive as respects qualifications and experience, or that he is failing to carry out the functions specified in sub-paragraph (3) above, and have notified the licence holder accordingly in writing, the licence holder shall not permit that person to act as a qualified person so long as the said notification has not been withdrawn by the licensing authority.

(5) The provisions of this paragraph shall not apply in relation to veterinary drugs or to medicinal products that are homoeopathic products.

(6) The provisions of this paragraph shall also not apply where the licence relates to manufacturing activity which:

(a) is limited to medicinal products to which Article 2 of the Medicines (Exemption from Licences) (Special and Transitional Cases) Order 1971 (SI 1971 No 1450) as amended (SI 1972 No 1200) applies, and consists solely of mixing together medicinal products and ingredients, other than active ingredients, on premises of which the licence holder is the occupier and which he is able to close so as to exclude the public, or

(b) is limited to assembly only, where all the products to be assembled are for sale or supply in the course of a business and are supplied, without any recommendation, for the purpose of administration to a particular person after the licence holder has been requested by or on behalf of that person, and in that person's presence, to use his judgement as to the treatment required.

(7) The provisions of this paragraph shall not have effect until 22nd November 1977 in relation to a licence which has been granted before the coming into operation of these regulations.

17 (1) Subject to sub-paragraph (5) below, the licence holder shall at all times have at his disposal the services of a person who as respects qualifications and experience satisfies the provisions of Articles 31 and 32 of the Council Directive, to carry out the functions specified in sub-paragraph (3) below ('qualified person'). For the purposes of this paragraph, but without prejudice to sub-paragraph (4) below, the licence holder may regard a person as satisfying the provisions of the said Article 32 as respects formal qualifications if he produces evidence that he is a member of the Royal Pharmaceutical Society of Great Britain or of the Royal Society of Chemistry or of such other body as may appear to the licensing authority to be an appropriate body for the purpose, and that he is regarded by the body of which he is a member as so satisfying those provisions.

(2) The licence holder shall at all times provide and maintain such staff, premises, equipment and facilities as will enable the qualified person who is at his disposal to carry out the said functions.

(3) The functions to be carried out by the qualified person shall be as follows:

(a) to ensure that each batch of the medicinal product to which the licence relates has been manufactured or assembled and checked in compliance with the provisions of the Act and regulations made thereunder, the provisions of the licence and the provisions of the product licence which relates to the product;

(b) to certify in a register, or other record appropriate for the purpose, whether each production batch of the medicinal product to which the licence relates satisfies the requirements set out in (a) above and to ensure that such register or other record is regularly maintained, in particular that the appropriate entries in such register or other record are made as soon as practicable after each such batch has been manufactured.

(4) Where, after giving the licence holder and the person acting as a qualified person the opportunity of making representations to them (orally or in writing), the licensing authority are of the opinion that the person so acting does not satisfy the provisions of the said Articles 31 and 32 of the Council Directive as respects qualifications and experience, or that he is failing to carry out the functions specified in sub-paragraph (3) above, and have notified the licence holder accordingly in writing, the licence holder shall not permit that person to act as a qualified person so long as the said notification has not been withdrawn by the licensing authority.

(5) The provisions of this paragraph shall not apply in relation to:–

(a) medicinal products which are manufactured, sold supplied, imported or exported for use by being administered to human beings;

(b) veterinary drugs which:–

(i) consist of vaccines, toxins or serums;

(ii) are based on radioactive isotopes;

(iii) are homoeopathic veterinary drugs; or

(iv) are additives for animal feeding stuffs to which the provisions of Council Directive 70/524/EEC apply.

(6) The provisions of this paragraph shall also not apply where the licence relates to manufacturing activity which:

(a) is limited to medicinal products to which Article 2 of the Medicines (Exemptions from Licences) (Special and Transitional Cases) Order 1971 (SI 1971 No 1450 as amended by SI 1972 No 1200) applies, and consists solely of mixing together medicinal products and ingredients, other than active ingredients, on premises of which the licence holder is the occupier and which he is able to close so as to exclude the public; or

(b) is limited to assembly only, where all products to be assembled are for sale or supply in the course of a business and are supplied, without any recommendation, for the purpose of administration to a particular animal or herd after the licence holder has been requested by the owner of that animal or herd to use his judgement as to the treatment required.

(7) The provisions of this paragraph shall not have effect until 9th October 1984 in relation to a licence which has been granted before the coming into operation of those regulations.

Schedule: prescribed conditions for manufacturer's undertakings for imported products (SI No 1038)

Extracts from:

The Medicines (Manufacturer's Undertakings for Imported Products) Regulations 1977 (SI 1977 No 1038) as amended by Amendment Regulations 1992 (SI 1992 No 2845).

Editor's note

This extract from the Regulations is presented for the reader's convenience. For any definitive information reference must be made to the original Regulations.

An additional Regulation (Regulation 4) is inserted by SI 1992 No 2845 to exclude from the scope of the Regulations applications for products coming from another Member State of the EU.

Schedule

1 The manufacturer shall provide and maintain such staff, premises and plant as are necessary for the carrying out in accordance with the relevant product licences of such stages of the manufacture and assembly of the medicinal products to which the relevant product licences relate as are undertaken by him.

2 The manufacturer shall provide and maintain such staff, premises, equipment and facilities for the handling, storage and distribution of the medicinal products to which the relevant product licences relate which he handles, stores or distributes as are necessary to avoid deterioration of the medicinal products.

2A In relation to medicinal products for human use, the manufacturer shall provide and maintain a designated quality control department having authority in relation to quality control and being independent of all other departments.

3 The manufacturer shall conduct all manufacture and assembly operations in such a way as to ensure that the medicinal products to which the relevant product licences relate conform with the standards of strength, quality and purity applicable to them under the relevant product licences.

3A In relation to medicinal products for human use, the manufacturer shall maintain an effective pharmaceutical quality assurance system involving the active participation of the management and personnel of the different services involved.

4   Where animals are used in the production of any medicinal product and the relevant product licences contain provisions relating to them the manufacturer shall arrange for the animals to be housed in premises of such a nature and to be managed in such a way as will facilitate compliance with such provisions.

5   The manufacturer shall make such adequate and suitable arrangements as are necessary for carrying out in accordance with the relevant product licences any tests of the strength, quality or purity of the medicinal products to which the licences relate.

6   The manufacturer shall inform the holder of the relevant product licences of any material alteration in the premises or plant used in connection with the manufacture or assembly of the medicinal products to which the relevant product licences relate or in the operations for which such premises or plant are so used and of any change, since the granting of the relevant product licences in respect of any person:

(a)   responsible for supervising the production operations; or

(b)   responsible for quality control of the medicinal products to which the relevant product licences relate; or

(c)   in charge of the animals from which are derived any substance used in the production of the medicinal products to which the relevant product licences relate; or

(d)   responsible for the culture of any living tissues used in the manufacture of the medicinal products to which the relevant product licences relate.

7   The manufacturer shall keep readily available for inspection by a person authorised by the Licensing Authority durable records of the details of manufacture and assembly of each batch of every medicinal product to which each relevant product licence relates and of the tests carried out thereon in such a form that the records will be easily identifiable from the number of the batch as shown on each container in which the medicinal product is exported from the country where it has been manufactured or assembled; the manufacturer shall permit the person authorised to take copies of or make extracts from such records. Such records shall not be destroyed –

(a)   in relation to a medicinal product for human use, for a period of five years from the date of release of the relevant batch, or for a period of one year after the expiry date of the relevant batch, whichever expires later,

(b)   in any other case.

7A In relation to medicinal products for human use to which a product licence relates, the manufacturer shall keep readily available for examination by a person authorised by the Licensing Authority, samples of –

(a) each batch of finished products for at least a period of one year after their expiry date; and

(b) starting materials (other than solvents, gases or water) for at least a period of two years after release of medicinal product of which the relevant starting materials formed part; except where the manufacturer is authorised by the licensing authority to destroy such samples earlier.

7B (1) The manufacturer shall implement a system for recording and reviewing complaints in relation to medicinal products for human use to which a product licence relates together with an effective system for recalling promptly and at any time the medicinal products in the distribution network.

(2) The manufacturer shall record and investigate all complaints described in sub-paragraph (1) of this paragraph and shall immediately inform the Licensing Authority of any defect which could result in a recall from sale, supply or exportation or in an abnormal restriction on such sale, supply or exportation.

8 The manufacturer shall inform the holder of the relevant product licence of any material change since the date upon which such licence was granted in respect of:

(a) the facilities and equipment available at each of the premises of the manufacturer for carrying out any stage of the manufacture or assembly of the medicinal products to which the relevant product licences relate; or

(b) the facilities and equipment available in each of the premises of the manufacturer for the storage of the medicinal products to which the relevant product licences relate on, and distribution of the products from or between, such premises; or

(c) any manufacturing operations, not being operations in relation to the medicinal products to which the relevant product licences relate, which are carried on by the manufacturer on or near any of the premises on which such medicinal products are manufactured or assembled and the substances or articles in respect of which such operations are carried on; or

(d) the arrangements for the identification and storage of materials and ingredients before and during manufacture of the medicinal products to which the relevant product licences relate and the arrangements for the storage of the medicinal products after they have been manufactured or assembled; or

(e)   the arrangements for ensuring satisfactory turnover of stocks of medicinal products to which the relevant product licences relate; or

(f)   the arrangements for maintaining production records and records of analytical and other testing procedures applied in the course of manufacture or assembly of the medicinal products to which the relevant product licences relate; or

(g)   the arrangements for keeping reference samples of materials used in the manufacture of any medicinal products to which the relevant product licences relate and reference samples of such medicinal products.

Manufacture and importation of unlicensed medicines for human use

Introduction

The Medicines Act contains certain exemptions from the requirement to hold a product licence (marketing authorisation) for medicinal products to be administered to humans. Two of the more important exemptions are outlined here: the manufacture and supply of unlicensed relevant medicinal products for individual patients ('specials') and the importation and supply of unlicensed relevant medicinal products for individual patients.

(A 'relevant medicinal product' is one to which the requirements of Directive 2001/83/EC apply unless subject to an exemption in that Directive.)

The manufacture and supply of unlicensed relevant medicinal products for individual patients ('specials')

The Medicines for Human Use (Marketing Authorisations Etc.) Regulations 1994 (SI 1994 No 3144) require that medicinal products are licensed before they are marketed in the UK. However some patients may have special clinical needs that cannot be met by licensed medicinal products. So that these special needs may be met the law allows manufacture and supply of unlicensed medicinal products (commonly known as 'specials'), subject to certain conditions.

The conditions, laid down in Schedule 1 of the Regulations, are that there is a bona fide unsolicited order, the product is formulated in accordance with the requirement of a doctor or dentist registered in the UK and the product is for use by one of their individual patients on their direct personal responsibility. If a 'special' is manufactured in the UK the manufacturer must hold a manufacturer's (specials) licence issued by the MCA. A 'special' may not be advertised and may not be supplied if an equivalent licensed product is available which could meet the patient's needs. Essential records must be kept and serious adverse drug reactions reported to the MCA.

The MCA Guidance Note 14 *The supply of unlicensed relevant medicinal products for individual patients* provides guidance to manufacturers about the conditions under which they may manufacture and supply 'specials' and their legal obligations.

The importation and supply of unlicensed relevant medicinal products for individual patients

An unlicensed relevant medicinal product may only be imported in accordance with The Medicines (Standard Provisions for Licences and Certificates) Amendment Regulations 1999 (SI 1999 No 4). An importer must hold the appropriate wholesale dealer's or wholesale dealer's import licence (for details please see the MCA Guidance Note 6, *Notes for applicants and holders of a wholesale dealer's licence* for further information) issued by the MCA and must comply with their licence conditions. Importer's licence conditions include the requirement that they must notify the MCA on each occasion that they intend to import such a product. Importation may proceed unless the importer has been informed by the MCA within 28 days that it objects to importation. The MCA may object and prevent importation because it has concerns about the safety or quality of the product or because there is an equivalent licensed medicinal product available and it is not satisfied that there is a 'special need' for the supply to an individual patient.

An imported unlicensed relevant medicinal product may only be supplied in accordance with Schedule 1 to The Medicines for Human Use (Marketing Authorisations Etc.) Regulations 1994 (SI 1994 No 3144). Schedule 1 exempts, under defined conditions (discussed in the previous section on 'specials') such a product when it is supplied to meet the 'special need' of an individual patient.

The MCA document *Interim Guidelines on the Import & Supply of Unlicensed Relevant Medicinal Products* provides guidance to importers about the conditions under which they may import and supply unlicensed relevant medicinal products and their legal obligations.

Qualified Persons

All holders of Manufacturer's or Wholesale dealer's (import) licences for licensed products are required to have available the services of a Qualified Person (QP), who must be named on the manufacturer's or wholesale dealer's licence. When considering a nomination, the Licensing Authority routinely takes into account the assessment of the nominee's eligibility made by the joint assessment panel of the Institute of Biology, the Royal Pharmaceutical Society of Great Britain and the Royal Society of Chemistry. Exceptionally, the Medicines Control Agency will assess a nominee directly if he or she is not a member of any of these professional bodies.

Title IV of Directive 2001/83/EC lays down the requirements for QPs in relation to products for human use. Article 51 defines the duties of the QP, Articles 49 and 50 define the requirements for eligibility under the permanent and transitional arrangements respectively, and Article 52 requires Member States to ensure that the duties of QPs are fulfilled, either through administrative measures or by making such persons subject to a professional code of conduct. Title IV of Directive 2001/82/EC lays down equivalent requirements in relation to veterinary products. Guidance on the duties of QPs is given in the EU Guide to GMP and in particular in its annex 16.

By inspection and other means the Licensing Authority routinely assesses whether or not QPs are fulfilling their duties. In making this assessment, reference is made to the *Code of Practice for Qualified Persons* produced jointly by the Institute of Biology, the Royal Pharmaceutical Society of Great Britain and the Royal Society of Chemistry in collaboration with the Medicines Control Agency and the Veterinary Medicines Directorate. This reference is made whether or not the QP in question is a member of one or more of these bodies (see next section).

All QPs should be guided in fulfilling their duties by the Code of Practice, although the references in sections 11.1 and 12.4 to the disciplinary machinery of the professional bodies, and in section 11.6 to the advice which professional bodies can give, would not be relevant in the case of a QP who is not a member of one of these bodies. The European Industrial Pharmacists Group adopted a similar Code[1] in 1995 for the guidance of its members.

---

(1) European Industrial Pharmacists Group. Code of Practice for Qualified Persons. June 1966. Available from the Industrial Pharmacists Group of the Royal Pharmaceutical Society of Great Britain.

Code of practice for Qualified Persons in the pharmaceutical industry [1]

1.0 Purpose of the Code

1.1 The legal functions of the Qualified Person (QP) are stated in SI 1971 No 972 (as amended) and reproduced in the preface to the Professional Bodies' Joint Register.

1.2 The aims and objectives of the Code of Practice are to provide operational guidelines for carrying out the functions of the QP within a professional code of conduct.

1.3 The Code is in the interests of Qualified Persons, their employers, patients, the Medicines Control Agency (MCA) of the Department of Health and the Veterinary Medicines Directorate (VMD) of the Ministry of Agriculture, Fisheries and Foods.

2.0 Application of the Code

2.1 The Code is equally applicable to Qualified Persons who have achieved that status under the transitional arrangements, and under the permanent provisions.

2.2 Qualified Persons have a professional duty to decline to act as Qualified Persons in the release of product types for which they do not possess the relevant experience and knowledge.

2.3 It should be noted that Qualified Persons are eligible to certify batches of medicinal product as follows:

i) those who have achieved Qualified Person status under the permanent provisions are eligible to certify batches of human or veterinary medicinal products in any member state within the European Union (EU);

ii) those who have achieved Qualified Person status under the transitional arrangements for human medicines are eligible to certify batches of human or veterinary medicinal products, and such certification is restricted to acting in the United Kingdom (UK) although such products, once certified, can legally be sold or supplied throughout the EU;

iii) those who have achieved Qualified Person status under the transitional arrangements for veterinary medicines are only eligible to certify batches of veterinary medicinal products, and such certification is restricted to acting in the UK although such products, once certified, can legally be sold or supplied throughout the EU.

2.4 The Code applies equally to Qualified Persons involved in human and/or veterinary medicines.

2.5 The Licensing Authority may refer to this Code in connection with disciplinary proceedings against a Qualified Person under Article 52 of Directive 2001/83/EC or Article 56 of Directive 2001/82/EC.

3.0 Terminology

3.1 The terminology used in this Code of Practice corresponds with that used in the current version of the EC directives on Good Pharmaceutical Manufacturing Practice (GMP) and the EC Guide to Good Pharmaceutical Manufacturing Practice.

3.2 Within the EU the terms Marketing Authorisation and Manufacturing Authorisation are generally used and shall henceforth be referred to throughout this Code.

The UK licensing system currently uses the equivalent terms Product Licence (= Marketing Authorisation) and Manufacturer's Licence (= Manufacturing Authorisation) or Wholesale dealer's (Import) Licence.

4.0 General Principles

4.1 Pharmaceutical Manufacturers and the Licensing Authorities have a duty to ensure that patients are properly protected and that medicinal products meet appropriate requirements for safety, quality and efficacy.

4.2 The legal framework is provided by the European Directives and 'The Rules Governing Medicinal Products in the European Union', the United Kingdom Medicines Act 1968, and by subsequent Regulations and Statutory Instruments, including the Medicines for Human Use (Marketing Authorisation etc.) Regulations SI 1994 No 3144.

4.3 An operational framework is provided in the current Volume 4 of the *Rules Governing Medicinal Products in the European Union 'Good Manufacturing Practices'*. In Chapter 1 of the Guidelines, Quality Management, it states that:

'The holder of a Manufacturing Authorisation must manufacture medicinal products so as to ensure that they are fit for their intended use, comply with the requirements of the Marketing Authorisation and do not place patients at risk due to inadequate safety, quality or efficacy. The attainment of this quality objective is the responsibility of senior management and requires the participation and commitment by staff in many different departments and at all levels within the company, the company's suppliers and the distributors.

To achieve the quality objective reliably there must be a comprehensively designed and correctly implemented system of Quality Assurance incorporating Good Manufacturing Practice and thus Quality Control. It should be fully documented and its effectiveness monitored. All parts of the Quality Assurance system should be adequately resourced with competent personnel, and suitable and sufficient premises, equipment and facilities. There are additional legal responsibilities for the holder of the Manufacturing Authorisation and for the Qualified Person(s).

The basic concepts of Quality Assurance, Good Manufacturing Practice and Quality Control are inter-related. They are described here in order to emphasise their relationships and their fundamental importance to the production and control of medicinal products.

4.4 Qualified Persons should be aware that whilst Quality Management applies to full-scale manufacture, it also extends to original product design, development, formulation and preparation of medicinal products for use in clinical trials. This includes the establishment of well-defined manufacturing processes, sampling programmes and analytical test methods and appropriate specifications for ingredients, printed and unprinted packaging components and finished dosage forms.

5.0   Routine Duties of a Qualified Person

Qualified Persons have routine duties, some of which may be delegated (see later), in line with the above general principles. Before certifying a batch prior to release the Qualified Person doing so should always ensure that the following requirements have been met:

The meaning of the word ensure in this context is that the Qualified Person must be confident that various actions, which may not be under his/her direct control, have in fact been taken. See also Section 6.

5.1 The Marketing Authorisation and Manufacturing Authorisation requirements for the medicinal product have been met for the batch concerned.

5.2 The principles and guidelines of GMP as stated in Directive 91/356/EEC (Human) or Directive 91/412/EEC (Veterinary) and as interpreted in the EC Guide to GMP have been followed.

5.3 The principal manufacturing and testing processes have been validated.

5.4 All the necessary Quality Control checks and tests have been performed, and account taken of the manufacturing and packaging conditions including a review of batch records.

The EC Guide to GMP suggests that the Head of Production and the Head of Quality Control assume line management responsibilities for these activities.

5.5 Any changes or deviations in manufacturing, packaging or Quality Control have been notified in accordance with a well-defined reporting system before any product is released. Such changes may need notification to and approval by the MCA or VMD.

5.6 Any additional sampling, inspection, tests and checks have been carried out or initiated, as appropriate, to cover changes or deviations.

5.7 All necessary manufacturing, packaging and associated documentation has been completed and endorsed by suitably authorised staff.

5.8 Regular audits, self-inspections and spot checks are being carried out by experienced staff.

5.9 All relevant factors have been considered including any not specifically associated with the output batch directly under review (e.g. calibration and maintenance records, environmental monitoring).

5.10 The legal requirements regarding imported products have been fully met.

For products imported from outside the EU or EEA the Qualified Person should ensure testing within the EU/EEA to the requirements of the Marketing Authorisation and any other tests to assure quality of the products, unless a mutual recognition agreement between the EU and the third country concerned allows the acceptance of manufacturer's batch certification in lieu. The Qualified Person should also be satisfied that the medicinal products have been manufactured in accordance with GMP standards which are equivalent to those of the EU or EEA.

5.11 The Qualified Person should also recognise the need to consult other company experts in the various areas of the Study Guide to reinforce his/her knowledge on appropriate points when a doubtful situation arises (e.g. increased levels of impurity, new impurities, environmental or microbiological factors, cross contamination etc).

5.12   In considering how to perform the above duties, 5.1 to 5.11, the Qualified Person will have to take account of the nature and size of the operations being performed. For example, in a very small company with a limited range of products it may be possible that the Qualified Person can take direct responsibility for some or all of the tasks outlined above. In larger organisations, the Qualified Person will be dependent upon the knowledge and expertise of his/her colleagues in undertaking some or all of the tasks. However, it is of paramount importance that the Qualified Person takes steps, within a well-planned Quality Management System, to assure himself or herself that the tasks allocated are in fact being performed satisfactorily. Hence the routine duties of the Qualified Person depend very much upon a team effort wherein the individuals concerned realise the position and responsibility of the Qualified Person and provide every support. What cannot be over emphasised in this context is the Qualified Person's commitment to regularly interact with professional colleagues in all functional groups and to understand their contribution and impact upon quality.

The certification of a batch prior to release must be performed by a Qualified Person.

6.0   Performance of Duties and Regulatory Compliance

6.1   Management, as a requirement of Quality Assurance, should clearly define the areas of work and the method of operating in the absence of the regular Qualified Person.

In the absence of one Qualified Person, the task of certifying batches can only be delegated to another Qualified Person nominated on the Manufacturing Authorisation and who is knowledgeable and experienced with regard to the medicinal products under review.

6.2   Whilst each Qualified Person has a personal and professional responsibility for being certain that the various checks and tests have been carried out, the detail of this work is described in the EC Guide to GMP as normally the responsibility of the Head of Production and the Head of Quality Control who must ensure that appropriately trained and experienced staff are available. Ultimately the Qualified Person must be satisfied either directly or, more usually, by the proper operation of quality systems which include appropriate approvals, audits, self-inspections and spot checks that manufacturing, packaging and Quality Control testing have complied with relevant requirements. Batch certification without such adequate steps may be professional misconduct.

6.3   It must be recognised that the Qualified Person depends upon many of his/her working colleagues for the achievement of quality and regulatory compliance in the manufacture of medicinal products. It is therefore of paramount importance that he or she achieves a good working relationship with other persons in positions of responsibility. These are likely to include those responsible for:

- production operations;

- Quality Control laboratories;

- application and maintenance of Manufacturing and Marketing Authorisations

- provision of engineering services;

- procurement of starting and packaging materials;

- storage and distribution.

6.4 It is recommended that the company and the Qualified Person take the necessary steps to appraise other functional groups, and the responsible people who belong to them, of the role of the Qualified Person within the company and how they should give proper support.

6.5 Ensuring compliance with the conditions of the Marketing Authorisation is a primary duty of the Qualified Person. It is, therefore, essential that the Qualified Person has access at all times to the dossiers upon which Marketing Authorisations have been granted, including any variations affecting such approval. The control of change needs to be rigorously monitored by the Qualified Person especially where there are implications for compliance, quality and patient safety. Particular attention needs to be paid to this when the manufacturer is making products for a Marketing Authorisation holder in a different company.

6.6 The Qualified Person should be present at the manufacturing site for a sufficient proportion of the working time in order to discharge the legal and professional obligations outlined in this Code and to ensure the proper operation of a Quality Management System including the control of any delegated duties.

6.7 Manufacturing Authorisations contain the names of the persons responsible for Production, Quality Control, and the name(s) of the Qualified Person(s). The duties of these members of staff must be clear in their respective job descriptions and they must have the authority required under the relevant EC directives.

7.0 Number and Location of Qualified Persons

7.1 The provisions of Statutory Instrument 1977, No 1053 (Human Medicines) and Statutory Instrument 1983, No 1730 (Veterinary Medicines) and the principles outlined in the EU Guide to GMP for

Medicinal Products only require a company or organisation to nominate one person on a Manufacturing Authorisation to carry out the duties of the Qualified Person provided that person is at the disposal of the company at all times and can carry out the required functions.

7.2 Some organisations may have a complex structure, or operate at several locations, or both, which would make it necessary, where justified, to nominate several Qualified Persons on its Manufacturing Authorisation.

7.3 It is acceptable and often helpful for the Quality Controller to be a Qualified Person.

8.0   Contracted Qualified Persons

8.1 In a number of cases, especially with smaller companies, a 'Contracted Qualified Person' provides the service. In such cases the duties and responsibilities of a 'Contracted Qualified Person' are the same as those Qualified Persons who are permanently employed by their company; the QP is not an employee of the company but provides his services under contract.

The term 'Contracted Qualified Person' is not a formal title and is used only in the sense of a Qualified Person providing an independent service under contract to a company.

8.2 In addition to compliance with the provisions applicable to all QPs including all the routine duties outlined in this Code of Practice, Contracted Qualified Persons should observe the following:

• have a clear written contract, which delineates the duties and responsibilities of the Qualified Person – as agreed between the company and the 'Contracted Qualified Person'. Both should sign and retain a copy of the contract;

• be readily available to the staff of the company for advice and discussion, and also be present during regulatory inspections and involved in communications with the inspectors;

• ensure that the company to whom the services are provided will allow free access to any people, information, documentation, premises, procedures etc which are relevant to the decision-making processes when certifying batches for sale. In addition the company should inform the Qualified Person of any deviations which need to be considered in relation to batch certification. Such deviations should be provided to the Qualified Person promptly and in writing;

- ensure that sufficient spot checks, inspections, and audits of the company (whether in the EU/UK or overseas) are carried out. In particular the 'Contracted Qualified Person' should satisfy himself/herself that an effective pharmaceutical Quality Management System is being operated.

8.3 Particularly for smaller companies, the person acting as contracted QP may agree with the company to provide some of the necessary services such as, for example, staff training, internal audits and maintenance of licences, personally in addition to performing strictly QP duties.

8.4 If any doubt exists concerning the duties and responsibilities between the Qualified Person and the company who requires his/her services, he or she should contact their local Medicines Inspector or their professional body for advice.

8.5 The Code of Practice should be brought to the attention of the Chief Executive Officer of the company who wishes to have the services of a 'Contracted Qualified Person'.

9.0 Contract Manufacture and/or Testing

9.1 Where products are manufactured and/or packed under contract there should be a clearly written technical agreement between the contract giver and the contract acceptor. Such an agreement should be reviewed and approved by the Qualified Persons engaged by the contract giver and acceptor. The agreement should clearly delineate the areas and responsibilities of both Qualified Persons.

9.2 The contract acceptor, who normally will be required to hold a manufacturing authorisation, may accept full responsibility for batch certification provided that the Qualified Person has all the appropriate information (including access to relevant details in the Marketing Authorisation(s)) and authority to fulfil these duties. Nevertheless the decision concerning responsibility for batch certification remains a matter between contract giver and acceptor depending on the circumstances.

9.3 The provision in 9.1 applies equally to the testing of samples under contract. The contract testing laboratory may not hold its own manufacturing authorisation but in this case must be authorised on the contract giver's authorisation.

10.0   Continuing Professional Development

10.1   Qualified Persons have a personal and professional duty to keep their knowledge and experience up to date. It is expected that this would cover the current state of pharmaceutical quality management, regulatory aspects and GMP guideline standards, product manufacturing and control technology, and general work practices.

10.2   Records of Continuing Professional Development (CPD) should be kept to reflect this important longer-term aspect of the Qualified Persons continued performance of professional duties.

10.3   Attention is drawn to the three professional bodies' statements on CPD which underline the importance of this aspect of a Qualified Person's performance of duties. These statements will also be of value to those Qualified Persons who are not members of any of the three professional bodies.

10.4   In the event of a Qualified Person making a major change in job responsibilities, for example from a company making only sterile dose forms to one with a wider range of products including solid dose forms, the Qualified Person and the senior management of the company involved should recognise the need for additional education and training and take adequate steps to demonstrate that proper provision is made for this. Such extra training should be undertaken before the Qualified Person acts in a new situation.

11.0   Codes of Conduct

11.1   Qualified Persons are subject to the overall jurisdiction of the Bye-laws, Charters and Regulations, Codes of Conduct, Disciplinary Regulations and any general guidelines of their own professional body, and should have access to them.

11.2   Qualified Persons have duties not only to their employer but also to the Licensing Authority and its Inspectorate. They must ensure that appropriate senior company executives are made fully aware of any manufacturing and/or testing difficulties which may cast doubt on the certification of batches or post facto might require a product recall.

11.3   If there is any aspect of the Quality Assurance system which is not in accordance with the Directives and Guidelines for Good Manufacturing Practice then the Qualified Person has a duty to bring this to the attention of Senior Management and ensure that appropriate corrective measures are taken.

11.4   Qualified Persons should establish a good working relationship with Medicines Inspectors and as far as possible provide information on request during site inspections.

There may be situations outside of site inspections where the Qualified Person may wish to consult with the local Medicines Inspector for advice or clarification in particular circumstances with which the Qualified Person is faced.

11.5   The following assumption is made by the professional bodies acting jointly when certifying the eligibility of a Qualified Person:

- in co-operation with their employers, Qualified Persons will undertake Continuing Professional Development to maintain and extend their technical and professional competence. (See also Section 10.0 above);

11.6   The following assumptions are made, firstly by the professional bodies acting jointly when certifying the eligibility of a Qualified Person and, secondly, by the Licensing Authority when accepting an eligible Qualified Person for nomination on a Manufacturing Authorisation:

- in cases where undue pressures to depart from professional obligations cannot be counterbalanced by reference to this and other relevant Codes of Practice, Qualified Persons, preferably having informed their employer first, should consult the appropriate professional body for confidential advice;

- management has a duty to provide Qualified Persons with appropriate resources and to ensure that Quality Management Systems and communications are working effectively. Qualified Persons also have a duty to make representations to management, if necessary in writing, whenever standards appear to be falling short of Good Manufacturing Practice(s). This duty should be reflected by appropriate wording in the Qualified Person's job description.

12.0   Disciplinary Procedures

12.1   Directives 2001/82/EC and 2001/83/EC read *inter alia*:

'Member States shall ensure that the duties of Qualified Persons … are fulfilled, either by means of appropriate administrative measures or by making such persons subject to a professional Code of Conduct.

Member States may provide for the temporary suspension of such a person upon the commencement of administrative or disciplinary procedures against him for failure to fulfil his obligations.'

12.2   SI 1977 No 1053 reads *inter alia*:

'Where, after giving the licence holder and the person acting as a Qualified Person the opportunity of making representations to them (orally or in writing), the Licensing Authority are of the opinion that the person so acting does not satisfy the provisions of the said Articles 23 and 24 of the Second Council Directive with respect to qualifications and experience, or that he is failing to carry out the functions specified ... and have notified the licence holder accordingly in writing, the licence holder shall not permit that person to act as a Qualified Person so long as the said notification has not been withdrawn by the Licensing Authority.'

12.3   MAL 45 and MAL 69 read *inter alia*:

'The Qualified Person has a personal and professional responsibility for ensuring that the various tests and checks have been carried out. This does not necessarily mean that he/she must himself/herself have carried out those tests or have directly supervised them, but in certifying in the register or equivalent document he/she is in effect indicating that he/she has satisfied himself/herself that the appropriate tests have been carried out specifically for that batch and that batch complies with the relevant requirements. If it were found that a person had certified in such a register without taking adequate steps so as to satisfy himself/herself, this failure might be a matter for consideration by the appropriate professional body to which he/she might belong as a matter of professional misconduct.'

12.4   The professional bodies have established disciplinary procedures to deal with cases of possible misconduct. One of the powers is to remove the name of an individual from the appropriate register or registers and they will act together as appropriate in the case of a Qualified Person who is a member of two or three of the Societies. In such cases, professional bodies will inform the Licensing Authority, the body with the power to delete the Qualified Person's name from the Manufacturing Authorisation.

---

(1) The Institute of Biology, the Royal Pharmaceutical Society of Great Britain, the Royal Society of Chemistry, 2001.

UK guidance on Certificates of Analysis

1   In certain circumstances a Certificate of Analysis from a third party may be used as part of a system to ensure the quality of materials. For such a certificate to be considered acceptable the following conditions should apply:

(a)   The person responsible for Quality Control (QC) in the purchasing company must assure himself that the organisation issuing the certificate is competent to do so, whether that organisation is part of the supplying company or is independent of it (e.g. is a contract analytical service).

(b)   The Certificate must:

(i)   Identify the organisation issuing it.

(ii)   Be authorised by a person competent to do so, and state his qualifications and position. 'Authorisation' may be by signature or acceptable electronic means (please refer to the guidance given for the similar situation when a Qualified Person (QP) releases a batch of finished products for sale (see paragraph 19 of Annex 11 to the guide to GMP).

(iii)   Name the material to which it refers and identify it by a batch number.

(iv)   State that the material has been tested, by whom, and when this was done.

(v)   State the specification (e.g. EP) and methods against which, and by which, the tests were performed.

vi)   Give the test results obtained, or declare that the results obtained showed compliance with the stated specification.

2   Certificates which merely carry such statements as 'a typical analysis is … ', or state that the material is of a particular quality with no supporting evidence, are not acceptable.

3   Possession of a Certificate of Analysis does not eliminate the need to confirm the identity of the material supplied.

4   Possession of a Certificate of Analysis does not absolve the purchaser from ultimate responsibility for the correctness of the material to which it refers.

5   The above paragraphs, whilst particularly relevant to the certification of starting materials, also apply as appropriate to other materials and products.

Note that the Certificate of Analysis described above is not *the Manufacturer's Batch Certificate used within the context of a Mutual Recognition Agreement (see Chapter 6).*

Directive 2001/83/EC of the European Parliament and of the Council of 6 November 2001 on the Community code relating to medicinal products for human use.

Editor's note

Title IV of this directive is reproduced below. Reference should be made to the full Directive for the preamble, definitions and the general and final provisions.

Title IV Manufacture and Importation

Article 40

1   Member States shall take all appropriate measures to ensure that the manufacture of the medicinal products within their territory is subject to the holding of an authorisation. This manufacturing authorisation shall be required notwithstanding that the medicinal products manufactured are intended for export.

2   The authorisation referred to in paragraph 1 shall be required for both total and partial manufacture, and for the various processes of dividing up, packaging or presentation.

However, such authorisation shall not be required for preparation, dividing up, changes in packaging or presentation where these processes are carried out, solely for retail supply, by pharmacists in dispensing pharmacies or by persons legally authorised in the Member States to carry out such processes.

3   Authorisation referred to in paragraph 1 shall also be required for imports coming from third countries into a Member State; this Title and Article 118 shall have corresponding application to such imports as they have to manufacture.

Article 41

In order to obtain the manufacturing authorisation, the applicant shall meet at least the following requirements:

(a) specify the medicinal products and pharmaceutical forms which are to be manufactured or imported and also the place where they are to be manufactured and/or controlled;

(b) have at his disposal, for the manufacture or import of the above, suitable and sufficient premises, technical equipment and control facilities complying with the legal requirements which the Member State concerned lays down as regards both manufacture and control and the storage of medicinal products, in accordance with Article 20;

(c) have at his disposal the services of at least one qualified person within the meaning of Article 48.

The applicant shall provide particulars in support of the above in his application.

Article 42

1 The competent authority of the Member State shall issue the manufacturing authorisation only after having made sure of the accuracy of the particulars supplied pursuant to Article 41, by means of an inquiry carried out by its agents.

2 In order to ensure that the requirements referred to in Article 41 are complied with, authorisation may be made conditional on the carrying out of certain obligations imposed either when authorisation is granted or at a later date.

3 The authorisation shall apply only to the premises specified in the application and to the medicinal products and pharmaceutical forms specified in that same application.

Article 43

The Member States shall take all appropriate measures to ensure that the time taken for the procedure for granting the manufacturing authorisation does not exceed 90 days from the day on which the competent authority receives the application.

Article 44

If the holder of the manufacturing authorisation requests a change in any of the particulars referred to in points (a) and (b) of the first paragraph of Article 41, the time taken for the procedure relating to this request shall not exceed 30 days. In exceptional cases this period of time may be extended to 90 days.

Article 45

The competent authority of the Member State may require from the applicant further information concerning the particulars supplied pursuant to Article 41 and concerning the qualified person referred to in Article 48; where the competent authority concerned exercises this right, application of the time-limits referred to in Article 43 and 44 shall be suspended until the additional data required have been supplied.

Article 46

The holder of a manufacturing authorisation shall at least be obliged:

(a) to have at his disposal the services of staff who comply with the legal requirements existing in the Member State concerned both as regards manufacture and controls;

(b) to dispose of the authorised medicinal products only in accordance with the legislation of the Member States concerned;

(c) to give prior notice to the competent authority of any changes he may wish to make to any of the particulars supplied pursuant to Article 41; the competent authority shall, in any event, be immediately informed if the qualified person referred to in Article 48 is replaced unexpectedly;

(d) to allow the agents of the competent authority of the Member State concerned access to his premises at any time;

(e) to enable the qualified person referred to in Article 48 to carry out his duties, for example by placing at his disposal all the necessary facilities;

(f) to comply with the principles and guidelines of good manufacturing practice for medicinal products as laid down by Community law.

Article 47

The principles and guidelines of good manufacturing practices for medicinal products referred to in Article 46(f) shall be adopted in the form of a directive, in accordance with the procedure referred to in Article 121(2).

Detailed guidelines in line with those principles will be published by the Commission and revised necessary to take account of technical and scientific progress.

Article 48

1   Member States shall take all appropriate measures to ensure that the holder of the manufacturing authorisation has permanently and continuously at his disposal the services of at least one qualified person, in accordance with the conditions laid down in Article 49, responsible in particular for carrying out the duties specified in Article 51.

2   If he personally fulfils the conditions laid down in Article 49, the holder of the authorisation may himself assume the responsibility referred to in paragraph 1.

Article 49

1   Member States shall ensure that the qualified person referred to in Article 48 fulfils the minimum conditions of qualification set out in paragraphs 2 and 3.

2   A qualified person shall be in possession of a diploma, certificate or other evidence of formal qualifications awarded on completion of a university course of study, or a course recognised as equivalent by the Member State concerned, extending over a period of at least four years of theoretical and practical study in one of the following scientific disciplines: pharmacy, medicine, veterinary medicine, chemistry, pharmaceutical chemistry and technology, biology.

However, the minimum duration of the university course may be three and a half years where the course is followed by a period of theoretical and practical training of a minimum duration of one year and including a training period of at least six months in a pharmacy open to the public, corroborated by an examination at university level.

Where two university courses or two courses recognised by the State as equivalent co-exist in a Member State and where one of these extends over four years and the other over three years, the three-year course leading to a diploma, certificate or other evidence of formal qualifications awarded on completion of a university course or its recognised equivalent shall be considered to fulfil the condition of duration referred to in the second subparagraph in so far as the diplomas, certificates or other evidence of formal qualifications awarded on completion of both courses are recognised as equivalent by the State in question.

The course shall include theoretical and practical study bearing upon at least the following basic subjects:

- Applied physics
- General and inorganic chemistry
- Organic chemistry
- Analytical chemistry
- Pharmaceutical chemistry, including analysis of medicinal products
- General and applied biochemistry (medical)
- Physiology
- Microbiology
- Pharmacology
- Pharmaceutical technology
- Toxicology
- Pharmacognosy (study of the composition and effects of the natural active substances of plant and animal origin).

Studies in these subjects should be so balanced as to enable the person concerned to fulfil the obligations specified in Article 51.

In so far as certain diplomas, certificates or other evidence of formal qualifications mentioned in the first subparagraph do not fulfil the criteria laid down in this paragraph, the competent authority of the Member State shall ensure that the person concerned provides evidence of adequate knowledge of the subjects involved.

3   The qualified person shall have acquired practical experience over at least two years, in one or more undertakings which are authorised to manufacture medicinal products, in the activities of qualitative analysis of medicinal products, of quantitative analysis of active substances and of the testing and checking necessary to ensure the quality of medicinal products.

The duration of practical experience may be reduced by one year where a university course lasts for at least five years and by a year and a half where the course lasts for at least six years.

Article 50

1   A person engaging in the activities of the person referred to in Article 48 from the time of the application of Directive 75/319/EEC, in a Member State without complying with the provisions of Article 49 shall be eligible to continue to engage in those activities in the State concerned.

2   The holder of a diploma, certificate or other evidence of formal qualifications awarded on completion of a university course – or a course recognised as equivalent by the Member State concerned – in a scientific discipline allowing him to engage in the activities of the person referred to in Article 48 in accordance with the laws of that State may – if he began his course prior to 21 May 1975 – be considered as qualified to carry out in that State the duties of the person referred to in Article 48 provided that he has previously engaged in the following activities for at least two years before 21 May 1985 following notification of this directive in one or more undertakings authorised to manufacture: production supervision and/or qualitative and quantitative analysis of active substances, and the necessary testing and checking under the direct authority of the person referred to in Article 48 to ensure the quality of the medicinal products.

If the person concerned has acquired the practical experience referred to in the first subparagraph before 21 May 1965, a further one year's practical experience in accordance with the conditions referred to in the first subparagraph will be required to be completed immediately before he engages in such activities.

Article 51

1   Member States shall take all appropriate measures to ensure that the qualified person referred to in Article 48, without prejudice to his relationship with the holder of the manufacturing authorisation, is responsible, in the context of the procedures referred to in Article 52, for securing:

(a)   in the case of medicinal products manufactured within the Member States concerned, that each batch of medicinal products has been manufactured and checked in compliance with the laws in force in that Member State and in accordance with the requirements of the marketing authorisation;

(b)   in the case of medicinal products coming from third countries, that each production batch has undergone in the importing Member State a full qualitative analysis, a quantitative analysis of at least all the active constituents and all the other tests or checks necessary to ensure the quality of medicinal products in accordance with the requirements of the marketing authorisation.

The batches of medicinal products which have undergone such controls in a Member State shall be exempt from the controls if they are marketed in another Member State, accompanied by the control reports signed by the qualified person.

2   In the case of medicinal products imported from a third country, where appropriate arrangements have been made by the Community with the exporting country to ensure that the manufacturer of the medicinal product applies standards of good manufacturing practice at least equivalent to those laid down by the Community, and to ensure that the controls referred to under point (b) of the first subparagraph of paragraph 1 have been carried out in the exporting country, the qualified person may be relieved of responsibility for carrying out those controls.

3   In all cases and particularly where the medicinal products are released for sale, the qualified person must certify in a register or equivalent document provided for that purpose, that each production batch satisfies the provisions of this Article; the said register or equivalent document must be kept up to date as operations are carried out and must remain at the disposal of the agents of the competent authority for the period specified in the provisions of the Member State concerned and in any event for at least five years.

Article 52

Member States shall ensure that the duties of qualified persons referred to in Article 48 are fulfilled, either by means of appropriate administrative measures or by making such persons subject to a professional code of conduct.

Member States may provide for the temporary suspension of such a person upon the commencement of administrative or disciplinary procedures against him for failure to fulfil his obligations.

Article 53

The provisions of this Title shall also apply to homeopathic medicinal products.

European Commission Directives 91/356/EEC and 91/412/EEC laying down the principles and guidelines of Good Manufacturing Practice

Editor's note

There are two Directives giving the principles and guidelines of Good Manufacturing Practice (GMP), one for medicinal products for human use (Directive 91/356/EEC of 13 June 1991) and one for veterinary medicinal products (Directive 91/412/EEC of 23 July 1991).

There are no differences of GMP between them, the main difference being in the cross-references to other Directives. For convenience of comparison, only one text is reproduced below but with the content of the veterinary Directive, where different from the human use Directive, italicised and in parenthesis.

The Directives 75/319/EEC and 81/851/EEC referred to below have since been replaced by Directives 2001/83/EC and 2001/82/EC respectively.

Commission Directive of 13 June (*23 July*) 1991 laying down the principles and guidelines of good manufacturing practice for medicinal products for human use (91/356/EEC) (*veterinary medicinal products*) (*91/412/EEC*)

The Commission of the European Communities,

Having regard to the Treaty establishing the European Economic Community,

Having regard to Council Directive 75/319/EEC of 20 May 1975 on the approximation of provisions laid down by law, regulation or administrative action relating to proprietary medicinal products, as last amended by Directive 89/381/EEC, and in particular Article 19a thereof,

(Having regard to Council Directive 81/851/EEC of 28 September 1981 concerning the approximation of the laws of the Member States relating to veterinary medicinal products, as last amended by Directive 90/676/EEC, and in particular Article 27a.

Having regard to Council Directive 90/677/EEC of 13 December 1990 extending the scope of Directive 81/851/EEC on the approximation of the laws of the Member States relating to veterinary medicinal products and laying down additional provisions for immunological veterinary medicinal products,)

Whereas all medicinal products for human use (*veterinary medicinal products*) manufactured or imported into the Community, including medicinal products intended for export, should be manufactured in accordance with the principles and guidelines of good manufacturing practice;

Whereas, in accordance with national legislation, Member States may require compliance with these principles of good manufacturing practice during the manufacture of products intended for use in clinical trials;

Whereas the detailed guidelines mentioned in Article 19a of Directive 75/319/EEC (*27a of Directive 81/851/EEC*) have been published by the Commission after consultation with the pharmaceutical inspection services of the Member States in the form of a *Guide to good manufacturing practice for medicinal products*;

Whereas it is necessary that all manufacturers should operate an effective quality management of their manufacturing operations, and that this requires the implementation of a pharmaceutical quality assurance system;

Whereas officials representing the competent authorities should report on whether the manufacturer complies with good manufacturing practice and that these reports should be communicated upon reasoned request to the competent authorities of another Member State;

Whereas the principles and guidelines of good manufacturing practice should primarily concern personnel, premises and equipment, documentation, production, quality control, contracting out, complaints and product recall, and self inspection;

Whereas the principles and guidelines envisaged by this Directive are in accordance (*conformity*) with the opinion of the Committee for the Adaptation to Technical Progress of the Directives on the Removal of Technical Barriers to Trade in the Proprietary (*Veterinary*) Medicinal Products Sector set up by Article 2b of Council Directive 75/318/EEC (81/852/EEC) of 20 May 1975 (*28 September 1981*) on (*concerning*) the approximation of the laws of Member States relating to analytical, pharmaco-toxicological and clinical standards and protocols in respect of the testing of proprietary (*veterinary*) medicinal products, as last amended by Directive 89/341/EEC (87/20/EEC),

has adopted this directive

CHAPTER I General Provisions

Article 1

This Directive lays down the principles and guidelines of good manufacturing practice for *(veterinary)* medicinal products whose manufacture requires the authorisation referred to in Article 16 of Directive 75/319/EEC *(Article 24 of Directive 81/851/EEC)*.

Article 2

For the purposes of this Directive, the definition of medicinal products set out in Article 1(2) of Council Directive 65/65/EEC (5), (*and the definition of veterinary medicinal products set out in Article 1 (2) of Directive 81/851/EEC*), shall apply.

In addition,

* 'manufacturer' shall mean any holder of the authorisation referred to in Article 16 of Directive 75/319/EEC (*Article 24 of Directive 81/851/EEC*).

* 'qualified person' shall mean the person referred to in Article 21 of Directive 75/319/EEC (*Article 29 of Directive 81/851/ EEC*).

* 'pharmaceutical quality assurance' shall mean the sum total of the organised arrangements made with the object of ensuring that (*veterinary*) medicinal products are of the quality required for their intended use,

* 'good manufacturing practice' shall mean the part of quality assurance which ensures that products are consistently produced and controlled to the quality standards appropriate to their intended use.

Article 3

By means of the repeated inspections referred to in Article 26 of Directive 75/319/EEC (*Article 34 of Directive 81/851/EEC*), the Member States shall ensure that manufacturers respect the principles and guidelines of good manufacturing practice laid down by this Directive.

For the interpretation of these principles and guidelines of good manufacturing practice, the manufacturers and the agents of the competent authorities shall refer to the detailed guidelines referred to in Article 19a of Directive 75/319/EEC (*Article 27a of Directive 81/851/EEC*). These detailed guidelines are published by the Commission in the *Guide to good manufacturing practice for medicinal products* and in its Annexes (Office for Official Publications of the European Communities, The rules governing medical products in the European Community, Volume IV).

Article 4

The manufacturer shall ensure that the manufacturing operations are carried out in accordance with good manufacturing practice and with the manufacturing authorisation.

For (*veterinary*) medicinal products imported from third countries, the importer shall ensure that the (*veterinary*) medicinal products have been manufactured by manufacturers duly authorised and conforming to good manufacturing practice standards, at least equivalent to those laid down by the Community.

Article 5

The manufacturer shall ensure that all manufacturing operations subject to an authorisation for marketing are carried out in accordance with the information given in the application for marketing authorisation as accepted by the competent authorities.

The manufacturer shall regularly review their manufacturing methods in the light of scientific and technical progress. When a modification to the marketing authorisation dossier is necessary, the application for modification must be submitted to the competent authorities.

CHAPTER II Principles and Guidelines of Good Manufacturing Practice

Article 6

Quality management

The manufacturer shall establish and implement an effective pharmaceutical quality assurance system, involving the active participation of the management and personnel of the different services involved.

Article 7

Personnel

1   At each manufacturing site, the manufacturer shall have competent and appropriately qualified personnel at his disposal in sufficient number to achieve the pharmaceutical quality assurance objective(s).

2   The duties of managerial and supervisory staff, including the qualified person(s), responsible for implementing and operating good manufacturing practice shall be defined in job descriptions. Their hierarchical relationships shall be defined in an organisation (*al*) chart. Organisation (*al*) charts and job descriptions shall be approved in accordance with the manufacturer's internal procedures.

3   Staff referred to in paragraph 2 shall be given sufficient authority to discharge (*carry out*) their responsibilities correctly.

4   Personnel shall receive initial and continuing training including the theory and application of the concept of quality assurance and good manufacturing practice.

5   Hygiene programmes adapted to the activities to be carried out shall be established and observed. These programmes include procedures relating to health, hygiene and clothing of personnel.

Article 8

Premises and equipment

1   Premises and manufacturing equipment shall be located, designed, constructed, adapted and maintained to suit the intended operations.

2   Lay out, design and operation must aim to minimise the risk of errors and permit effective cleaning and maintenance in order to avoid contamination, cross contamination and, in general, any adverse effect on the quality of the product.

3   Premises and equipment intended to be used for manufacturing operations which are critical for the quality of the products shall be subjected to appropriate qualification.

Article 9

Documentation

1   The manufacturer shall have a system of documentation based upon specifications, manufacturing formulae and processing and packaging instructions, procedures and records covering the various manufacturing operations that they perform. Documents shall be clear, free from errors and kept up to date. Pre-established procedures for general manufacturing operations and conditions shall be available, together with specific documents for the manufacture of each batch. This set of documents shall make it possible to trace the history of the manufacture of each batch. The batch documentation shall be retained for at least one year after the expiry date of the batches to which it relates or at least five years after the certification referred to in Article 22(2) of Directive 75/319/EEC *(Article 30(2) of Directive 81/851/EEC)* whichever is the longer.

2 When electronic, photographic or other data processing systems are used instead of written documents, the manufacturer shall have validated the systems by proving that the data will be appropriately stored during the anticipated period of storage. Data stored by these systems shall be made readily available in legible form. The electronically stored data shall be protected against loss or damage of data (e.g. by duplication or back-up and transfer onto another storage system).

Article 10

Production

The different production operations shall be carried out according to pre-established instructions and procedures and in accordance with good manufacturing practice. Adequate and sufficient resources shall be made available for the in-process controls.

Appropriate technical and/or organisational measures shall be taken to avoid cross contamination and mix-ups.

Any new manufacture or important modification of a manufacturing process shall be validated. Critical phases of manufacturing processes shall be regularly revalidated.

Article 11

Quality Control

1 The manufacturer shall establish and maintain a Quality Control department. This department shall be placed under the authority of a person having the required qualifications and shall be independent of the other departments.

2 The quality control department shall have at its disposal one or more quality control laboratories appropriately staffed and equipped to carry out the necessary examination and testing of starting materials, packaging materials and intermediate and finished products testing. Resorting to outside laboratories may be authorised in accordance with Article 12 of this Directive after the authorisation referred to in Article 5b of Directive 75/319/EEC (*Article 10(2) of Directive 81/851/EEC*) has been granted.

3 During the final control of finished products before their release for sale or distribution, in addition to analytical results, the quality control department shall take into account essential information such as the production conditions, the results of in-process controls, the examination of the manufacturing documents and the conformity of the products to their specifications (including the final finished pack).

4   Samples of each batch of finished products shall be retained for at least one year after the expiry date. Unless in the Member States (*State*) of manufacture a longer period is required, samples of starting materials (other than solvents, gases and water) used shall be retained for at least two years after the release of the product. This period may be shortened if their stability, as mentioned in the relevant specification, is shorter. All these samples shall be maintained at the disposal of the competent authorities.

For certain (*veterinary*) medicinal products manufactured individually or in small quantities, or when their storage could raise special problems, other sampling and retaining conditions may be defined in agreement with the competent authority.

Article 12

Work contracted out

1   Any manufacturing operation or operation linked with the manufacture which is carried out under contract, shall be the subject of a written contract between the contract giver and the contract acceptor.

2   The contract shall clearly define the responsibilities of each party and in particular the observance of good manufacturing practice by the contract acceptor and the manner in which the qualified person responsible for releasing each batch shall undertake his full responsibilities.

3   The contract acceptor shall not subcontract any of the work entrusted to him by the contract giver without the written authorisation of the contract giver.

4   The contract acceptor shall respect the principles and guidelines of good manufacturing practice and shall submit to inspections carried out by the competent authorities as provided for by Article 26 of Directive 75/319/EEC (*Article 34 of Directive 81/851/EEC*).

Article 13

Complaints and product recall

The manufacturer shall implement a system for recording and reviewing complaints together with an effective system for recalling promptly and at any time the (*veterinary*) medicinal products in the distribution network. Any complaint concerning a defect shall be recorded and investigated by the manufacturer. The competent authority shall be informed by the manufacturer of any defect that could result in a recall or abnormal restriction on the supply. In so far as possible, the countries of destination shall also be indicated.

Any recall shall be made in accordance with the requirements referred to in Article 33 of Directive 75/319/EEC (*Article 42 of Directive 81/851/EEC*).

Article 14

Self-inspection

The manufacturer shall conduct repeated self-inspections as part of the quality assurance system in order to monitor the implementation and respect of good manufacturing practice and to propose any necessary corrective measures. Records of such self-inspections and any subsequent (*further*) corrective action shall be maintained.

CHAPTER III   Final Provisions

Article 15

Member States shall bring into force the laws, regulations and administrative provision necessary to comply with this Directive not later than 1 January 1992 (*before 23 July 1993*). They shall forthwith inform the Commission thereof.

When Member States adopt these provisions, these shall contain a reference to this Directive or shall be accompanied by such reference at the time of their official publication. The procedure for such reference shall be adopted by Member States.

Article 16

This Directive is addressed to the Member States.

Done at Brussels, 13 June 1991 (*23 July 1991*).

EC Guide to Good Manufacturing Practice

Editor's note

The Foreword (below) to the EC guidance for GMP [1] was written by the Commission for the 1998 edition and is reproduced without change. Since then:

Article 16 of Directive 75/319/EEC has been replaced by Article 40 of Directive 2001/83/EC;

Article 24 of Directive 81/851/EEC has been replaced by Article 44 of Directive 2001/82/EC;

Annexes 1, 6 and 14 to the EC Guide to GMP have been revised. Annexes 15, 16, 17 and 18 have been added.

These revisions and additions have been included in this publication.

Annex 13 is currently undergoing revision.

Foreword

The pharmaceutical industry of the European Community maintains high standards of Quality Assurance in the development, manufacture and control of medicinal products. A system of marketing authorisations ensures that all medicinal products are assessed by a competent authority to ensure compliance with contemporary requirements of safety, quality and efficacy. A system of manufacturing authorisations ensures that all products authorised on the European market are manufactured only by authorised manufacturers, whose activities are regularly inspected by the competent authorities. Manufacturing authorisations are required by all pharmaceutical manufacturers in the European Community whether the products are sold within or outside the Community.

Two directives laying down principles and guidelines of Good Manufacturing Practice (GMP) for medicinal products were adopted by the Commission in 1991, the first for medicinal products for human use (Directive 91/356/EEC), the second one for veterinary use (Directive 91/412/EEC). Detailed guidelines in accordance with those principles are published in the Guide to Good Manufacturing Practice[1] which will be used in assessing applications for manufacturing authorisations and as a basis for inspection of manufacturers of medicinal products.

The principles of GMP and the detailed guidelines are applicable to all operations which require the authorisation referred to in Article 16 of Directive 75/319/EEC and in Article 24 of Directive 81/851/EEC as modified. They are also relevant for all other large scale pharmaceutical manufacturing processes, such as that undertaken in hospitals, for the preparation of products for use in clinical trials, and for wholesaling, where applicable.

All Member States and the industry itself are agreed that GMP requirements applicable to the manufacture of veterinary medicinal products are the same as those applicable to the manufacture of medicinal products for human use. Certain detailed adjustments to the GMP guidelines are set out in two annexes specific to veterinary medicinal products and to immunological veterinary medicinal products.

This Guide is presented in chapters, each headed by a principle. Chapter 1 on Quality Management outlines the fundamental concept of Quality Assurance as applied to the manufacture of medicinal products. Thereafter each chapter has a principle outlining the Quality Assurance objectives of that chapter and a text which provides sufficient detail for manufacturers to be made aware of the essential matters to be considered when implementing the principle.

In addition to the general matters of GMP outlined in the nine chapters of this Guide, a series of annexes providing detail about specific areas of activity is included. For some manufacturing processes, different annexes will apply simultaneously (e.g. annex on sterile preparations and on radiopharmaceuticals and/or on biological medicinal products).

A glossary of some terms used in the Guide has been incorporated after the annexes.

The first edition of the Guide was published in 1989, including an annex on the manufacture of sterile medicinal products.

Neither the basic requirements nor this first annex have been modified in this new issue and manufacturers should come into compliance with their provisions by at least 1 January 1992. Nine additional annexes on the manufacture of medicinal products intended for human use have been included in this second edition.

They were adopted in 1991, and, although they were widely circulated before their adoption, it was agreed that manufacturers would have until 1 January 1993 to comply with their provisions. Directive 91/412/EEC on GMP for veterinary medicinal products comes into force on 23 July 1993, and manufacturers of veterinary medicinal products should comply with the provisions of the Guide, including two new annexes on veterinary medicinal products, not later than this date.

With regard to the manufacture of active ingredients, it was agreed that the Guideline for the manufacture of active pharmaceutical ingredients published by the Pharmaceutical Inspection Convention on 6 June 1987 would be an appropriate reference for manufacturers and a basis for inspection by competent authorities (available from the EFTA Secretariat, Geneva).

The Guide is not intended to cover security aspects for the personnel engaged in manufacture. This may be particularly important in the manufacture of certain medicinal product such as highly active, biological and radioactive medicinal products, but they are governed by other provisions of Community or national law.

Throughout the Guide it is assumed that the requirements of the marketing authorisation relating to the safety, quality and efficacy of the products, are systematically incorporated into all the manufacturing, control and release for sale arrangements of the holder of the manufacturing authorisation.

The Guide has been written with the intention that it should replace national guidelines or other relevant GMP requirements.

It is recognised that there are acceptable methods, other than those described in the Guide, which are capable of achieving the principles of Quality Assurance. The Guide is not intended to place any restraint upon the development of any new concepts or new technologies which have been validated and which provide a level of Quality Assurance at least equivalent to those set out in this Guide.

It will be regularly revised.

---

(1)   COMMISSION OF THE EUROPEAN COMMUNITIES.
      The rules governing medicinal products in the EC. Vol IV.
      Good Manufacturing Practice for medicinal products. Luxembourg:
      Office for Official Publications of the EC, 1998. ISBN 92-828-2029-X.

Contents

1 Quality Management

Principle

The holder of a manufacturing authorisation must manufacture medicinal products so as to ensure that they are fit for their intended use, comply with the requirements of the marketing authorisation and do not place patients at risk due to inadequate safety, quality or efficacy. The attainment of this quality objective is the responsibility of senior management and requires the participation and commitment by staff in many different departments and at all levels within the company, by the company's suppliers and by the distributors. To achieve the quality objective reliably there must be a comprehensively designed and correctly implemented system of Quality Assurance (QA) incorporating Good Manufacturing Practice (GMP) and thus Quality Control (QC). It should be fully documented and its effectiveness monitored. All parts of the QA system should be adequately resourced with competent personnel, and suitable and sufficient premises, equipment and facilities. There are additional legal responsibilities for the holder of the manufacturing authorisation and for the Qualified Person(s) (QP).

1.1   The basic concepts of QA, GMP and QC are inter-related. They are described here in order to emphasise their relationships and their fundamental importance to the production and control of medicinal products.

Quality Assurance (QA)

1.2   QA is a wide ranging concept which covers all matters which individually or collectively influence the quality of the product. It is the sum total of the organised arrangements made with the object of ensuring that medicinal products are of the quality required for their intended use. QA therefore incorporates GMP plus other factors outside the scope of this Guide.

The system of QA appropriate for the manufacture of medicinal products should ensure that:

(i)   Medicinal products are designed and developed in a way that takes account of the requirements of GMP and Good Laboratory Practice (GLP).

(ii)   Production and control operations are clearly specified and GMP adopted.

(iii)   Managerial responsibilities are clearly specified.

(iv)   Arrangements are made for the manufacture, supply and use of the correct starting and packaging arrangements.

(v)   All necessary controls on intermediate products, and any other in-process controls and validations are carried out.

(vi)   The finished product is correctly processed and checked, according to the defined procedures.

(vii)   Medicinal products are not sold or supplied before a QP has certified that each production batch has been produced and controlled in accordance with the requirements of the marketing authorisation and any other regulations relevant to the production, control and release of medicinal products.

(viii)   Satisfactory arrangements exist to ensure, as far as possible, that the medicinal products are stored, distributed and subsequently handled so that quality is maintained throughout their shelf life.

(ix)   There is a procedure for self-inspection and/or quality audit which regularly appraises the effectiveness and applicability of the QA system.

Good Manufacturing Practice for medicinal products (GMP)

1.3   GMP is that part of QA which ensures that products are consistently produced and controlled to the quality standards appropriate to their intended use and as required by the marketing authorisation or product specification.

GMP is concerned with both production and QC. The basic requirements of GMP are that:

(i)   All manufacturing processes are clearly defined, systematically reviewed in the light of experience and shown to be capable of consistently manufacturing medicinal products of the required quality and complying with their specifications.

(ii)   Critical steps of manufacturing processes and significant changes to the process are validated.

(iii)   All necessary facilities for GMP are provided including:

.   (a)   appropriately qualified and trained personnel;

(b)   adequate premises and space;

(c)   suitable equipment and services;

(d)   correct materials, containers and labels;

(e)   approved procedures and instructions;

(f)   suitable storage and transport.

(iv)   Instructions and procedures are written in an instructional form in clear and unambiguous language, specifically applicable to the facilities provided.

(v)   Operators are trained to carry out procedures correctly.

(vi)   Records are made, manually and/or by recording instruments, during manufacture which demonstrate that all steps required by the defined procedures and instructions were in fact taken and that the quantity and quality of the product was as expected. Any significant deviations are fully recorded and investigated.

(vii) Records of manufacture including distribution which enable the complete history of a batch to be traced, are retained in a comprehensible and accessible form.

(viii) The distribution (wholesaling) of the products minimises any risk to their quality.

(ix)   A system is available to recall any batch of product, from sale or supply.

(x)   Complaints about marketed products are examined, the cause of quality defects investigated and appropriate measures taken in respect of the defective products and to prevent reoccurrence.

Quality Control (QC)

1.4   QC is that part of GMP which is concerned with sampling, specifications and testing, and with the organisation, documentation and release procedures which ensure that the necessary and relevant tests are actually carried out and that materials are not released for use, nor products released for sale or supply, until their quality has been judged to be satisfactory.

The basic requirements of QC are that:

(i)   Adequate facilities, trained personnel and approved procedures are available for sampling, inspecting and testing starting materials, packaging materials, intermediate, bulk and finished products, and, where appropriate, for monitoring environmental conditions for GMP purposes.

(ii)   Samples of starting materials, packaging materials, intermediate products, bulk products and finished products are taken by personnel and by methods approved by QC.

(iii) Test methods are validated.

(iv)   Records are made, manually and/or by recording instruments, which demonstrate that all the required sampling, inspecting and testing procedures were actually carried out. Any deviations are fully recorded and investigated.

(v)   The finished products contain active ingredients complying with the qualitative and quantitative composition of the marketing authorisation, are of the purity required, and are enclosed within their proper containers and correctly labelled.

(vi)   Records are made of the results of inspection and that testing of materials, intermediate, bulk and finished products is formally assessed against specification. Product assessment includes a review and evaluation of relevant production documentation and an assessment of deviations from specified procedures.

(vii)   No batch of product is released for sale or supply, prior to certification by a QP that it is in accordance with the requirements of the marketing authorisation.

(viii) Sufficient reference samples of starting materials and products are retained to permit future examination of the product if necessary and that the product is retained in its final pack unless exceptionally large packs are produced.

2 Personnel

Principle

The establishment and maintenance of a satisfactory system of Quality Assurance (QA) and the correct manufacture of medicinal products relies upon people. For this reason there must be sufficient qualified personnel to carry out all the tasks which are the responsibility of the manufacturer. Individual responsibilities should be clearly understood by the individuals and recorded. All personnel should be aware of the principles of Good Manufacturing Practice (GMP) that affect them and receive initial and continuing training, including hygiene instructions, relevant to their needs.

General

2.1 The manufacturer should have an adequate number of personnel with the necessary qualifications and practical experience. The responsibilities placed on any one individual should not be so extensive as to present any risk to quality.

2.2 The manufacturer must have an organisation chart. People in responsible positions should have specific duties recorded in written job descriptions and adequate authority to carry out their responsibilities. Their duties may be delegated to designated deputies of a satisfactory qualification level. There should be no gaps or unexplained overlaps in the responsibilities of those personnel concerned with the application of GMP.

Key personnel

2.3 Key personnel include the Head of Production, the Head of Quality Control (QC) and if at least one of these persons is not responsible for the duties described in Article 22 of Directive 75/319/EEC, the Qualified Person(s) (QP) designated for the purpose. Normally key posts should be occupied by full time personnel. The Heads of Production and QC must be independent from each other. In large organisations, it may be necessary to delegate some of the functions listed in 2.5, 2.6 and 2.7.

2.4 The duties of the QP(s) are fully described in Article 22 of Directive 75/319/EEC, and can be summarised as follows:

(a) For medicinal products manufactured within the European Community, a QP must ensure that each batch has been produced and tested/checked in accordance with the directives and the marketing authorisation[1].

(b) For medicinal products manufactured outside the European Community, a QP must ensure that each imported batch has undergone, in the importing country, the testing specified in paragraph 1 (b) of Article 22.

(c) A QP must certify in a register or equivalent document, as operations are carried out and before any release, that each production batch satisfies the provisions of Article 22.

The persons responsible for these duties must meet the qualification requirements laid down in Article 23 of the same Directive, they shall be permanently and continuously at the disposal of the holder of the manufacturing authorisation to carry out their responsibilities. Their responsibilities may be delegated, but only to other QP(s).

2.5 The Head of the Production Department generally has the following responsibilities:

(i) To ensure that products are produced and stored according to the appropriate documentation in order to obtain the required quality.

(ii) To approve the instructions relating to production operations and to ensure their strict implementation.

(iii) To ensure that the production records are evaluated and signed by an authorised person before they are sent to the QC Department.

(iv) To check the maintenance of his department, premises and equipment.

(v) To ensure that the appropriate validations are done.

(vi) To ensure that the required initial and continuing training of his department personnel is carried out and adapted according to need.

2.6 The Head of the QC Department generally has the following responsibilities:

(i) To approve or reject, as he sees fit, starting materials, packaging materials, and intermediate, bulk and finished products.

(ii) To evaluate batch records.

(iii) To ensure that all necessary testing is carried out.

(iv) To approve specifications, sampling instructions, test methods and other QC procedures.

(v) To approve and monitor any contract analysts.

(vi) To check the maintenance of his department, premises and equipment.

(vii) To ensure that the appropriate validations are done.

(viii) To ensure that the required initial and continuing training of his department personnel is carried out and adapted according to need.

Other duties of the QC Department are summarised in Chapter 6.

2.7 The Heads of Production and QC generally have some shared, or jointly exercised, responsibilities relating to quality. These may include, subject to any national regulations:

- The authorisation of written procedures and other documents, including amendments;

- The monitoring and control of the manufacturing environment;

- Plant hygiene;

- Process validation;

- Training;

- The approval and monitoring of suppliers of materials;

- The approval and monitoring of contract manufacturers;

- The designation and monitoring of storage conditions for materials and products;

- The retention of records;

- The monitoring of compliance with the requirements of GMP;

- The inspection, investigation, and taking of samples, in order to monitor factors which may affect product quality.

Training

2.8 The manufacturer should provide training for all the personnel whose duties take them into production areas or into control laboratories (including the technical, maintenance and cleaning personnel), and for other personnel whose activities could affect the quality of the product.

2.9 Besides the basic training on the theory and practice of GMP, newly recruited personnel should receive training appropriate to the duties assigned to them. Continuing training should also be given, and its practical effectiveness should be periodically assessed. Training programmes should be available, approved by either the Head of Production or the Head of QC, as appropriate. Training records should be kept.

2.10 Personnel working in areas where contamination is a hazard, e.g. clean areas or areas where highly active, toxic, infectious or sensitising materials are handled, should be given specific training.

2.11 Visitors or untrained personnel should, preferably, not be taken into the production and QC areas. If this is unavoidable, they should be given information in advance, particularly about personal hygiene and the prescribed protective clothing. They should be closely supervised.

2.12 The concept of QA and all the measures capable of improving its understanding and implementation should be fully discussed during the training sessions.

Personnel hygiene

2.13 Detailed hygiene programmes should be established and adapted to the different needs within the factory. They should include procedures relating to the health, hygiene practices and clothing of personnel. These procedures should be understood and followed in a very strict way by every person whose duties take him into production and control areas. Hygiene programmes should be promoted by management and widely discussed during training sessions.

2.14 All personnel should receive medical examination upon recruitment. It must be the manufacturer's responsibility that there are instructions ensuring that health conditions that can be of relevance to the quality of products come to the manufacturer's knowledge. After the first medical examination, examinations should be carried out when necessary for the work and personal health.

2.15 Steps should be taken to ensure as far as is practicable that no person affected by an infectious disease or having open lesions on the exposed surface of the body is engaged in the manufacture of medicinal products.

2.16 Every person entering the manufacturing areas should wear protective garments appropriate to the operations to be carried out.

2.17 Eating, drinking, chewing or smoking, or the storage of food, drink, smoking materials or personal medication in the production and storage areas should be prohibited. In general, any unhygienic practice within the manufacturing areas or in any other area where the product might be adversely affected, should be forbidden.

2.18   Direct contact should be avoided between the operator's hands and the exposed product as well as with any part of the equipment that comes into contact with the products.

2.19   Personnel should be instructed to use the hand-washing facilities.

2.20   Any specific requirements for the manufacture of special groups, e.g. sterile preparations, are covered in the annexes.

---

(1)   According to Directive 75/319/EEC and the Ruling (Case 247/81) of the Court of Justice of the European Communities, medicinal products which have been properly controlled in the EEC by a QP do not have to be recontrolled or rechecked in any other Member State of the Community.

3 Premises and Equipment

Principle

Premises and equipment must be located, designed, constructed, adapted and maintained to suit the operations to be carried out. Their layout and design must aim to minimise the risk of errors and permit effective cleaning and maintenance in order to avoid cross-contamination, build up of dust or dirt and, in general, any adverse effect on the quality of products.

Premises

General

3.1   Premises should be situated in an environment which, when considered together with measures to protect the manufacture, presents minimal risk of causing contamination of materials or products.

3.2   Premises should be carefully maintained, ensuring that repair and maintenance operations do not present any hazard to the quality of products. They should be cleaned and, where applicable, disinfected according to detailed written procedures.

3.3   Lighting, temperature, humidity and ventilation should be appropriate and such that they do not adversely affect, directly or indirectly, either the medicinal products during their manufacture and storage, or the accurate functioning of equipment.

3.4   Premises should be designed and equipped so as to afford maximum protection against the entry of insects or other animals.

3.5   Steps should be taken in order to prevent the entry of unauthorised people. Production, storage and Quality Control (QC) areas should not be used as a right of way by personnel who do not work in them.

Production area

3.6   In order to minimise the risk of a serious medical hazard due to cross-contamination, dedicated and self-contained facilities must be available for the production of particular medicinal products, such as highly sensitising materials (e.g. penicillins) or biological preparations (e.g. from live microorganisms). The production of certain additional products, such as certain antibiotics, certain hormones, certain cytotoxics, certain highly active drugs and non-medicinal products should not be conducted in the same facilities. For those products, in exceptional cases, the principle of campaign working in the same facilities can be accepted provided that specific precautions are taken and the necessary validations are made. The manufacture of technical poisons, such as pesticides and herbicides, should not be allowed in premises used for the manufacture of medicinal products.

3.7   Premises should preferably be laid out in such a way as to allow the production to take place in areas connected in a logical order corresponding to the sequence of the operations and to the requisite cleanliness levels.

3.8   The adequacy of the working and in-process storage space should permit the orderly and logical positioning of equipment and materials so as to minimise the risk of confusion between different medicinal products or their components, to avoid cross-contamination and to minimise the risk of omission or wrong application of any of the manufacturing or control steps.

3.9   Where starting and primary packaging materials, intermediate or bulk products are exposed to the environment, interior surfaces (walls, floors and ceilings) should be smooth, free from cracks and open joints, and should not shed particulate matter and should permit easy and effective cleaning and, if necessary, disinfection.

3.10   Pipework, light fittings, ventilation points and other services should be designed and sited to avoid the creation of recesses which are difficult to clean. As far as possible, for maintenance purposes, they should be accessible from outside the manufacturing areas.

3.11   Drains should be of adequate size, and have trapped gullies. Open channels should be avoided where possible, but if necessary, they should be shallow to facilitate cleaning and disinfection.

3.12   Production areas should be effectively ventilated, with air control facilities (including temperature and, where necessary, humidity and filtration) appropriate both to the products handled, to the operations undertaken within them and to the external environment.

3.13   Weighing of starting materials usually should be carried out in a separate weighing room designed for that use.

3.14   In cases where dust is generated (e.g. during sampling, weighing, mixing and processing operations, packaging of dry products), specific provisions should be taken to avoid cross-contamination and facilitate cleaning.

3.15   Premises for the packaging of medicinal products should be specifically designed and laid out so as to avoid mix-ups or cross-contamination.

3.16   Production areas should be well lit, particularly where visual on-line controls are carried out.

3.17   In-process controls may be carried out within the production area provided they do not carry any risk for the production.

Storage areas

3.18   Storage areas should be of sufficient capacity to allow orderly storage of the various categories of materials and products: starting and packaging materials, intermediate, bulk and finished products, products in quarantine, released, rejected, returned or recalled.

3.19   Storage areas should be designed or adapted to ensure good storage conditions. In particular, they should be clean and dry and maintained within acceptable temperature limits. Where special storage conditions are required (e.g. temperature, humidity) these should be provided, checked and monitored.

3.20   Receiving and dispatch bays should protect materials and products from the weather. Reception areas should be designed and equipped to allow containers of incoming materials to be cleaned where necessary before storage.

3.21   Where quarantine status is ensured by storage in separate areas, these areas must be clearly marked and their access restricted to authorised personnel. Any system replacing the physical quarantine should give equivalent security.

3.22   There should normally be a separate sampling area for starting materials. If sampling is performed in the storage area, it should be conducted in such a way as to prevent contamination or cross-contamination.

3.23   Segregated areas should be provided for the storage of rejected, recalled or returned materials or products.

3.24   Highly active materials or products should be stored in safe and secure areas.

3.25   Printed packaging materials are considered critical to the conformity of the medicinal product and special attention should be paid to the safe and secure storage of these materials.

Quality Control (QC) areas

3.26   Normally, QC laboratories should be separated from production areas. This is particularly important for laboratories for the control of biologicals, microbiologicals and radioisotopes, which should also be separated from each other.

3.27   Control laboratories should be designed to suit the operations to be carried out in them. Sufficient space should be given to avoid mix-ups and cross-contamination. There should be adequate suitable storage space for samples and records.

3.28   Separate rooms may be necessary to protect sensitive instruments from vibration, electrical interference, humidity etc.

3.29   Special requirements are needed in laboratories handling particular substances, such as biological or radioactive samples.

Ancillary areas

3.30   Rest and refreshment rooms should be separate from other areas.

3.31   Facilities for changing clothes, and for washing and toilet purposes should be easily accessible and appropriate for the number of users. Toilets should not directly communicate with production or storage areas.

3.32   Maintenance workshops should as far as possible be separate from production areas. Whenever parts and tools are stored in the production area, they should be kept in rooms or lockers reserved for that use.

3.33   Animal houses should be well isolated from other areas, with separate entrance (animal access) and air handling facilities.

Equipment

3.34   Manufacturing equipment should be designed, located and maintained to suit its intended purpose.

3.35   Repair and maintenance operations should not present any hazard to the quality of the products.

3.36   Manufacturing equipment should be designed so that it can be easily and thoroughly cleaned. It should be cleaned according to detailed and written procedures and stored only in a clean and dry condition.

3.37   Washing and cleaning equipment should be chosen and used in order not to be a source of contamination.

3.38   Equipment should be installed in such a way as to prevent any risk of error or of contamination.

3.39   Production equipment should not present any hazard to the products. The parts of the production equipment that come into contact with the product must not be reactive, additive or absorptive to such an extent that it will affect the quality of the product and thus present any hazard.

3.40   Balances and measuring equipment of an appropriate range and precision should be available for production and control operations.

3.41   Measuring, weighing, recording and control equipment should be calibrated and checked at defined intervals by appropriate methods. Adequate records of such tests should be maintained.

3.42   Fixed pipework should be clearly labelled to indicate the contents and, where applicable, the direction of flow.

3.43   Distilled, deionised and, where appropriate, other water pipes should be sanitised according to written procedures that detail the action limits for microbiological contamination and the measures to be taken.

3.44   Defective equipment should, if possible, be removed from production and QC areas, or at least be clearly labelled as defective.

4 Documentation

Principle

Good documentation constitutes an essential part of the Quality Assurance (QA) system. Clearly written documentation prevents errors from spoken communication and permits tracing of batch history. Specifications, manufacturing formulae and instructions, procedures, and records must be free from errors and available in writing. The legibility of documents is of paramount importance.

General

4.1 *Specifications* describe in detail the requirement with which the products or materials used or obtained during manufacture have to conform. They serve as a basis for quality evaluation.

Manufacturing formula, processing and packaging instructions state all the starting materials used and lay down all processing and packaging operations.

Procedures give directions for performing certain operations, e.g. cleaning, clothing, environmental control, sampling, testing, equipment operation.

Records provide a history of each batch of product, including its distribution, and also of all other relevant circumstances pertinent to the quality of the final product.

4.2 Documents should be designed, prepared, reviewed and distributed with care. They should comply with the relevant parts of the manufacturing and marketing authorisation dossiers.

4.3 Documents should be approved, signed and dated by appropriate and authorised persons.

4.4 Documents should have unambiguous contents; title, nature and purpose should be clearly stated. They should be laid out in an orderly fashion and be easy to check. Reproduced documents should be clear and legible. The reproduction of working documents from master documents must not allow any error to be introduced through the reproduction process.

4.5 Documents should be regularly reviewed and kept up-to-date. When a document has been revised, systems should be operated to prevent inadvertent use of superseded documents.

4.6 Documents should not be handwritten; although, where documents require the entry of data, these entries may be made in clear, legible, indelible handwriting. Sufficient space should be provided for such entries.

4.7 Any alteration made to the entry on a document should be signed and dated; the alteration should permit the reading of the original information. Where appropriate, the reason for the alteration should be recorded.

4.8 The records should be made or completed at the time each action is taken and in such a way that all significant activities concerning the manufacture of medicinal products are traceable. They should be retained for at least one year after the expiry date of the finished product.

4.9 Data may be recorded by electronic data processing systems, photographic or other reliable means, but detailed procedures relating to the system in use should be available and the accuracy of the records should be checked. If documentation is handled by electronic data processing methods, only authorised persons should be able to enter or modify data in the computer and there should be a record of changes and deletions; access should be restricted by passwords or other means and the result of entry of critical data should be independently checked. Batch records electronically stored should be protected by back-up transfer on magnetic tape, microfilm, paper or other means. It is particularly important that the data are readily available throughout the period of retention.

Documents required

4.10 *Specifications*

There should be appropriately authorised and dated specifications for starting and packaging materials and finished products; where appropriate, they should be also available for intermediate or bulk products.

Specifications for starting and packaging materials

4.11 Specifications for starting and primary or printed packaging materials should include, if applicable:

(a) A description of the materials, including:

- the designated name and the internal code reference;
- the reference, if any, to a pharmacopoeial monograph;

- the approved suppliers and, if possible, the original producer of the products;

- specimen of printed materials.

(b) Directions for sampling and testing or reference to procedures.

(c) Qualitative and quantitative requirements with acceptance limits.

(d) Storage conditions and precautions.

(e) The maximum period of storage before re-examination.

Specifications for intermediate and bulk products

4.12 Specifications for intermediate and bulk products should be available if these are purchased or dispatched, or if data obtained from intermediate products are used for the evaluation of the finished product. The specifications should be similar to specifications for starting materials or for finished products, as appropriate.

Specifications for finished products

4.13 Specifications for finished products should include:

(a) The designated name of the product and the code reference where applicable.

(b) The formula or a reference to.

(c) A description of the pharmaceutical form and package details.

(d) Directions for sampling and testing or a reference to procedures.

(e) The qualitative and quantitative requirements, with the acceptance limits.

(f) The storage conditions and any handling precautions, where applicable.

(g) The shelf life.

Manufacturing formula and processing instructions

Formally authorised manufacturing formula and processing instructions should exist for each product and batch size to be manufactured. They are often combined in one document.

4.14 The manufacturing formula should include:

(a) The name of the product, with a product reference code relating to its specification.

(b) A description of the pharmaceutical form, strength of the product and batch size.

(c)   A list of all starting materials to be used, with the amount of each, described using the designated name and a reference which is unique to that material; mention should be made of any substance that may disappear in the course of processing.

(d)   A statement of the expected final yield with the acceptable limits, and of relevant intermediate yields, where applicable.

4.15   The processing instructions should include:

(a)   A statement of the processing location and the principal equipment to be used.

(b)   The methods, or reference to the methods, to be used for preparing the critical equipment (e.g. cleaning, assembling, calibrating, sterilising).

(c)   Detailed stepwise processing instructions (e.g. checks on materials, pretreatments, sequence for adding materials, mixing times, temperatures).

(d)   The instructions for any in-process controls with their limits.

(e)   Where necessary, the requirements for bulk storage of the products, including the container, labelling and special storage conditions where applicable.

(f)   Any special precautions to be observed.

Packaging instructions

4.16   There should be formally authorised packaging instructions for each product, pack size and type. These should normally include, or have a reference to, the following:

(a)   Name of the product.

(b)   Description of its pharmaceutical form, and strength where applicable.

(c)   The pack size expressed in terms of the number, weight or volume of the product in the final container.

(d)   A complete list of all the packaging materials required for a standard batch size, including quantities, sizes and types, with the code or reference number relating to the specifications of each packaging material.

(e)   Where appropriate, an example or reproduction of the relevant printed packaging materials, and specimens indicating where to apply batch number references, and shelf life of the product.

(f)   Special precautions to be observed, including a careful examination of the area and equipment in order to ascertain the line clearance before operations begin.

(g) A description of the packaging operation, including any significant subsidiary operations, and equipment to be used.

(h) Details of in-process controls with instructions for sampling and acceptance limits.

Batch processing records

4.17 A batch processing record should be kept for each batch processed. It should be based on the relevant parts of the currently approved manufacturing formula and processing instructions. The method of preparation of such records should be designed to avoid transcription errors. The record should carry the number of the batch being manufactured.

Before any processing begins, there should be recorded checks that the equipment and work station are clear of previous products, documents or materials not required for the planned process, and that equipment is clean and suitable for use.

During processing, the following information should be recorded at the time each action is taken and, after completion, the record should be dated and signed in agreement by the person responsible for the processing operations:

(a) The name of the product.

(b) Dates and times of commencement of significant intermediate stages and of completion of production.

(c) Name of the person responsible for each stage of production.

(d) Initials of the operator of different significant steps of production and, where appropriate, of the person who checked each of these operations (e.g. weighing).

(e) The batch number and/or analytical control number as well as the quantities of each starting material actually weighed (including the batch number and amount of any recovered or reprocessed material added).

(f) Any relevant processing operation or event and major equipment used.

(g) A record of the in-process controls and the initials of the person(s) carrying them out, and the results obtained.

(h) The product yield obtained at different and pertinent stages of manufacture.

(i) Notes on special problems including details, with signed authorisation for any deviation from the manufacturing formula and processing instructions.

Batch packaging records

4.18   A batch packaging record should be kept for each batch or part batch processed. It should be based on the relevant parts of the packaging instructions and the method of preparation of such records should be designed to avoid transcription errors. The record should carry the batch number and the quantity of bulk product to be packed, as well as the batch number and the planned quantity of finished product that will be obtained.

Before any packaging operation begins, there should be recorded checks that the equipment and work station are clear of previous products, documents or materials not required for the planned packaging operations, and that equipment is clean and suitable for use.

The following information should be entered at the time each action is taken and, after completion, the record should be dated and signed in agreement by the person(s) responsible for the packaging operations:

(a)   The name of the product.

(b)   The date(s) and times of the packaging operations.

(c)   The name of the Responsible Person carrying out the packaging operation.

(d)   The initials of the operators of the different significant steps.

(e)   Records of checks for identity and conformity with the packaging instructions including the results of in-process controls.

(f)   Details of the packaging operations carried out, including references to equipment and the packaging lines used.

(g)   Whenever possible, samples of printed packaging materials used, including specimens of the batch coding, expiry dating and any additional overprinting.

(h)   Notes on any special problems or unusual events including details, with signed authorisation for any deviation from the manufacturing formula and processing instructions.

(i)   The quantities and reference number or identification of all printed packaging materials and bulk product issued, used, destroyed or returned to stock and the quantities of obtained product, in order to provide for an adequate reconciliation.

Procedures and records

Receipt

4.19   There should be written procedures and records for the receipt of each delivery of each starting and primary and printed packaging material.

4.20   The records of the receipts should include:

   (a)   The name of the material on the delivery note and the containers;

   (b)   The in-house name and/or code of material (if different from (a));

   (c)   Date of receipt;

   (d)   Supplier's name and, if possible, manufacturer's name;

   (e)   Manufacturer's batch or reference number;

   (f)   Total quantity, and number of containers received;

   (g)   The batch number assigned after receipt;

   (h)   Any relevant comment (e.g. state of the containers).

4.21   There should be written procedures for the internal labelling, quarantine and storage of starting materials, packaging materials and other materials, as appropriate.

Sampling

4.22   There should be written procedures for sampling, which include the person(s) authorised to take samples, the methods and equipment to be used, the amounts to be taken and any precautions to be observed to avoid contamination of the material or any deterioration in its quality (see Chapter 6: **Quality Control**, paragraph 13).

Testing

4.23   There should be written procedures for testing materials and products at different stages of manufacture, describing the methods and equipment to be used. The tests performed should be recorded (see Chapter 6: **Quality Control**, paragraph 17).

Other

4.24   Written release and rejection procedures should be available for materials and products, and in particular for the release for sale of the finished product by the Qualified Person(s) (QP) in accordance with the requirements of Article 22 of Directive 75/319/EEC.

4.25   Records should be maintained of the distribution of each batch of a product in order to facilitate the recall of the batch if necessary (see Chapter 8: **Complaints and product recall**).

4.26   There should be written procedures and the associated records of actions taken or conclusions reached, where appropriate, for:

   •   Validation;

   •   Equipment assembly and calibration;

- Maintenance, cleaning and sanitisation;
- Personnel matters including training, clothing, hygiene;
- Environmental monitoring;
- Pest control;
- Complaints;
- Recalls;
- Returns.

4.27 Clear operating procedures should be available for major items of manufacturing and test equipment.

4.28 Log books should be kept for major or critical equipment recording, as appropriate, any validations, calibrations, maintenance, cleaning or repair operations, including the dates and identity of people who carried these operations out.

4.29 Log books should also record in chronological order the use of major or critical equipment and the areas where the products have been processed.

5   Production

Principle

Production operations must follow clearly defined procedures; they must comply with the principles of Good Manufacturing Practice (GMP) in order to obtain products of the requisite quality and be in accordance with the relevant manufacturing and marketing authorisations.

General

5.1   Production should be performed and supervised by competent people.

5.2   All handling of materials and products, such as receipt and quarantine, sampling, storage, labelling, dispensing, processing, packaging and distribution should be done in accordance with written procedures or instructions and, where necessary, recorded.

5.3   All incoming materials should be checked to ensure that the consignment corresponds to the order. Containers should be cleaned where necessary and labelled with the prescribed data.

5.4   Damage to containers and any other problem which might adversely affect the quality of a material should be investigated, recorded and reported to the Quality Control (QC) Department.

5.5   Incoming materials and finished products should be physically or administratively quarantined immediately after receipt or processing, until they have been released for use or distribution.

5.6   Intermediate and bulk products purchased as such should be handled on receipt as though they were starting materials.

5.7   All materials and products should be stored under the appropriate conditions established by the manufacturer and in an orderly fashion to permit batch segregation and stock rotation.

5.8   Checks on yields, and reconciliation of quantities, should be carried out as necessary to ensure that there are no discrepancies outside acceptable limits.

5.9 Operations on different products should not be carried out simultaneously or consecutively in the same room unless there is no risk of mix-up or cross-contamination.

5.10 At every stage of processing, products and materials should be protected from microbial and other contamination.

5.11 When working with dry materials and products, special precautions should be taken to prevent the generation and dissemination of dust. This applies particularly to the handling of highly active or sensitising materials.

5.12 At all times during processing, all materials, bulk containers, major items of equipment and, where appropriate, rooms used should be labelled or otherwise identified with an indication of the product or material being processed, its strength (where applicable) and batch number. Where applicable, this indication should also mention the stage of production.

5.13 Labels applied to containers, equipment or premises should be clear, unambiguous and in the company's agreed format. It is often helpful in addition to the wording on the labels to use colours to indicate status (e.g. quarantined, accepted, rejected, clean etc.).

5.14 Checks should be carried out to ensure that pipelines and other pieces of equipment used for the transportation of products from one area to another are connected in a correct manner.

5.15 Any deviation from instructions or procedures should be avoided as far as possible. If a deviation occurs, it should be approved in writing by a competent person, with the involvement of the QC Department when appropriate.

5.16 Access to production premises should be restricted to authorised personnel.

5.17 Normally, the production of non-medicinal products should be avoided in areas and with the equipment destined for the production of medicinal products.

Prevention of cross-contamination in production

5.18 Contamination of a starting material or of a product by another material or product must be avoided. This risk of accidental cross-contamination arises from the uncontrolled release of dust, gases, vapours, sprays or organisms from materials and products in-process, from residues on equipment, and from operators' clothing. The significance of this risk varies with the type of contaminant and of product being contaminated. Amongst the most hazardous contaminants are highly sensitising materials, biological preparations containing living organisms, certain hormones, cytotoxics and other highly active materials. Products in which contamination is likely to be most significant are those administered by injection, those given in large doses and/or over a long time.

5.19 Cross-contamination should be avoided by appropriate technical or organisational measures, for example:

(a) Production in segregated areas (required for products such as penicillins, live vaccines, live bacterial preparations and some other biologicals), or by campaign (separation in time) followed by appropriate cleaning;

(b) Providing appropriate air locks and air extraction;

(c) Minimising the risk of contamination caused by recirculation or re-entry of untreated or insufficiently treated air;

(d) Keeping protective clothing inside areas where products with special risk of cross-contamination are processed;

(e) Using cleaning and decontamination procedures of known effectiveness, as ineffective cleaning of equipment is a common source of cross-contamination;

(f) Using 'closed systems' of production;

(g) Testing for residues and use of cleaning status labels on equipment.

5.20 Measures to prevent cross-contamination and their effectiveness should be checked periodically according to set procedures.

Validation

5.21 Validation studies should reinforce GMP and be conducted in accordance with defined procedures. Results and conclusions should be recorded.

5.22 When any new manufacturing formula or method of preparation is adopted, steps should be taken to demonstrate its suitability for routine processing. The defined process, using the materials and equipment specified, should be shown to yield a product consistently of the required quality.

5.23 Significant amendments to the manufacturing process, including any change in equipment or materials, which may affect product quality and/or the reproducibility of the process should be validated.

5.24 Processes and procedures should undergo periodic critical re-validation to ensure that they remain capable of achieving the intended results.

Starting materials

5.25 The purchase of starting materials is an important operation which should involve staff who have a particular and thorough knowledge of the suppliers.

5.26 Starting materials should only be purchased from approved suppliers named in the relevant specification and, where possible, directly from the producer. It is recommended that the specifications established by the manufacturer for the starting materials be discussed with the suppliers. It is of benefit that all aspects of the production and control of the starting material in question, including handling, labelling and packaging requirements, as well as complaints and rejection procedures are discussed with the manufacturer and the supplier.

5.27 For each delivery, the containers should be checked for integrity of package and seal and for correspondence between the delivery note and the supplier's labels.

5.28 If one material delivery is made up of different batches, each batch must be considered as separate for sampling, testing and release.

5.29 Starting materials in the storage area should be appropriately labelled (see Chapter 5: **Production**, paragraph 13). Labels should bear at least the following information:

- The designated name of the product and the internal code reference where applicable;

- A batch number given at receipt;

- Where appropriate, the status of the contents (e.g. in quarantine, on test, released, rejected);

- Where appropriate, an expiry date or a date beyond which retesting is necessary.

When fully computerised storage systems are used, all the above information need not necessarily be in a legible form on the label.

5.30 There should be appropriate procedures or measures to assure the identity of the contents of each container of starting material. Bulk containers from which samples have been drawn should be identified (see Chapter 6: **Quality Control**, paragraph 13).

5.31 Only starting materials which have been released by the QC Department and which are within their shelf life should be used.

5.32 Starting materials should only be dispensed by designated persons, following a written procedure, to ensure that the correct materials are accurately weighed or measured into clean and properly labelled containers.

5.33   Each dispensed material and its weight or volume should be independently checked and the check recorded.

5.34   Materials dispensed for each batch should be kept together and conspicuously labelled as such.

Processing operations: intermediate and bulk products

5.35   Before any processing operation is started, steps should be taken to ensure that the work area and equipment are clean and free from any starting materials, products, product residues or documents not required for the current operation.

5.36   Intermediate and bulk products should be kept under appropriate conditions.

5.37   Critical processes should be validated (see **Validation** in this Chapter).

5.38   Any necessary in-process controls and environmental controls should be carried out and recorded.

5.39   Any significant deviation from the expected yield should be recorded and investigated.

Packaging materials

5.40   The purchase, handling and control of primary and printed packaging materials shall be accorded attention similar to that given to starting materials.

5.41   Particular attention should be paid to printed materials. They should be stored in adequately secure conditions such as to exclude unauthorised access. Cut-labels and other loose printed materials should be stored and transported in separate closed containers so as to avoid mix-ups. Packaging materials should be issued for use only by authorised personnel following an approved and documented procedure.

5.42   Each delivery or batch of printed or primary packaging material should be given a specific reference number or identification mark.

5.43   Outdated or obsolete primary packaging material or printed packaging material should be destroyed and this disposal recorded.

Packaging operations

5.44   When setting up a programme for the packaging operations, particular attention should be given to minimising the risk of cross-contamination, mix-ups or substitutions. Different products should not be packaged in close proximity unless there is physical segregation.

5.45   Before packaging operations are begun, steps should be taken to ensure that the work area, packaging lines, printing machines and other equipment are clean and free from any products, materials or documents previously used, if these are not required for the current operation. The line clearance should be performed accordingly to an appropriate check list.

5.46   The name and batch number of the product being handled should be displayed at each packaging station or line.

5.47   All products and packaging materials to be used should be checked on delivery to the Packaging Department for quantity, identity and conformity with the packaging instructions.

5.48   Containers for filling should be clean before filling. Attention should be given to avoiding and removing any contaminants such as glass fragments and metal particles.

5.49   Normally, filling and sealing should be followed as quickly as possible by labelling. If it is not the case, appropriate procedures should be applied to ensure that no mix-ups or mislabelling can occur.

5.50   The correct performance of any printing operation (e.g. code numbers, expiry dates) to be done separately or in the course of the packaging should be checked and recorded. Attention should be paid to printing by hand which should be re-checked at regular intervals.

5.51   Special care should be taken when using cut-labels and when over-printing is carried out off-line. Roll-feed labels are normally preferable to cut-labels, in helping to avoid mix-ups.

5.52   Checks should be made to ensure that any electronic code readers, label counters or similar devices are operating correctly.

5.53   Printed and embossed information on packaging materials should be distinct and resistant to fading or erasing.

5.54   On-line control of the product during packaging should include at least checking the following:

      (a)   General appearance of the packages;

      (b)   Whether the packages are complete;

(c)   Whether the correct products and packaging materials are used;

(d)   Whether any over-printing is correct;

(e)   Correct functioning of line monitors.

Samples taken away from the packaging line should not be returned.

5.55   Products which have been involved in an unusual event should only be reintroduced into the process after special inspection, investigation and approval by authorised personnel. Detailed records should be kept of this operation.

5.56   Any significant or unusual discrepancy observed during reconciliation of the amount of bulk product and printed packaging materials and the number of units produced should be investigated and satisfactorily accounted for before release.

5.57   Upon completion of a packaging operation, any unused batch-coded packaging materials should be destroyed and the destruction recorded. A documented procedure should be followed if uncoded printed materials are returned to stock.

Finished products

5.58   Finished products should be held in quarantine until their final release under conditions established by the manufacturer.

5.59   The evaluation of finished products and documentation which is necessary before release of product for sale are described in Chapter 6: **Quality Control**.

5.60   After release, finished products should be stored as usable stock under conditions established by the manufacturer.

Rejected, recovered and returned materials

5.61   Rejected materials and products should be clearly marked as such and stored separately in restricted areas. They should either be returned to the suppliers or, where appropriate, reprocessed or destroyed. Whatever action is taken should be approved and recorded by authorised personnel.

5.62   The reprocessing of rejected products should be exceptional. It is only permitted if the quality of the final product is not affected, if the specifications are met and if it is done in accordance with a defined and authorised procedure after evaluation of the risks involved. Records should be kept of the reprocessing.

5.63   The recovery of all or part of earlier batches which conform to the required quality by incorporation into a batch of the same product at a defined stage of manufacture should be authorised beforehand. This recovery should be carried out in accordance with a defined procedure after evaluation of the risks involved, including any possible effect on shelf life. The recovery should be recorded.

5.64   The need for additional testing of any finished product which has been reprocessed, or into which a recovered product has been incorporated, should be considered by the QC Department.

5.65   Products returned from the market and which have left the control of the manufacturer should be destroyed unless there is no doubt that their quality is satisfactory; they may be considered for resale, relabelling or recovery in a subsequent batch only after they have been critically assessed by the QC Department in accordance with a written procedure. The nature of the product, any special storage conditions it requires, its condition and history, and the time elapsed since it was issued should all be taken into account in this assessment. Where any doubt arises over the quality of the product, it should not be considered suitable for reissue or reuse, although basic chemical reprocessing to recover active ingredient may be possible. Any action taken should be appropriately recorded.

6 Quality Control

Principle

Quality Control (QC) is concerned with sampling, specifications and testing as well as the organisation, documentation and release procedures which ensure that the necessary and relevant tests are carried out, and that materials are not released for use, nor products released for sale or supply, until their quality has been judged satisfactory. QC is not confined to laboratory operations, but must be involved in all decisions which may concern the quality of the product. The independence of QC from production is considered fundamental to the satisfactory operation of QC (see also Chapter 1: **Quality management**).

General

6.1   Each holder of a manufacturing authorisation should have a QC Department. This department should be independent from other departments, and under the authority of a person with appropriate qualifications and experience, who has one or several control laboratories at his disposal. Adequate resources must be available to ensure that all the QC arrangements are effectively and reliably carried out.

6.2   The principal duties of the Head of QC are summarised in Chapter 2: **Personnel**. The QC Department as a whole will also have other duties, such as to establish, validate and implement all QC procedures, keep the reference samples of materials and products, ensure the correct labelling of containers of materials and products, ensure the monitoring of the stability of the products, participate in the investigations of complaints related to the quality of the product etc. All these operations should be carried out in accordance with written procedures and, where necessary, recorded.

6.3   Finished product assessment should embrace all relevant factors, including production conditions, results of in-process testing, a review of manufacturing (including packaging) documentation, compliance with Finished Product Specification and examination of the final finished pack.

6.4   QC personnel should have access to production areas for sampling and investigation as appropriate.

Good Quality Control Laboratory Practice

6.5   Control laboratory premises and equipment should meet the general and specific requirements for QC areas given in Chapter 3: **Premises and equipment**.

6.6   The personnel, premises, and equipment in the laboratories should be appropriate to the tasks imposed by the nature and the scale of the manufacturing operations. The use of outside laboratories, in conformity with the principles detailed in Chapter 7: **Contract manufacture and analysis** can be accepted for particular reasons, but this should be stated in the QC records.

Documentation

6.7   Laboratory documentation should follow the principles given in Chapter 4: **Documentation**. An important part of this documentation deals with QC and the following details should be readily available to the QC Department:

- Specifications;

- Sampling procedures;

- Testing procedures and records (including analytical worksheets and/or laboratory notebooks);

- Analytical reports and/or certificates;

- Data from environmental monitoring, where required;

- Validation records of test methods, where applicable;

- Procedures for and records of the calibration of instruments and maintenance of equipment.

6.8   Any QC documentation relating to a batch record should be retained for one year after the expiry date of the batch and at least five years after the certification referred to in article 22.2 of Directive 75/319/EEC.

6.9   For some kinds of data (e.g. analytical tests results, yields, environmental controls etc.) it is recommended that records be kept in a manner permitting trend evaluation.

6.10   In addition to the information which is part of the batch record, other original data such as laboratory notebooks and/or records should be retained and readily available.

Sampling

6.11   The sample taking should be done in accordance with approved written procedures that describe:

- The method of sampling;

- The equipment to be used;

- The amount of the sample to be taken;

- Instructions for any required sub-division of the sample;

- The type and condition of the sample container to be used;

- The identification of containers sampled;

- Any special precautions to be observed, especially with regard to the sampling of sterile or noxious materials;

- The storage conditions;

- Instructions for the cleaning and storage of sampling equipment.

6.12   Reference samples should be representative of the batch of materials or products from which they are taken. Other samples may also be taken to monitor the most stressed part of a process (e.g. beginning or end of a process).

6.13   Sample containers should bear a label indicating the contents, with the batch number, the date of sampling and the containers from which samples have been drawn.

6.14   Reference samples from each batch of finished products should be retained until one year after the expiry date. Finished products should usually be kept in their final packaging and stored under the recommended conditions. Samples of starting materials (other than solvents, gases and water) should be retained for at least two years[1] after the release of the product if their stability allows. This period may be shortened if their stability, as mentioned in the relevant specification, is shorter. Reference samples of materials and products should be of a size sufficient to permit at least a full re-examination.

Testing

6.15   Analytical methods should be validated. All testing operations described in the marketing authorisation should be carried out according to the approved methods.

6.16   The results obtained should be recorded and checked to make sure that they are consistent with each other. Any calculations should be critically examined.

6.17 The tests performed should be recorded and the records should include at least the following data:

(a) Name of the material or product and, where applicable, dosage form.

(b) Batch number and, where appropriate, the manufacturer and/or supplier.

(c) References to the relevant specifications and testing procedures.

(d) Test results, including observations and calculations, and reference to any Certificates of Analysis.

(e) Dates of testing.

(f) Initials of the persons who performed the testing.

(g) Initials of the persons who verified the testing and the calculations, where appropriate.

(h) A clear statement of release or rejection (or other status decision) and the dated signature of the designated Responsible Person.

6.18 All the in-process controls, including those made in the production area by production personnel, should be performed according to methods approved by QC and the results recorded.

6.19 Special attention should be given to the quality of laboratory reagents, volumetric glassware and solutions, reference standards and culture media. They should be prepared in accordance with written procedures.

6.20 Laboratory reagents intended for prolonged use should be marked with the preparation date and the signature of the person who prepared them. The expiry date of unstable reagents and culture media should be indicated on the label, together with specific storage conditions. In addition, for volumetric solutions, the last date of standardisation and the last current factor should be indicated.

6.21 Where necessary, the date of receipt of any substance used for testing operations (e.g. reagents and reference standards) should be indicated on the container. Instructions for use and storage should be followed. In certain cases it may be necessary to carry out an identification test and/or other testing of reagent materials upon receipt or before use.

6.22 Animals used for testing components, materials or products, should, where appropriate, be quarantined before use. They should be maintained and controlled in a manner that assures their suitability for the intended use. They should be identified, and adequate records should be maintained, showing the history of their use.

---

(1) In Germany, France, Belgium and Greece, samples of starting materials should be retained for as long as the corresponding finished

7 Contract manufacture and analysis

Principle

Contract manufacture and analysis must be correctly defined, agreed and controlled in order to avoid misunderstandings which could result in a product or work of unsatisfactory quality. There must be a written contract between the Contract Giver and the Contract Acceptor which clearly establishes the duties of each party. The contract must clearly state the way in which the Qualified Person (QP) releasing each batch of product for sale exercises his full responsibility.

Note

This Chapter deals with the responsibilities of manufacturers towards the competent authorities of the Member States with respect to the granting of marketing and manufacturing authorisations. It is not intended in any way to affect the respective liability of Contract Acceptors and Contract Givers to consumers; this is governed by other provisions of Community and national law.

General

7.1 There should be a written contract covering the manufacture and/or analysis arranged under contract and any technical arrangements made in connection with it.

7.2 All arrangements for contract manufacture and analysis including any proposed changes in technical or other arrangements should be in accordance with the marketing authorisation for the product concerned.

The Contract Giver

7.3 The Contract Giver is responsible for assessing the competence of the Contract Acceptor to carry out successfully the work required and for ensuring by means of the contract that the principles and guidelines of Good Manufacturing Practice (GMP) as interpreted in this Guide are followed.

7.4 The Contract Giver should provide the Contract Acceptor with all the information necessary to carry out the contracted operations correctly in accordance with the marketing authorisation and any other legal requirements. The Contract Giver should ensure that the Contract Acceptor is fully aware of any problems associated with the product or the work which might pose a hazard to his premises, equipment, personnel, other materials or other products.

7.5 The Contract Giver should ensure that all processed products and materials delivered to him by the Contract Acceptor comply with their specifications or that the products have been released by a QP.

The Contract Acceptor

7.6 The Contract Acceptor must have adequate premises and equipment, knowledge and experience, and competent personnel to carry out satisfactorily the work ordered by the Contract Giver. Contract manufacture may be undertaken only by a manufacturer who is the holder of a manufacturing authorisation.

7.7 The Contract Acceptor should ensure that all products or materials delivered to him are suitable for their intended purpose.

7.8 The Contract Acceptor should not pass to a third party any of the work entrusted to him under the contract without the Contract Giver's prior evaluation and approval of the arrangements. Arrangements made between the Contract Acceptor and any third party should ensure that the manufacturing and analytical information is made available in the same way as between the original Contract Giver and Contract Acceptor.

7.9 The Contract Acceptor should refrain from any activity which may adversely affect the quality of the product manufactured and/or analysed for the Contract Giver.

The Contract

7.10 A contract should be drawn up between the Contract Giver and the Contract Acceptor which specifies their respective responsibilities relating to the manufacture and control of the product. Technical aspects of the contract should be drawn up by competent persons suitably knowledgeable in pharmaceutical technology, analysis and GMP. All arrangements for manufacture and analysis must be in accordance with the marketing authorisation and agreed by both parties.

7.11 The contract should specify the way in which the QP releasing the batch for sale ensures that each batch has been manufactured and checked for compliance with the requirements of marketing authorisation.

7.12 The contract should describe clearly who is responsible for purchasing materials, testing and releasing materials, undertaking production and quality controls, including in-process controls, and who has responsibility for sampling and analysis. In the case of contract analysis, the contract should state whether or not the Contract Acceptor should take samples at the premises of the manufacturer.

7.13 Manufacturing, analytical and distribution records, and reference samples should be kept by, or be available to, the Contract Giver. Any records relevant to assessing the quality of a product in the event of complaints or a suspected defect must be accessible and specified in the defect/recall procedures of the Contract Giver.

7.14 The contract should permit the Contract Giver to visit the facilities of the Contract Acceptor.

7.15 In the case of contract analysis, the Contract Acceptor should understand that he is subject to inspection by the competent authorities.

8 Complaints and product recall

Principle

All complaints and other information concerning potentially defective products must be reviewed carefully according to written procedures. In order to provide for all contingencies, and in accordance with Article 28 of Directive 75/319/EEC, a system should be designed to recall, if necessary, promptly and effectively products known or suspected to be defective from the market.

Complaints

8.1 A person should be designated responsible for handling the complaints and deciding the measures to be taken together with sufficient supporting staff to assist him. If this person is not the Qualified Person (QP), the latter should be made aware of any complaint, investigation or recall.

8.2 There should be written procedures describing the action to be taken, including the need to consider a recall, in the case of a complaint concerning a possible product defect.

8.3 Any complaint concerning a product defect should be recorded with all the original details and thoroughly investigated. The person responsible for Quality Control (QC) should normally be involved in the study of such problems.

8.4 If a product defect is discovered or suspected in a batch, consideration should be given to checking other batches in order to determine whether they are also affected. In particular, other batches which may contain reworks of the defective batch should be investigated.

8.5 All the decisions and measures taken as a result of a complaint should be recorded and referenced to the corresponding batch records.

8.6 Complaints records should be reviewed regularly for any indication of specific or recurring problems requiring attention and possibly the recall of marketed products.

8.7 The competent authorities should be informed if a manufacturer is considering action following possibly faulty manufacture, product deterioration, or any other serious quality problems with a product.

Recalls

8.8   A person should be designated as responsible for execution and co-ordination of recalls and should be supported by sufficient staff to handle all the aspects of the recalls with the appropriate degree of urgency. This Responsible Person should normally be independent of the sales and marketing organisation. If this person is not the QP, the latter should be made aware of any recall operation.

8.9   There should be established written procedures, regularly checked and updated when necessary, in order to organise any recall activity.

8.10   Recall operations should be capable of being initiated promptly and at any time.

8.11   All competent authorities of all countries to which products may have been distributed should be informed promptly if products are intended to be recalled because they are, or are suspected of being, defective.

8.12   The distribution records should be readily available to the person(s) responsible for recalls, and should contain sufficient information on wholesalers and directly supplied customers (with addresses, telephone and/or fax numbers inside and outside working hours, batches and amounts delivered), including those for exported products and medical samples.

8.13   Recall products should be identified and stored separately in a secure way while awaiting a decision on their fate.

8.14   The progress of the recall process should be recorded and a final report issued, including a reconciliation between the delivered and recovered quantities of the products.

8.15   The effectiveness of the arrangements for recalls should be evaluated from time to time.

9 Self-inspection

Principle

Self-inspections should be conducted in order to monitor the implementation and compliance with Good Manufacturing Practice (GMP) principles and to propose necessary corrective measures.

9.1 Personnel matters, premises, equipment, documentation, production, Quality Control (QC), distribution of the medicinal products, arrangements for dealing with complaints and recalls, and self-inspection, should be examined at intervals following a pre-arranged programme in order to verify their conformity with the principles of Quality Assurance (QA).

9.2 Self-inspections should be conducted in an independent and detailed way by designated competent person(s) from the company. Independent audits by external experts may also be useful.

9.3 All self-inspections should be recorded. Reports should contain all the observations made during the inspections and, where applicable, proposals for corrective measures. Statements on the actions subsequently taken should also be recorded.

Manufacture of Sterile Medicinal Products

Principle

The manufacture of sterile products is subject to special requirements in order to minimise risks of microbiological contamination, and of particulate and pyrogen contamination. Much depends on the skill, training and attitudes of the personnel involved. Quality Assurance is particularly important, and this type of manufacture must strictly follow carefully established and validated methods of preparation and procedure. Sole reliance for sterility or other quality aspects must not be placed on any terminal process or finished product test.

Note:

The present guidance does not lay down detailed methods for determining the microbiological and particulate cleanliness of air, surfaces etc. Reference is made to other compendia such as the CEN/ISO Standards.

General

1   The manufacture of sterile products should be carried out in clean areas entry to which should be through airlocks for personnel and/or for equipment and materials. Clean areas should be maintained to an appropriate cleanliness standard and supplied with air which has passed through filters of an appropriate efficiency.

2   The various operations of component preparation, product preparation and filling should be carried out in separate areas within the clean area.

Manufacturing operations are divided into two categories; firstly those where the product is terminally sterilised, and secondly those which are conducted aseptically at some or all stages.

3   Clean areas for the manufacture of sterile products are classified according to the required characteristics of the environment. Each manufacturing operation requires an appropriate environmental cleanliness level in the operational state in order to minimise the risks of particulate or microbial contamination of the product or materials being handled.

In order to meet 'in operation' conditions these areas should be designed to reach certain specified air-cleanliness levels in the 'at rest' occupancy state. The 'at-rest' state is the condition where the installation is installed and operating, complete with production equipment but with no operating personnel present. The 'in operation' state is the condition where the installation is functioning in the defined operating mode with the specified number of personnel working.

For the manufacture of sterile medicinal products there are normally 4 grades of clean areas.

Grade A: The local zone for high risk operations, e.g. filling zone, stopper bowls, open ampoules and vials, making aseptic connections. Normally such conditions are provided by a laminar air flow work station. Laminar air flow systems should provide a homogeneous air speed of 0.45 m/s ± 20 % (guidance value) at the working position.

Grade B: For aseptic preparation and filling, this is the background environment for grade A zone.

Grade C and D: Clean areas for carrying out less critical stages in the manufacture of sterile products.

The airborne particulate classification for these grades is given in the following table.

	maximum permitted number of particles/m³ equal to or above			
Grade	at rest (b)		in operation	
	0.5 µm	5 µm	0.5 µm	5 µm
A	3 500	0	3 500	0
B (a)	3 500	0	350 000	2 000
C (a)	350 000	2 000	3 500 000	20 000
D (a)	3 500 000	20 000	not defined (c)	not defined (c)

Notes

(a) *In order to reach the B, C and D air grades, the number of air changes should be related to the size of the room and the equipment and personnel present in the room. The air system should be provided with appropriate filters such as HEPA for grades A, B and C.*

(b) *The guidance given for the maximum permitted number of particles in the 'at rest' condition corresponds approximately to the US Federal Standard 209 E and the ISO classifications as follows:*

grades A and B correspond with class 100, M 3.5, ISO 5; grade C with class 10.000, M 5.5, ISO 7 and grade D with class 100.000, M 6.5, ISO 8.

(c)   *The requirement and limit for this area will depend on the nature of the operations carried out.*

Examples of operations to be carried out in the various grades are given in the table below. (see also par. 11 and 12)

Grade	Examples of operations for terminally sterilised products. (see par. 11)
A	Filling of products, when unusually at risk.
C	Preparation of solutions, when unusually at risk. Filling of products.
D	Preparation of solutions and components for subsequent filling.

Grade	Examples of operations for aseptic preparations. (see par. 12)
A	Aseptic preparation and filling.
C	Preparation of solutions to be filtered.
D	Handling of components after washing.

The particulate conditions given in the table for the 'at rest' state should be achieved in the unmanned state after a short 'clean up' period of 15-20 minutes (guidance value), after completion of operations. The particulate conditions for grade A in operation given in the table should be maintained in the zone immediately surrounding the product whenever the product or open container is exposed to the environment. It is accepted that it may not always be possible to demonstrate conformity with particulate standards at the point of fill when filling is in progress, due to the generation of particles or droplets from the product itself.

4   The areas should be monitored during operation, in order to control the particulate cleanliness of the various grades.

5   Where aseptic operations are performed monitoring should be frequent using methods such as settle plates, volumetric air and surface sampling (e.g. swabs and contact plates). Sampling methods used in operation should not interfere with zone protection. Results from monitoring should be considered when reviewing batch documentation for finished product release. Surfaces and personnel should be monitored after critical operations. Additional microbiological monitoring is also required outside production operations, e.g. after validation of systems, cleaning and sanitisation.

Recommended limits for microbiological monitoring of clean areas during operation.

Grade	Recommended limits for microbial contamination (a)			
	air sample cfu/m³	settle plates (diam. 9 0 mm), cfu/4 hours (b)	contact plates (diam. 55 mm), cfu/plate	glove print 5 fingers cfu/glove
A	< 1	< 1	< 1	< 1
B	10	5	5	5
C	100	50	25	–
D	200	100	50	–

Notes
(a)   These are average values.
(b)   Individual settle plates may be exposed for less than 4 hours.

6   Appropriate alert and action limits should be set for the results of particulate and microbiological monitoring. If these limits are exceeded operating procedures should prescribe corrective action.

Isolator Technology

7   The utilisation of isolator technology to minimise human interventions in processing areas may result in a significant decrease in the risk of microbiological contamination of aseptically manufactured products from the environment. There are many possible designs of isolators and transfer devices. The isolator and the background environment should be designed so that the required air quality for the respective zones can be realised. Isolators are constructed of various materials more or less prone to puncture and leakage. Transfer devices may vary from a single door to double door designs to fully sealed systems incorporating sterilisation mechanisms.

The transfer of materials into and out of the unit is one of the greatest potential sources of contamination. In general the area inside the isolator is the local zone for high risk manipulations, although it is recognised that laminar air flow may not exist in the working zone of all such devices. The air classification required for the background environment depends on the design of the isolator and its application. It should be controlled and for aseptic processing it should be at least grade D.

8   Isolators should be introduced only after appropriate validation. Validation should take into account all critical factors of isolator technology, for example the quality of the air inside and outside (background) the isolator, sanitisation of the isolator, the transfer process and isolator integrity.

9   Monitoring should be carried out routinely and should include frequent leak testing of the isolator and glove/sleeve system.

Blow/Fill/Seal Technology

10   Blow/fill/seal units are purpose built machines in which, in one continuous operation, containers are formed from a thermoplastic granulate, filled and then sealed, all by the one automatic machine. Blow/fill/seal equipment used for aseptic production which is fitted with an effective grade A air shower may be installed in at least a grade C environment, provided that grade A/B clothing is used. The environment should comply with the viable and non viable limits at rest and the viable limit only when in operation. Blow/fill/seal equipment used for the production of products which are terminally sterilised should be installed in at least a grade D environment.

Because of this special technology particular attention should be paid to at least the following: equipment design and qualification, validation and reproducibility of cleaning-in-place and sterilisation-in-place, background cleanroom environment in which the equipment is located, operator training and clothing, and interventions in the critical zone of the equipment including any aseptic assembly prior to the commencement of filling.

Terminally Sterilised Products

11   Preparation of components and most products should be done in at least a grade D environment in order to give low risk of microbial and particulate contamination, suitable for filtration and sterilisation. Where the product is at a high or unusual risk of microbial contamination, (for example, because the product actively supports microbial growth or must be held for a long period before sterilisation or is necessarily processed not mainly in closed vessels), then preparation should be carried out in a grade C environment.

Filling of products for terminal sterilisation should be carried out in at least a grade C environment.

Where the product is at unusual risk of contamination from the environment, for example because the filling operation is slow or the containers are wide-necked or are necessarily exposed for more than a few seconds before sealing, the filling should be done in a grade A zone with at least a grade C background. Preparation and filling of ointments, creams, suspensions and emulsions should generally be carried out in a grade C environment before terminal sterilisation.

Aseptic Preparation

12   Components after washing should be handled in at least a grade D environment. Handling of sterile starting materials and components, unless subjected to sterilisation or filtration through a micro-organism-retaining filter later in the process, should be done in a grade A environment with grade B background.

Preparation of solutions which are to be sterile filtered during the process should be done in a grade C environment; if not filtered, the preparation of materials and products should be done in a grade A environment with a grade B background.

Handling and filling of aseptically prepared products should be done in a grade A environment with a grade B background.

Prior to the completion of stoppering, transfer of partially closed containers, as used in freeze drying should be done either in a grade A environment with grade B background or in sealed transfer trays in a grade B environment.

Preparation and filling of sterile ointments, creams, suspensions and emulsions should be done in a grade A environment, with a grade B background, when the product is exposed and is not subsequently filtered.

Personnel

13   Only the minimum number of personnel required should be present in clean areas; this is particularly important during aseptic processing. Inspections and controls should be conducted outside the clean areas as far as possible.

14   All personnel (including those concerned with cleaning and maintenance) employed in such areas should receive regular training in disciplines relevant to the correct manufacture of sterile products. This training should include reference to hygiene and to the basic elements of microbiology. When outside staff who have not received such training (e.g. building or maintenance contractors) need to be brought in, particular care should be taken over their instruction and supervision.

15   Staff who have been engaged in the processing of animal tissue materials or of cultures of micro-organisms other than those used in the current manufacturing process should not enter sterile-product areas unless rigorous and clearly defined entry procedures have been followed.

16   High standards of personal hygiene and cleanliness are essential. Personnel involved in the manufacture of sterile preparations should be instructed to report any condition which may cause the shedding of abnormal numbers or types of contaminants; periodic health checks for such conditions are desirable. Actions to be taken about personnel who could be introducing undue microbiological hazard should be decided by a designated competent person.

17   Changing and washing should follow a written procedure designed to minimise contamination of clean area clothing or carry-through of contaminants to the clean areas.

18   Wristwatches, make-up and jewellery should not be worn in clean areas.

19   The clothing and its quality should be appropriate for the process and the grade of the working area. It should be worn in such a way as to protect the product from contamination.

The description of clothing required for each grade is given below:

Grade D: Hair and, where relevant, beard should be covered. A general protective suit and appropriate shoes or overshoes should be worn. Appropriate measures should be taken to avoid any contamination coming from outside the clean area.

Grade C: Hair and where relevant beard and moustache should be covered. A single or two-piece trouser suit, gathered at the wrists and with high neck and appropriate shoes or overshoes should be worn. They should shed virtually no fibres or particulate matter.

Grade A/B: Headgear should totally enclose hair and, where relevant, beard and moustache; it should be tucked into the neck of the suit; a face mask should be worn to prevent the shedding of droplets. Appropriate sterilised, non-powdered rubber or plastic gloves and sterilised or disinfected footwear should be worn. Trouser-legs should be tucked inside the footwear and garment sleeves into the gloves. The protective clothing should shed virtually no fibres or particulate matter and retain particles shed by the body.

20   Outdoor clothing should not be brought into changing rooms leading to grade B and C rooms. For every worker in a grade A/B area, clean sterile (sterilised or adequately sanitised) protective garments should be provided at each work session, or at least once a day if monitoring results justify this. Gloves should be regularly disinfected during operations. Masks and gloves should be changed at least at every working session.

21   Clean area clothing should be cleaned and handled in such a way that it does not gather additional contaminants which can later be shed. These operations should follow written procedures. Separate laundry facilities for such clothing are desirable. Inappropriate treatment of clothing will damage fibres and may increase the risk of shedding of particles.

Premises

22   In clean areas, all exposed surfaces should be smooth, impervious and unbroken in order to minimise the shedding or accumulation of particles or micro-organisms and to permit the repeated application of cleaning agents, and disinfectants where used.

23   To reduce accumulation of dust and to facilitate cleaning there should be no uncleanable recesses and a minimum of projecting ledges, shelves, cupboards and equipment. Doors should be designed to avoid those uncleanable recesses; sliding doors may be undesirable for this reason.

24   False ceilings should be sealed to prevent contamination from the space above them.

25   Pipes and ducts and other utilities should be installed so that they do not create recesses, unsealed openings and surfaces which are difficult to clean.

26   Sinks and drains should be prohibited in grade A/B areas used for aseptic manufacture. In other areas air breaks should be fitted between the machine or sink and the drains. Floor drains in lower grade clean rooms should be fitted with traps or water seals to prevent back-flow.

27   Changing rooms should be designed as airlocks and used to provide physical separation of the different stages of changing and so minimise microbial and particulate contamination of protective clothing. They should be flushed effectively with filtered air. The final stage of the changing room should, in the at-rest state, be the same grade as the area into which it leads. The use of separate changing rooms for entering and leaving clean areas is sometimes desirable. In general hand washing facilities should be provided only in the first stage of the changing rooms.

28   Both airlock doors should not be opened simultaneously. An interlocking system or a visual and/or audible warning system should be operated to prevent the opening of more than one door at a time.

29   A filtered air supply should maintain a positive pressure and an air flow relative to surrounding areas of a lower grade under all operational conditions and should flush the area effectively. Adjacent rooms of different grades should have a pressure differential of 10 –15 pascals (guidance values). Particular attention should be paid to the protection of the zone of greatest risk, that is, the immediate environment to which a product and cleaned components which contact the product are exposed. The various recommendations regarding air supplies and pressure differentials may need to be modified where it becomes necessary to contain some materials, e.g. pathogenic, highly toxic, radioactive or live viral or bacterial materials or products. Decontamination of facilities and treatment of air leaving a clean area may be necessary for some operations.

30   It should be demonstrated that air-flow patterns do not present a contamination risk, e.g. care should be taken to ensure that air flows do not distribute particles from a particle-generating person, operation or machine to a zone of higher product risk.

31   A warning system should be provided to indicate failure in the air supply. Indicators of pressure differences should be fitted between areas where these differences are important. These pressure differences should be recorded regularly or otherwise documented.

Equipment

32   A conveyor belt should not pass through a partition between a grade A or B area and a processing area of lower air cleanliness, unless the belt itself is continually sterilised (e.g. in a sterilising tunnel).

33   As far as practicable equipment, fittings and services should be designed and installed so that operations, maintenance and repairs can be carried out outside the clean area. If sterilisation is required, it should be carried out, wherever possible, after complete reassembly.

34   When equipment maintenance has been carried out within the clean area, the area should be cleaned, disinfected and/or sterilised where appropriate, before processing recommences if the required standards of cleanliness and/or asepsis have not been maintained during the work.

35   Water treatment plants and distribution systems should be designed, constructed and maintained so as to ensure a reliable source of water of an appropriate quality. They should not be operated beyond their designed capacity. Water for injections should be produced, stored and distributed in a manner which prevents microbial growth, for example by constant circulation at a temperature above 70°C.

36   All equipment such as sterilisers, air handling and filtration systems, air vent and gas filters, water treatment, generation, storage and distribution systems should be subject to validation and planned maintenance; their return to use should be approved.

Sanitation

37   The sanitation of clean areas is particularly important. They should be cleaned thoroughly in accordance with a written programme. Where disinfectants are used, more than one type should be employed. Monitoring should be undertaken regularly in order to detect the development of resistant strains.

38   Disinfectants and detergents should be monitored for microbial contamination; dilutions should be kept in previously cleaned containers and should only be stored for defined periods unless sterilised. Disinfectants and detergents used in Grades A and B areas should be sterile prior to use.

39   Fumigation of clean areas may be useful for reducing microbiological contamination in inaccessible places.

Processing

40   Precautions to minimise contamination should be taken during all processing stages including the stages before sterilisation.

41   Preparations of microbiological origin should not be made or filled in areas used for the processing of other medicinal products; however, vaccines of dead organisms or of bacterial extracts may be filled, after inactivation, in the same premises as other sterile medicinal products.

42   Validation of aseptic processing should include a process simulation test using a nutrient medium (media fill). Selection of the nutrient medium should be made based on dosage form of the product and selectivity, clarity, concentration and suitability for sterilisation of the nutrient medium. The process simulation test should imitate as closely as possible the routine aseptic manufacturing process and include all the critical subsequent manufacturing steps. It should also take into account various interventions known to occur during normal production as well as worst case situations. Process simulation tests should be performed as initial validation with three consecutive satisfactory simulation tests per shift and repeated at defined intervals and after any significant modification to the HVAC-system, equipment, process and number of shifts. Normally process simulation tests should be repeated twice a year per shift and process. The number of containers used for media fills should be sufficient to

enable a valid evaluation. For small batches, the number of containers for media fills should at least equal the size of the product batch. The target should be zero growth but a contamination rate of less than 0.1% with 95% confidence limit is acceptable. The manufacturer should establish alert and action limits. Any contamination should be investigated.

43 Care should be taken that any validation does not compromise the processes.

44 Water sources, water treatment equipment and treated water should be monitored regularly for chemical and biological contamination and, as appropriate, for endotoxins. Records should be maintained of the results of the monitoring and of any action taken.

45 Activities in clean areas and especially when aseptic operations are in progress should be kept to a minimum and movement of personnel should be controlled and methodical, to avoid excessive shedding of particles and organisms due to over-vigorous activity. The ambient temperature and humidity should not be uncomfortably high because of the nature of the garments worn.

46 Microbiological contamination of starting materials should be minimal. Specifications should include requirements for microbiological quality when the need for this has been indicated by monitoring.

47 Containers and materials liable to generate fibres should be minimised in clean areas.

48 Where appropriate, measures should be taken to minimise the particulate contamination of the end product.

49 Components, containers and equipment should be handled after the final cleaning process in such a way that they are not recontaminated.

50 The interval between the washing and drying and the sterilisation of components, containers and equipment as well as between their sterilisation and use should be minimised and subject to a time-limit appropriate to the storage conditions.

51 The time between the start of the preparation of a solution and its sterilisation or filtration through a micro-organism-retaining filter should be minimised. There should be a set maximum permissible time for each product that takes into account its composition and the prescribed method of storage.

52 The bioburden should be monitored before sterilisation. There should be working limits on contamination immediately before

sterilisation which are related to the efficiency of the method to be used. Where appropriate the absence of pyrogens should be monitored. All solutions, in particular large volume infusion fluids, should be passed through a micro-organism-retaining filter, if possible sited immediately before filling.

53   Components, containers, equipment and any other article required in a clean area where aseptic work takes place should be sterilised and passed into the area through double-ended sterilisers sealed into the wall, or by a procedure which achieves the same objective of not introducing contamination. Non-combustible gases should be passed through micro-organism retentive filters.

54   The efficacy of any new procedure should be validated, and the validation verified at scheduled intervals based on performance history or when any significant change is made in the process or equipment.

Sterilisation

55   All sterilisation processes should be validated. Particular attention should be given when the adopted sterilisation method is not described in the current edition of the European Pharmacopoeia, or when it is used for a product which is not a simple aqueous or oily solution. Where possible, heat sterilisation is the method of choice. In any case, the sterilisation process must be in accordance with the marketing and manufacturing authorisations.

56   Before any sterilisation process is adopted its suitability for the product and its efficacy in achieving the desired sterilising conditions in all parts of each type of load to be processed should be demonstrated by physical measurements and by biological indicators where appropriate. The validity of the process should be verified at scheduled intervals, at least annually, and whenever significant modifications have been made to the equipment. Records should be kept of the results.

57   For effective sterilisation the whole of the material must be subjected to the required treatment and the process should be designed to ensure that this is achieved.

58   Validated loading patterns should be established for all sterilisation processes.

59   Biological indicators should be considered as an additional method for monitoring the sterilisation. They should be stored and used according to the manufacturers instructions, and their quality checked by positive controls.

If biological indicators are used, strict precautions should be taken to avoid transferring microbial contamination from them.

60 There should be a clear means of differentiating products which have not been sterilised from those which have. Each basket, tray or other carrier of products or components should be clearly labelled with the material name, its batch number and an indication of whether or not it has been sterilised. Indicators such as autoclave tape may be used, where appropriate, to indicate whether or not a batch (or sub-batch) has passed through a sterilisation process, but they do not give a reliable indication that the lot is, in fact, sterile.

61 Sterilisation records should be available for each sterilisation run. They should be approved as part of the batch release procedure.

Sterilisation by Heat

62 Each heat sterilisation cycle should be recorded on a time/temperature chart with a sufficiently large scale or by other appropriate equipment with suitable accuracy and precision. The position of the temperature probes used for controlling and/or recording should have been determined during the validation, and where applicable also checked against a second independent temperature probe located at the same position.

63 Chemical or biological indicators may also be used, but should not take the place of physical measurements.

64 Sufficient time must be allowed for the whole of the load to reach the required temperature before measurement of the sterilising time-period is commenced. This time must be determined for each type of load to be processed.

65 After the high temperature phase of a heat sterilisation cycle, precautions should be taken against contamination of a sterilised load during cooling. Any cooling fluid or gas in contact with the product should be sterilised unless it can be shown that any leaking container would not be approved for use.

Moist Heat

66 Both temperature and pressure should be used to monitor the process. Control instrumentation should normally be independent of monitoring instrumentation and recording charts. Where automated control and monitoring systems are used for these applications they should be validated to ensure that critical process requirements are met. System and cycle faults should be registered by the system and

observed by the operator. The reading of the independent temperature indicator should be routinely checked against the chart recorder during the sterilisation period. For sterilisers fitted with a drain at the bottom of the chamber, it may also be necessary to record the temperature at this position, throughout the sterilisation period. There should be frequent leak tests on the chamber when a vacuum phase is part of the cycle.

67   The items to be sterilised, other than products in sealed containers, should be wrapped in a material which allows removal of air and penetration of steam but which prevents recontamination after sterilisation. All parts of the load should be in contact with the sterilising agent at the required temperature for the required time.

68   Care should be taken to ensure that steam used for sterilisation is of suitable quality and does not contain additives at a level which could cause contamination of product or equipment.

Dry Heat

69   The process used should include air circulation within the chamber and the maintenance of a positive pressure to prevent the entry of non-sterile air. Any air admitted should be passed through a HEPA filter. Where this process is also intended to remove pyrogens, challenge tests using endotoxins should be used as part of the validation.

Sterilisation by Radiation

70   Radiation sterilisation is used mainly for the sterilisation of heat sensitive materials and products. Many medicinal products and some packaging materials are radiation-sensitive, so this method is permissible only when the absence of deleterious effects on the product has been confirmed experimentally. Ultraviolet irradiation is not normally an acceptable method of sterilisation.

71   During the sterilisation procedure the radiation dose should be measured. For this purpose, dosimetry indicators which are independent of dose rate should be used, giving a quantitative measurement of the dose received by the product itself. Dosimeters should be inserted in the load in sufficient number and close enough together to ensure that there is always a dosimeter in the irradiator. Where plastic dosimeters are used they should be used within the time-limit of their calibration. Dosimeter absorbances should be read within a short period after exposure to radiation.

72   Biological indicators may be used as an additional control.

73   Validation procedures should ensure that the effects of variations in density of the packages are considered.

74   Materials handling procedures should prevent mix-up between irradiated and non-irradiated materials. Radiation sensitive colour disks should also be used on each package to differentiate between packages which have been subjected to irradiation and those which have not.

75   The total radiation dose should be administered within a predetermined time span.

Sterilisation with Ethylene Oxide

76   This method should only be used when no other method is practicable. During process validation it should be shown that there is no damaging effect on the product and that the conditions and time allowed for degassing are such as to reduce any residual gas and reaction products to defined acceptable limits for the type of product or material.

77   Direct contact between gas and microbial cells is essential; precautions should be taken to avoid the presence of organisms likely to be enclosed in material such as crystals or dried protein. The nature and quantity of packaging materials can significantly affect the process.

78   Before exposure to the gas, materials should be brought into equilibrium with the humidity and temperature required by the process. The time required for this should be balanced against the opposing need to minimise the time before sterilisation.

79   Each sterilisation cycle should be monitored with suitable biological indicators, using the appropriate number of test pieces distributed throughout the load. The information so obtained should form part of the batch record.

80   For each sterilisation cycle, records should be made of the time taken to complete the cycle, of the pressure, temperature and humidity within the chamber during the process and of the gas concentration and of the total amount of gas used. The pressure and temperature should be recorded throughout the cycle on a chart. The record(s) should form part of the batch record.

81   After sterilisation, the load should be stored in a controlled manner under ventilated conditions to allow residual gas and reaction products to reduce to the defined level. This process should be validated.

Filtration of Medicinal Products which cannot be Sterilised in their Final Container

82 Filtration alone is not considered sufficient when sterilisation in the final container is possible. With regard to methods currently available, steam sterilisation is to be preferred. If the product cannot be sterilised in the final container, solutions or liquids can be filtered through a sterile filter of nominal pore size of 0.22 micron (or less), or with at least equivalent micro-organism retaining properties, into a previously sterilised container. Such filters can remove most bacteria and moulds, but not all viruses or mycoplasmas. Consideration should be given to complementing the filtration process with some degree of heat treatment.

83 Due to the potential additional risks of the filtration method as compared with other sterilisation processes, a second filtration via a further sterilised micro-organism retaining filter, immediately prior to filling, may be advisable. The final sterile filtration should be carried out as close as possible to the filling point.

84 Fibre shedding characteristics of filters should be minimal.

85 The integrity of the sterilised filter should be verified before use and should be confirmed immediately after use by an appropriate method such as a bubble point, diffusive flow or pressure hold test. The time taken to filter a known volume of bulk solution and the pressure difference to be used across the filter should be determined during validation and any significant differences from this during routine manufacturing should be noted and investigated. Results of these checks should be included in the batch record. The integrity of critical gas and air vent filters should be confirmed after use. The integrity of other filters should be confirmed at appropriate intervals.

86 The same filter should not be used for more than one working day unless such use has been validated.

87 The filter should not affect the product by removal of ingredients from it or by release of substances into it.

Finishing of Sterile Products

88 Containers should be closed by appropriately validated methods. Containers closed by fusion, e.g. glass or plastic ampoules should be subject to 100% integrity testing. Samples of other containers should be checked for integrity according to appropriate procedures.

89 Containers sealed under vacuum should be tested for maintenance of that vacuum after an appropriate, pre-determined period.

90   Filled containers of parenteral products should be inspected individually for extraneous contamination or other defects. When inspection is done visually, it should be done under suitable and controlled conditions of illumination and background. Operators doing the inspection should pass regular eyesight checks, with spectacles if worn, and be allowed frequent breaks from inspection. Where other methods of inspection are used, the process should be validated and the performance of the equipment checked at intervals. Results should be recorded.

Quality Control

91   The sterility test applied to the finished product should only be regarded as the last in a series of control measures by which sterility is assured. The test should be validated for the product(s) concerned.

92   In those cases where parametric release has been authorised, special attention should be paid to the validation and the monitoring of the entire manufacturing process.

93   Samples taken for sterility testing should be representative of the whole of the batch, but should in particular include samples taken from parts of the batch considered to be most at risk of contamination, e.g.

    a.   for products which have been filled aseptically, samples should include containers filled at the beginning and end of the batch and after any significant intervention,

    b.   for products which have been heat sterilised in their final containers, consideration should be given to taking samples from the potentially coolest part of the load.

Manufacture of Biological Medicinal Products for Human Use

Scope

The methods employed in the manufacture of biological medicinal products are a critical factor in shaping the appropriate regulatory control. Biological medicinal products can be defined therefore largely by reference to their method of manufacture. Biological medicinal products prepared by the following methods of manufacture will fall under the scope of this annex[1]:

(a)   Microbial cultures, excluding those resulting from r-DNA techniques;

(b)   Microbial and cell cultures, including those resulting from recombinant DNA or hybridoma techniques;

(c)   Extraction from biological tissues;

(d)   Propagation of live agents in embryos or animals.

(Not all of the aspects of this annex may necessarily apply to products in category (a)).

Note

In drawing up this guidance, due consideration has been given to the general requirements for manufacturing establishments and control laboratories proposed by the WHO.

The present guidance does not lay down detailed requirements for specific classes of biological products, and attention is therefore directed to other guidelines issued by the Committee for Proprietary Medicinal Products (CPMP), for example the note for guidance on monoclonal antibodies and the note for guidance on products of recombinant DNA technology[2].

Principle

The manufacture of biological medicinal products involves certain specific considerations arising from the nature of the products and the processes. The way in which biological medicinal products are produced, controlled and administered make some particular precautions necessary.

Unlike conventional medicinal products, which are reproduced using chemical and physical techniques capable of a high degree of consistency, the production of biological medicinal products involves biological processes and materials, such as cultivation of cells or extraction of material from living organisms. These biological processes may display inherent variability, so that the range and nature of by-products are variable. Moreover, the materials used in these cultivation processes provide good substrates for growth of microbial contaminants.

Control of biological medicinal products usually involves biological analytical techniques which have a greater variability than physico-chemical determinations. In-process controls therefore take on a great importance in the manufacture of biological medicinal products.

Personnel

1   All personnel (including those concerned with cleaning, maintenance or quality control) employed in areas where biological medicinal products are manufactured should receive additional training specific to the products manufactured and to their work. Personnel should be given relevant information and training in hygiene and microbiology.

2   Persons responsible for production and quality control should have an adequate background in relevant scientific disciplines, such as bacteriology, biology, biometry, chemistry, medicine, pharmacy, pharmacology, virology, immunology and veterinary medicine, together with sufficient practical experience to enable them to exercise their management function for the process concerned.

3   The immunological status of personnel may have to be taken into consideration for product safety. All personnel engaged in production, maintenance, testing and animal care (and inspectors) should be vaccinated where necessary with appropriate specific vaccines and have regular health checks. Apart from the obvious problem of exposure of staff to infectious agents, potent toxins or allergens, it is necessary to avoid the risk of contamination of a production batch with infectious agents. Visitors should generally be excluded from production areas.

4   Any changes in the immunological status of personnel which could adversely affect the quality of the product should preclude work in the production area. Production of BCG vaccine and tuberculin products should be restricted to staff who are carefully monitored by regular checks of immunological status or chest X-ray.

5   In the course of a working day, personnel should not pass from areas where exposure to live organisms or animals is possible to areas where other products or different organisms are handled. If such passage is unavoidable, clearly defined decontamination measures, including change of clothing and shoes and, where necessary, showering should be followed by staff involved in any such production.

Premises and Equipment

6   The degree of environmental control of particulate and microbial contamination of the production premises should be adapted to the product and the production step, bearing in mind the level of contamination of the starting materials and the risk to the finished product.

7   The risk of cross-contamination between biological medicinal products, especially during those stages of the manufacturing process in which live organisms are used, may require additional precautions with respect to facilities and equipment, such as the use of dedicated facilities and equipment, production on a campaign basis and the use of closed systems. The nature of the product as well as the equipment used will determine the level of segregation needed to avoid cross-contamination.

8   In principle, dedicated facilities should be used for the production of BCG vaccine and for the handling of live organisms used in production of tuberculin products.

9   Dedicated facilities should be used for the handling of *Bacillus anthracis*, of *Clostridium botulinum* and of *Clostridium tetani* until the inactivation process is accomplished.

10   Production on a campaign basis may be acceptable for other spore forming organisms provided that the facilities are dedicated to this group of products and not more than one product is processed at any one time.

11   Simultaneous production in the same area using closed systems of biofermenters may be acceptable for products such as monoclonal antibodies and products prepared by r-DNA techniques.

12   Processing steps after harvesting may be carried out simultaneously in the same production area provided that adequate precautions are taken to prevent cross-contamination. For killed vaccines and toxoids, such parallel processing should only be performed after inactivation of the culture or after detoxification.

13   Positive pressure areas should be used to process sterile products but negative pressure in specific areas at point of exposure of pathogens is acceptable for containment reasons.

     Where negative pressure areas or safety cabinets are used for aseptic processing of pathogens, they should be surrounded by a positive pressure sterile zone.

14   Air filtration units should be specific to the processing area concerned and recirculation of air should not occur from areas handling live pathogenic organisms.

15   The layout and design of production areas and equipment should permit effective cleaning and decontamination (e.g. by fumigation). The adequacy of cleaning and decontamination procedures should be validated.

16   Equipment used during handling of live organisms should be designed to maintain cultures in a pure state and uncontaminated by external sources during processing.

17   Pipework systems, valves and vent filters should be properly designed to facilitate cleaning and sterilisation. The use of 'clean in place' and 'sterilise in place' systems should be encouraged. Valves on fermentation vessels should be completely steam sterilisable. Air vent filters should be hydrophobic and validated for their scheduled life span.

18   Primary containment should be designed and tested to demonstrate freedom from leakage risk.

19   Effluents which may contain pathogenic microorganisms should be effectively decontaminated.

20   Due to the variability of biological products or processes, some additives or ingredients have to be measured or weighed during the production process (e.g. buffers). In these cases, small stocks of these substances may be kept in the production area.

Animal Quarters and Care

21   Animals are used for the manufacture of a number of biological products, for example polio vaccine (monkeys), snake antivenoms (horses and goats), rabies vaccine (rabbits, mice and hamsters) and serum gonadotrophin (horses). In addition, animals may also be used in the quality control of most sera and vaccines, e.g. pertussis vaccine (mice), pyrogenicity (rabbits), BCG vaccine (guinea pigs).

22   General requirements for animal quarters, care and quarantine are laid down in Directive 86/609/EEC. Quarters for animals used in production and control of biological products should be separated from production and control areas. The health status of animals from which some starting materials are derived and of those used for quality control and safety testing should be monitored and recorded. Staff employed in such areas must be provided with special clothing

and changing facilities. Where monkeys are used for the production or quality control of biological medicinal products, special consideration is required as laid down in the current WHO *Requirements for biological substances no 7.*

Documentation

23 Specifications for biological starting materials may need additional documentation on the source, origin, method of manufacture and controls applied, particularly microbiological controls.

24 Specifications are routinely required for intermediate and bulk biological medicinal products.

Production

Starting materials

25 The source, origin and suitability of starting materials should be clearly defined. Where the necessary tests take a long time, it may be permissible to process starting materials before the results of the tests are available. In such cases, release of a finished product is conditional on satisfactory results of these tests.

26 Where sterilisation of starting materials is required, it should be carried out where possible by heat. Where necessary, other appropriate methods may also be used for inactivation of biological materials (e.g. irradiation).

Seed lot and cell bank system

27 In order to prevent the unwanted drift of properties which might ensue from repeated subcultures or multiple generations, the production of biological medicinal products obtained by microbial culture, cell culture or propagation in embryos and animals should be based on a system of master and working seed lots and/or cell banks.

28 The number of generations (doublings, passages) between the seed lot or cell bank and the finished product should be consistent with the marketing authorisation dossier. Scaling up of the process should not change this fundamental relationship.

29 Seed lots and cell banks should be adequately characterised and tested for contaminants. Their suitability for use should be further demonstrated by the consistency of the characteristics and quality of the successive batches of product. Seed lots and cell banks should be established, stored and used in such a way as to minimise the risks of contamination or alteration.

30   Establishment of the seed lot and cell bank should be performed in a suitably controlled environment to protect the seed lot and the cell bank and, if applicable, the personnel handling it. During the establishment of the seed lot and cell bank, no other living or infectious material (e.g. virus, cell lines or cell strains) should be handled simultaneously in the same area or by the same persons.

31   Evidence of the stability and recovery of the seeds and banks should be documented. Storage containers should be hermetically sealed, clearly labelled and kept at an appropriate temperature. An inventory should be meticulously kept. Storage temperature should be recorded continuously for freezers and properly monitored for liquid nitrogen. Any deviation from set limits and any corrective action taken should be recorded.

32   Only authorised personnel should be allowed to handle the material and this handling should be done under the supervision of a responsible person. Access to stored material should be controlled. Different seed lots or cell banks should be stored in such a way as to avoid confusion or cross-contamination. It is desirable to split the seed lots and cell banks and to store the parts at different locations so as to minimise the risks of total loss.

33   All containers of master or working cell banks and seed lots should be treated identically during storage. Once removed from storage, the containers should not be returned to the stock.

Operating principles

34   The growth promoting properties of culture media should be demonstrated.

35   Addition of materials or cultures to fermenters and other vessels and the taking of samples should be carried out under carefully controlled conditions to ensure that absence of contamination is maintained. Care should be taken to ensure that vessels are correctly connected when addition or sampling take place.

36   Centrifugation and blending of products can lead to aerosol formation and containment of such activities to prevent transfer of live microorganisms is necessary.

37   If possible, media should be sterilised in situ. In-line sterilising filters for routine addition of gases, media, acids or alkalis, defoaming agents etc. to fermenters should be used where possible.

38   Careful consideration should be given to the validation of any necessary virus removal or inactivation undertaken (see CPMP notes for guidance).

39   In cases where a virus inactivation or removal process is performed during manufacture, measures should be taken to avoid the risk of recontamination of treated products by non-treated products.

40   A wide variety of equipment is used for chromatography, and in general such equipment should be dedicated to the purification of one product and should be sterilised or sanitised between batches. The use of the same equipment at different stages of processing should be discouraged. Acceptance criteria, life span and sanitisation or sterilisation method of columns should be defined.

Quality Control

41   In-process controls play a specially important role in ensuring the consistency of the quality of biological medicinal products. Those controls which are crucial for quality (e.g. virus removal) but which cannot be carried out on the finished product, should be performed at an appropriate stage of production.

42   It may be necessary to retain samples of intermediate products in sufficient quantities and under appropriate storage conditions to allow the repetition or confirmation of a batch control.

43   Continuous monitoring of certain production processes is necessary, for example fermentation. Such data should form part of the batch record.

44   Where continuous culture is used, special consideration should be given to the quality control requirements arising from this type of production method.

---

(1)   Biological medicinal products manufactured by these methods include vaccines, immunosera, antigens, hormones, cytokines, enzymes and other products of fermentation (including monoclonal antibodies and products derived from r-DNA).

(2)   In: COMMISSION OF THE EUROPEAN COMMUNITIES.
Rules governing medicinal products in the EC.
Luxembourg: Office for Official Publications of the EC.

Manufacture of Radiopharmaceuticals

Principle

The manufacturing and handling of radiopharmaceuticals is potentially hazardous. The level of risk depends in particular upon the types of radiation emitted and the half-lives of the radioactive isotopes. Particular attention must be paid to the prevention of cross-contamination, to the retention of radionuclide contaminants, and to waste disposal. Special consideration may be necessary with reference to the small batch sizes made frequently for many radiopharmaceuticals. Due to their short half-life, some radiopharmaceuticals are released before completion of certain Quality Control tests. In this case, the continuous assessment of the effectiveness of the Quality Assurance system becomes very important.

Note

Manufacture must comply with the requirements of EURATOM Directives laying down the basic standards for the health protection of the general public and workers against the dangers of ionising radiation, as well as complying with other relevant national requirements.

Personnel

1   All personnel (including those concerned with cleaning and maintenance) employed in areas where radioactive products are manufactured should receive additional training specific to this class of products. In particular, they should be given detailed information and appropriate training on radiation protection.

Premises and Equipment

2   Radioactive products should be stored, processed, packaged and controlled in dedicated and self-contained facilities. The equipment used for manufacturing operations should be reserved exclusively for radiopharmaceuticals.

3   In order to contain the radioactive particles, it may be necessary for the air pressure to be lower where products are exposed than in surrounding areas. However, it is still necessary to protect the product from environmental contamination.

4   For sterile products the working zone where products or containers may be exposed should comply with the environmental requirements described in the annex on sterile products. This may be achieved by the provision within the work station of a laminar flow of HEPA-filtered air and by fitting air-locks to entry ports. Total containment work stations may provide these requirements. They should be in an environment conforming to at least grade D.

5   Air extracted from areas where radioactive products are handled should not be recirculated; air outlets should be designed to avoid possible environmental contamination by radioactive particles and gases.

     There should be a system to prevent air entering the clean area through extract ducts e.g. when the extract fan is not operating.

Production

6   Production of different radioactive products in the same work stations and at the same time should be avoided in order to minimise the risk of cross-contamination or mix-up.

7   Process validation, in-process controls and monitoring of process parameters and environment assume particular importance in cases where it is necessary to take the decision to release or reject a batch or a product before all tests are completed.

Quality Control

8   When products have to be dispatched before all tests are completed this does not obviate the need for a formal recorded decision to be taken by the Qualified Person on the conformity of the batch. In this case there should be a written procedure detailing all production and Quality Control data which should be considered before the batch is dispatched. A procedure should also describe the measures to be taken by the Qualified Person if unsatisfactory test results are obtained after dispatch.

9   Unless otherwise specified in the marketing authorisation, reference samples of every batch should be retained.

Distribution and Recalls

10   Detailed distribution records should be maintained and there should be procedures which describe the measures to be taken for stopping the use of defective radiopharmaceuticals. Recall operations should be shown to be operable within a very short time.

Manufacture of Veterinary Medicinal Products other than Immunological Veterinary Medicinal Products

Note

This annex applies to all veterinary medicinal products falling within the scope of Directive 81/851/EEC other than immunological veterinary medicinal products, which are the subject of a separate annex.

Manufacture of Premixes for Medicated Feedingstuffs

For the purposes of these paragraphs,

- *a medicated feedingstuff* is any mixture of a veterinary medicinal product or products and feed or feeds which is ready prepared for marketing and intended to be fed to animals without further processing because of its curative or preventative properties as a medicinal product covered by Article 1(2) of Directive 65/65/EEC;

- *a premix for medicated feedingstuffs* is any veterinary medicinal product prepared in advance with a view to the subsequent manufacture of medicated feedingstuffs.

1   The manufacture of premixes for medicated feedingstuffs requires the use of large quantities of vegetable matter which is likely to attract insects and rodents. Premises should be designed, equipped and operated to minimise this risk (point 3.4 of the Guide) and should also be subject to a regular pest control programme.

2   Because of the large volume of dust generated during the production of bulk material for premixes, specific attention should be given to the need to avoid cross contamination and facilitate cleaning (point 3.14 of the Guide), for example through the installation of sealed transport systems and dust extraction, whenever possible. The installation of such systems does not, however, eliminate the need for regular cleaning of production areas.

3   Parts of the process likely to have a significant adverse influence on the stability of the active ingredient(s) (e.g. use of steam in pellet manufacture) should be carried out in a uniform manner from batch to batch.

4   Consideration should be given to undertake the manufacture of premixes in dedicated areas which, if at all possible, do not form part of a main manufacturing plant. Alternatively, such dedicated areas should be surrounded by a buffer zone in order to minimise the risk of contamination of other manufacturing areas.

The manufacture of Ectoparasiticides

5   In derogation from point 3.6 of the Guide, ectoparasiticides for external application to animals, which are veterinary medicinal products, and subject to marketing authorisation, may be produced and filled on a campaign basis in pesticide specific areas. However other categories of veterinary medicinal products should not be produced in such areas.

6   Adequate validated cleaning procedures should be employed to prevent cross contamination, and steps should be taken to ensure the secure storage of the veterinary medicinal product in accordance with the Guide.

The Manufacture of Veterinary Medicinal Products Containing Penicillins

7   The use of penicillins in veterinary medicine does not present the same risks of hypersensitivity in animals as in humans. Although incidents of hypersensitivity have been recorded in horses and dogs, there are other materials which are toxic to certain species, e.g. the ionophore antibiotics in horses. Although desirable, the requirements that such products be manufactured in dedicated, self-contained facilities (point 3.6 of the Guide) may be dispensed with in the case of facilities dedicated to the manufacture of veterinary medicinal products only. However, all necessary measures should be taken to avoid cross contamination and any risk to operator safety in accordance with the Guide. In such circumstances, penicillin-containing products should be manufactured on a campaign basis and should be followed by appropriate, validated decontamination and cleaning procedures.

Retention of Samples (point 1.4 viii and point 6.14 of the Guide)

8   It is recognised that because of the large volume of certain veterinary medicinal products in their final packaging, in particular premixes, it may not be feasible for manufacturers to retain samples from each batch in its final packaging. However, manufacturers should ensure that sufficient representative samples of each batch are retained and stored in accordance with the Guide.

9   In all cases, the container used for storage should be composed of the same materials as the market primary container in which the product is marketed.

Sterile Veterinary Medicinal Products

10   Where this has been accepted by the competent authorities, terminally sterilised veterinary medicinal products may be manufactured in a clean area of a lower grade than the grade required in the annex on sterile preparations but at least in a grade D environment.

ANNEX 5 Manufacture of Immunological Veterinary Medicinal Products

Principle

The manufacture of immunological veterinary medicinal products has special characteristics which should be taken into consideration when implementing and assessing the quality assurance system.

Due to the large number of animal species and related pathogenic agents, the variety of products manufactured is very wide and the volume of manufacture is often low; hence work on a campaign basis is common. Moreover, because of the very nature of this manufacture (cultivation steps, lack of terminal sterilisation etc.), the products must be particularly well-protected against contamination and cross-contamination. The environment also must be protected especially when the manufacture involves the use of pathogenic or exotic biological agents and the worker must be particularly well-protected when the manufacture involves the use of biological agents pathogenic to man.

These factors, together with the inherent variability of immunological products and the relative inefficiency in particular of final product quality control tests in providing adequate information about products, means that the role of the quality assurance system is of the utmost importance. The need to maintain control over all of the following aspects of GMP, as well as those outlined in this Guide, cannot be overemphasised. In particular, it is important that the data generated by the monitoring of the various aspects of GMP (equipment, premises, product etc.) are rigorously assessed and informed decisions, leading to appropriate action, are made and recorded.

Personnel

1   All personnel (including those concerned with cleaning and maintenance) employed in areas where immunological products are manufactured should be given training in and information on hygiene and microbiology. They should receive additional training specific to the products with which they work.

2   Responsible personnel should be formally trained in some or all of the following fields: bacteriology, biology, biometry, chemistry, immunology, medicine, parasitology, pharmacy, pharmacology, virology and veterinary medicine and should also have an adequate knowledge of environmental protection measures.

3   Personnel should be protected against possible infection with the biological agents used in manufacture. In the case of biological agents known to cause disease in humans, adequate measures should be taken to prevent infection of personnel working with the agent or with experimental animals.

     Where relevant, the personnel should be vaccinated and subject to medical examination.

4   Adequate measures should be taken to prevent biological agents being taken outside the manufacturing plant by personnel acting as a carrier. Dependent on the type of biological agent, such measures may include complete change of clothes and compulsory showering before leaving the production area.

5   For immunological products, the risk of contamination or cross-contamination by personnel is particularly important.

     Prevention of **contamination** by personnel should be achieved by a set of measures and procedures to ensure that appropriate protective clothing is used during the different stages of the production process.

     Prevention of **cross-contamination** by personnel involved in production should be achieved by a set of measures and procedures to ensure that they do not pass from one area to another unless they have taken appropriate measures to eliminate the risk of contamination. In the course of a working day, personnel should not pass from areas where contamination with live microorganisms is likely or where animals are housed to premises where other products or organisms are handled. If such passage is unavoidable, clearly defined decontamination procedures including change of clothing and shoes and, where necessary, showering, should be followed by staff involved in any such production.

     Personnel entering a contained area where organisms had not been handled in open circuit operations in the previous twelve hours to check on cultures in sealed, surface decontaminated flasks would not be regarded as being at risk of contamination, unless the organism involved was an exotic.

Premises

6   Premises should be designed in such a way as to control both the risk to the product and to the environment.

This can be achieved by the use of containment, clean, clean/ contained or controlled areas.

7   Live biological agents should be handled in contained areas. The level of containment should depend on the pathogenicity of the microorganism and whether it has been classified as exotic. (Other relevant legislation, such as Directives 90/219/EEC and 90/220/EEC, also applies.)

8   Inactivated biological agents should be handled in clean areas. Clean areas should also be used when handling non-infected cells isolated from multicellular organisms and, in some cases, filtration-sterilised media.

9   Open circuit operations involving products or components not subsequently sterilised should be carried out within a laminar air flow work station (grade A) in a grade B area.

10   Other operations where live biological agents are handled (quality control, research and diagnostic services etc.) should be appropriately contained and separated if production operations are carried out in the same building. The level of containment should depend on the pathogenicity of the biological agent and whether they have been classified as exotic. Whenever diagnostic activities are carried out, there is the risk of introducing highly pathogenic organisms. Therefore, the level of containment should be adequate to cope with all such risks. Containment may also be required if quality control or other activities are carried out in buildings in close proximity to those used for production.

11   Containment premises should be easily disinfected and should have the following characteristics:

(a)   the absence of direct venting to the outside;

(b)   a ventilation with air at negative pressure. Air should be extracted through HEPA filters and not be recirculated except to the same area, and provided further HEPA filtration is used (normally this condition would be met by routing the recirculated air through the normal supply HEPAs for that area). However, recycling of air between areas may be permissible provided that it passes through two exhaust HEPAs, the first of which is continuously monitored for integrity, and there are adequate measures for safe venting of exhaust air should this filter fail;

(c)   air from manufacturing areas used for the handling of exotic organisms should be vented through 2 sets of HEPA filters in series, and that from production areas not recirculated;

(d)   a system for the collection and disinfection of liquid effluents including contaminated condensate from sterilisers, biogenerators etc. Solid wastes, including animal carcasses, should be disinfected, sterilised or incinerated as appropriate. Contaminated filters should be removed using a safe method;

(e)   changing rooms designed and used as air locks, and equipped with washing and showering facilities if appropriate. Air pressure differentials should be such that there is no flow of air between the work area and the external environment or risk of contamination of outer clothing worn outside the area;

(f)   an air lock system for the passage of equipment, which is constructed so that there is no flow of contaminated air between the work area and the external environment or risk of contamination of equipment within the lock. The air lock should be of a size which enables the effective surface decontamination of materials being passed through it. Consideration should be given to having a timing device on the door interlock to allow sufficient time for the decontamination process to be effective;

(g)   in many instances, a barrier double-door autoclave for the secure removal of waste materials and introduction of sterile items.

12   Equipment passes and changing rooms should have an interlock mechanism or other appropriate system to prevent the opening of more than one door at a time. Changing rooms should be supplied with air filtered to the same standard as that for the work area, and equipped with air extraction facilities to produce an adequate air circulation independent of that of the work area. Equipment passes should normally be ventilated in the same way, but unventilated passes, or those equipped with supply air only, may be acceptable.

13   Production operations such as cell maintenance, media preparation, virus culture etc. likely to cause contamination should be performed in separate areas. Animals and animal products should be handled with appropriate precautions.

14   Production areas where biological agents particularly resistant to disinfection (e.g. spore-forming bacteria) are handled should be separated and dedicated to that particular purpose until the biological agents have been inactivated.

15   With the exception of blending and subsequent filling operations, one biological agent only should be handled at a time within an area.

16   Production areas should be designed to permit disinfection between campaigns, using validated methods.

17   Production of biological agents may take place in controlled areas provided it is carried out in totally enclosed and heat sterilised equipment, all connections being also heat sterilised after making and before breaking. It may be acceptable for connections to be made under local laminar air flow provided these are few in number and proper aseptic techniques are used and there is no risk of leakage. The sterilisation parameters used before breaking the connections must be validated for the organisms being used. Different products may be placed in different biogenerators, within the same area, provided that there is no risk of accidental cross-contamination. However, organisms generally subject to special requirements for containment should be in areas dedicated to such products.

18   Animal houses where animals intended or used for production are accommodated, should be provided with the appropriate containment and/or clean area measures and should be separate from other animal accommodation.

      Animal houses where animals used for quality control, involving the use of pathogenic biological agents, are accommodated, should be adequately contained.

19   Access to manufacturing areas should be restricted to authorised personnel. Clear and concise written procedures should be posted as appropriate.

20   Documentation relating to the premises should be readily available in a plant master file.

      The manufacturing site and buildings should be described in sufficient detail (by means of plans and written explanations) so that the designation and conditions of use of all the rooms are correctly identified as well as the biological agents which are handled in them. The flow of people and product should also be clearly marked.

      The animal species accommodated in the animal houses or otherwise on the site should be identified.

      The activities carried out in the vicinity of the site should also be indicated.

      Plans of contained and/or clean area premises, should describe the ventilation system indicating inlets and outlets, filters and their specifications, the number of air changes per hour, and pressure gradients. They should indicate which pressure gradients are monitored by pressure indicator.

Equipment

21 The equipment used should be designed and constructed so that it meets the particular requirements for the manufacture of each product.

Before being put into operation the equipment should be qualified and validated and subsequently be regularly maintained and validated.

22 Where appropriate, the equipment should ensure satisfactory primary containment of the biological agents.

Where appropriate, the equipment should be designed and constructed as to allow easy and effective decontamination and/or sterilisation.

23 Closed equipment used for the primary containment of the biological agents should be designed and constructed as to prevent any leakage or the formation of droplets and aerosols.

Inlets and outlets for gases should be protected so as to achieve adequate containment e.g. by the use of sterilising hydrophobic filters.

The introduction or removal of material should take place using a sterilisable closed system, or possibly in an appropriate laminar air flow.

24 Equipment where necessary should be properly sterilised before use, preferably by pressurised dry steam. Other methods can be accepted if steam sterilisation cannot be used because of the nature of the equipment. It is important not to overlook such individual items as bench centrifuges and water baths.

Equipment used for purification, separation or concentration should be sterilised or disinfected at least between use for different products. The effect of the sterilisation methods on the effectiveness and validity of the equipment should be studied in order to determine the life span of the equipment.

All sterilisation procedures should be validated.

25 Equipment should be designed so as to prevent any mix-ups between different organisms or products. Pipes, valves and filters should be identified as to their function.

Separate incubators should be used for infected and non-infected containers and also generally for different organisms or cells. Incubators containing more than one organism or cell type will only be acceptable if adequate steps are taken to seal, surface decontaminate and segregate the containers. Culture vessels etc. should be individually labelled. The cleaning and disinfection of the items can be particularly difficult and should receive special attention.

Equipment used for the storage of biological agents or products should be designed and used in such a manner as to prevent any possible mix-up. All stored items should be clearly and unambiguously labelled and in leak-proof containers. Items such as cells and organisms seed stock should be stored in dedicated equipment.

26   Relevant equipment, such as that requiring temperature control, should be fitted with recording and/or alarm systems.

To avoid breakdowns, a system of preventative maintenance, together with trend analysis of recorded data, should be implemented.

27   The loading of freeze driers requires an appropriate clean/contained area.

Unloading freeze driers contaminates the immediate environment. Therefore, for single-ended freeze driers, the clean room should be decontaminated before a further manufacturing batch is introduced into the area, unless this contains the same organisms, and double door freeze driers should be sterilised after each cycle unless opened in a clean area.

Sterilisation of freeze driers should be done in accordance with item 24. In case of campaign working, they should at least be sterilised after each campaign.

Animals and Animal Houses

28   General requirements for animal quarters, care and quarantine are laid down in Directive 86/609/EEC.

29   Animal houses should be separated from the other production premises and suitably designed.

30   The sanitary status of the animals used for production should be defined, monitored, and recorded. Some animals should be handled as defined in specific monographs (e.g. Specific Pathogens Free flocks).

31   Animals, biological agents, and tests carried out should be the subject of an identification system so as to prevent any risk of confusion and to control all possible hazards.

Disinfection – Waste Disposal

32   Disinfection and/or wastes and effluents disposal may be particularly important in the case of manufacture of immunological products. Careful consideration should therefore be given to procedures and equipment aiming at avoiding environmental contamination as well as to their validation or qualification.

Production

33   Because of the wide variety of products, the frequently large number of stages involved in the manufacture of immunological veterinary medicinal products and the nature of the biological processes, careful attention must be paid to adherence to validated operating procedures, to the constant monitoring of production at all stages and to in-process controls.

Additionally, special consideration should be given to starting materials, media and the use of a seed lot system.

Starting Materials

34   The suitability of starting materials should be clearly defined in written specifications. These should include details of the supplier, the method of manufacture, the geographical origin and the animal species from which the materials are derived. The controls to be applied to starting materials must be included. Microbiological controls are particularly important.

35   The results of tests on starting materials must comply with the specifications. Where the tests take a long time (e.g. eggs from SPF flocks) it may be necessary to process starting materials before the results of analytical controls are available. In such cases, the release of a finished product is conditional upon satisfactory results of the tests on starting materials.

36   Special attention should be paid to a knowledge of the supplier's quality assurance system in assessing the suitability of a source and the extent of quality control testing required.

37   Where possible, heat is the preferred method for sterilising starting materials. If necessary, other validated methods, such as irradiation, may be used.

Media

38 The ability of media to support the desired growth should be properly validated in advance.

39 Media should preferably be sterilised in situ or in line. Heat is the preferred method. Gases, media, acids, alkalis, defoaming agents and other materials introduced into sterile biogenerators should themselves be sterile.

Seed Lot and Cell Bank System

40 In order to prevent the unwanted drift of properties which might ensue from repeated subcultures or multiple generations, the production of immunological veterinary medicinal products obtained by microbial, cell or tissue culture, or propagation in embryos and animals, should be based on a system of seed lots or cell banks.

41 The number of generations (doublings, passages) between the seed lot or cell bank and the finished product should be consistent with the dossier of authorisation for marketing.

42 Seed lots and cell banks should be adequately characterised and tested for contaminants. Acceptance criteria for new seed lots should be established. Seed lots and cell banks shall be established, stored and used in such a way as to minimise the risks of contamination, or any alteration. During the establishment of the seed lot and cell bank, no other living or infectious material (e.g. virus or cell lines) shall be handled simultaneously in the same area or by the same person.

43 Establishment of the seed lot and cell bank should be performed in a suitable environment to protect the seed lot and the cell bank and, if applicable, the personnel handling it and the external environment.

44 The origin, form and storage conditions of seed material should be described in full. Evidence of the stability and recovery of the seeds and cells should be provided. Storage containers should be hermetically sealed, clearly labelled and stored at an appropriate temperature. Storage conditions shall be properly monitored. An inventory should be kept and each container accounted for.

45 Only authorised personnel should be allowed to handle the material and this handling should be done under the supervision of a responsible person. Different seed lots or cell banks shall be stored in such a way to avoid confusion or cross-contamination errors. It is desirable to split the seed lots and cell banks and to store the parts at different locations so as to minimise the risk of total loss.

Operating Principles

46   The formation of droplets and the production of foam should be avoided or minimised during manufacturing processes. Centrifugation and blending procedures which can lead to droplet formation should be carried out in appropriate contained or clean/ contained areas to prevent transfer of live organisms.

47   Accidental spillages, especially of live organisms, must be dealt with quickly and safely. Validated decontamination measures should be available for each organism. Where different strains of single bacteria species or very similar viruses are involved, the process need be validated against only one of them, unless there is reason to believe that they may vary significantly in their resistance to the agent(s) involved.

48   Operations involving the transfer of materials such as sterile media, cultures or product should be carried out in pre-sterilised closed systems wherever possible. Where this is not possible, transfer operations must be protected by laminar airflow work stations.

49   Addition of media or cultures to biogenerators and other vessels should be carried out under carefully controlled conditions to ensure that contamination is not introduced. Care must be taken to ensure that vessels are correctly connected when addition of cultures takes place.

50   Where necessary, for instance when two or more fermentors are within a single area, sampling and addition ports, and connectors (after connection, before the flow of product, and again before disconnection) should be sterilised with steam. In other circumstances, chemical disinfection of ports and laminar air flow protection of connections may be acceptable.

51   Equipment, glassware, the external surfaces of product containers and other such materials must be disinfected before transfer from a contained area using a validated method (see 47 above). Batch documentation can be a particular problem. Only the absolute minimum required to allow operations to GMP standards should enter and leave the area. If obviously contaminated, such as by spills or aerosols, or if the organism involved is an exotic, the paperwork must be adequately disinfected through an equipment pass, or the information transferred out by such means as photocopy or fax.

52   Liquid or solid wastes such as the debris after harvesting eggs, disposable culture bottles, unwanted cultures or biological agents, are best sterilised or disinfected before transfer from a contained area. However, alternatives such as sealed containers or piping may be appropriate in some cases.

53 Articles and materials, including documentation, entering a production room should be carefully controlled to ensure that only articles and materials concerned with production are introduced. There should be a system which ensures that articles and materials entering a room are reconciled with those leaving so that their accumulation within the room does not occur.

54 Heat stable articles and materials entering a clean area or clean/contained area should do so through a double-ended autoclave or oven. Heat labile articles and materials should enter through an airlock with interlocked doors where they are disinfected. Sterilisation of articles and materials elsewhere is acceptable provided that they are double wrapped and enter through an airlock with the appropriate precautions.

55 Precautions must be taken to avoid contamination or confusion during incubation. There should be a cleaning and disinfection procedure for incubators. Containers in incubators should be carefully and clearly labelled.

56 With the exception of blending and subsequent filling operations (or when totally enclosed systems are used) only one live biological agent may be handled within a production room at any given time. Production rooms must be effectively disinfected between the handling of different live biological agents.

57 Products should be inactivated by the addition of inactivant accompanied by sufficient agitation. The mixture should then be transferred to a second sterile vessel, unless the container is of such a size and shape as to be easily inverted and shaken so as to wet all internal surfaces with the final culture/inactivant mixture.

58 Vessels containing inactivated product should not be opened or sampled in areas containing live biological agents. All subsequent processing of inactivated products should take place in clean areas grade A–B or enclosed equipment dedicated to inactivated products.

59 Careful consideration should be given to the validation of methods for sterilisation, disinfection, virus removal and inactivation.

60 Filling should be carried out as soon as possible following production. Containers of bulk product prior to filling should be sealed, appropriately labelled and stored under specified conditions of temperature.

61 There should be a system to assure the integrity and closure of containers after filling.

62   The capping of vials containing live biological agents must be performed in such a way that ensures that contamination of other products or escape of the live agents into other areas or the external environment does not occur.

63   For various reasons there may be a delay between the filling of final containers and their labelling and packaging. Procedures should be specified for the storage of unlabelled containers in order to prevent confusion and to ensure satisfactory storage conditions. Special attention should be paid to the storage of heat labile or photosensitive products. Storage temperatures should be specified.

64   For each stage of production, the yield of product should be reconciled with that expected from that process. Any significant discrepancies should be investigated.

Quality Control

65   In-process controls play a specially important role in ensuring the consistency of the quality of biological medicinal products. Those controls which are crucial for the quality (e.g. virus removal) but which cannot be carried out on the finished product, should be performed at an appropriate stage of production.

66   It may be necessary to retain samples of intermediate products in sufficient amount and under appropriate storage conditions to allow repetition or confirmation of a batch control.

67   There may be a requirement for the continuous monitoring of data during a production process, for example monitoring of physical parameters during fermentation.

68   Continuous culture of biological products is a common practice and special consideration needs to be given to the quality control requirements arising from this type of production method.

ANNEX 6 Manufacture of Medicinal Gases

1 Principle

This annex deals with industrial manufacturing of medicinal gases, which is a specialised industrial process not normally undertaken by pharmaceutical companies. It does not cover manufacturing and handling of medicinal gases in hospitals, which will be subject to national legislation. However relevant parts of this annex may be used as a basis for such activities.

The manufacture of medicinal gases is generally carried out in closed equipment. Consequently, environmental contamination of the product is minimal. However, there is a risk of cross-contamination with other gases.

Manufacture of medicinal gases should comply with the basic requirements of GMP, with applicable annexes, Pharmacopoeial standards and the following detailed guidelines.

2 Personnel

2.1 The qualified person responsible for release of medicinal gases should have a thorough knowledge of the production and control of medicinal gases.

2.2 All personnel involved in the manufacture of medicinal gases should understand the GMP requirements relevant to medicinal gases and should be aware of the critically important aspects and potential hazards for patients from products in the form of medicinal gases.

3 Premises and Equipment

3.1 *Premises*

3.1.1 Medicinal gases should be filled in a separate area from non-medicinal gases and there should be no exchange of containers between these areas. In exceptional cases, the principal of campaign filling in the same area can be accepted provided that specific precautions are taken and necessary validation is done.

3.1.2 Premises should provide sufficient space for manufacturing, testing and storage operations to avoid the risk of mix-up. Premises should be clean and tidy to encourage orderly working and adequate storage.

3.1.3 Filling areas should be of sufficient size and have an orderly layout to provide:

a. separate marked areas for different gases;

b. clear identification and segregation of empty cylinders and cylinders at various stages of processing (e.g. 'awaiting filling', 'filled', 'quarantine', 'approved' 'rejected ').

The method used to achieve these various levels of segregation will depend on the nature, extent and complexity of the overall operation, but marked-out floor areas, partitions, barriers and signs could be used or other appropriate means.

3.2 *Equipment*

3.2.1 All equipment for manufacture and analyses should be qualified and calibrated regularly as appropriate.

3.2.2 It is necessary to ensure that the correct gas is put into the correct container. Except for validated automated filling processes there should be no interconnections between pipelines carrying different gases. The manifolds should be equipped with fill connections that correspond only to the valve for that particular gas or particular mixture of gases so that only the correct containers can be attached to the manifold. (The use of manifold and container valve connections may be subject to international or national standards.)

3.2.3 Repair and maintenance operations should not affect the quality of the medicinal gases.

3.2.4 Filling of non-medicinal gases should be avoided in areas and with equipment destined for the production of medicinal gases. Exceptions can be acceptable if the quality of the gas used for non-medicinal purposes is at least equal to the quality of the medicinal gas and GMP-standards are maintained. There should be a validated method of backflow prevention in the line supplying the filling area for non-medicinal gases to prevent contamination of the medicinal gas.

3.2.5 Storage tanks and mobile delivery tanks should be dedicated to one gas and a well-defined quality of this gas. However liquefied medicinal gases may be stored or transported in the same tanks as the same non-medicinal gas provided that the quality of the latter is at least equal to the quality of the medicinal gas.

4 Documentation

4.1 Data included in the records for each batch of cylinders filled must ensure that each filled cylinder is traceable to significant aspects of the relevant filling operations. As appropriate, the following should be entered:

- the name of the product;
- the date and the time of the filling operations;
- a reference to the filling station used;
- equipment used;
- name and reference to the specification of the gas or each gas in a mixture;
- pre-filling operations performed (see point 5.3.5);
- the quantity and size of cylinders before and after filling;
- the name of the person carrying out the filling operation;
- the initials of the operators for each significant step (line clearance, receipt of cylinders, emptying of cylinders etc);
- key parameters that are needed to ensure correct fill at standard conditions;
- the results of quality control tests and where test equipment is calibrated before each test, the reference gas specification and calibration check results;
- results of appropriate checks to ensure the containers have been filled;
- a sample of the batch code label;
- details of any problems or unusual events, and signed authorisation for any deviation from filling instructions;
- to indicate agreement, the date and signature of the supervisor responsible for the filling operation.

5 Production

5.1 All critical steps in the different manufacturing processes should be subject to validation.

5.2 *Bulk production*

5.2.1 Bulk gases intended for medicinal use could be prepared by chemical synthesis or obtained from natural resources followed by purification steps if necessary (as for example in an air separation plant). These gases could be regarded as Active Pharmaceutical Ingredients (API) or as bulk pharmaceutical products as decided by the national competent authority.

5.2.2 Documentation should be available specifying the purity, other components and possible impurities that may be present in the source gas and at purification steps, as applicable. Flow charts of each different process should be available.

5.2.3 All separation and purification steps should be designed to operate at optimal effectiveness. For example, impurities that may adversely affect a purification step should be removed before this step is reached.

5.2.4 Separation and purification steps should be validated for effectiveness and monitored according to the results of the validation. Where necessary, in-process controls should include continuous analysis to monitor the process. Maintenance and replacement of expendable equipment components, e.g. purification filters, should be based on the results of monitoring and validation.

5.2.5 If applicable, limits for process temperatures should be documented and in-process monitoring should include temperature measurement.

5.2.6 Computer systems used in controlling or monitoring processes should be validated.

5.2.7 For continuous processes, a definition of a batch should be documented and related to the analysis of the bulk gas.

5.2.8 Gas production should be continuously monitored for quality and impurities.

5.2.9 Water used for cooling during compression of air should be monitored for microbiological quality when in contact with the medicinal gas.

5.2.10 All the transfer operations, including controls before transfers, of liquefied gases from primary storage should be in accordance with written procedures designed to avoid any contamination. The transfer line should be equipped with a non-return valve or other suitable alternative. Particular attention should be paid to purge the flexible connections and to coupling hoses and connectors.

5.2.11 Deliveries of gas may be added to bulk storage tanks containing the same gas from previous deliveries. The results of a sample must show that the quality of the delivered gas is acceptable. Such a sample could be taken from:

- the delivered gas before the delivery is added; or

- from the bulk tank after adding and mixing.

5.2.12 Bulk gases intended for medicinal use should be defined as a batch, controlled in accordance with relevant Pharmacopoeial monographs and released for filling.

5.3 *Filling and labelling*

5.3.1 For filling of medicinal gases the batch should be defined.

5.3.2 Containers for medicinal gases should conform to appropriate technical specifications. Valve outlets should be equipped with tamper-evident seals after filling. Cylinders should preferably have minimum pressure retention valves in order to get adequate protection against contamination.

5.3.3 The medicinal gases filling manifold as well as the cylinders should be dedicated to a single medicinal gas or to a given mixture of medicinal gases (see also 3.2.2). There should be a system in place ensuring traceability of cylinders and valves.

5.3.4 Cleaning and purging of filling equipment and pipelines should be carried out according to written procedures. This is especially important after maintenance or breaches of system integrity. Checks for the absence of contaminants should be carried out before the line is released for use. Records should be maintained.

5.3.5 Cylinders should be subject to an internal visual inspection when:

- they are new;

- in connection with any hydrostatic pressure test or equivalent test.

After fitting of the valve, the valve should be maintained in a closed position to prevent any contamination from entering the cylinder.

5.3.6 Checks to be performed before filling should include:

- a check to determine the residual pressure (>3 to 5 bar) to ensure that the cylinder is not emptied;

- Cylinders with no residual pressure should be put aside for additional measures to make sure they are not contaminated with water or other contaminants. These could include cleaning with validated methods or visual inspection as justified;

- Assuring that all batch labels and other labels if damaged have been removed;

- visual external inspection of each valve and container for dents, arc burns, debris, other damage and contamination with oil or grease; Cylinders should be cleaned, tested and maintained in an appropriate manner;

- a check of each cylinder or cryogenic vessel valve connection to determine that it is the proper type for the particular medicinal gas involved;

- a check of the cylinder 'test code date' to determine that the hydrostatic pressure test or equivalent test has been conducted and still is valid as required by national or international guidelines;

- a check to determine that each container is colour-coded according to the relevant standard.

5.3.7   Cylinders which have been returned for refilling should be prepared with great care in order to minimise risks for contamination. For compressed gases a maximum theoretical impurity of 500 ppm v/v should be obtained for a filling pressure of 200 bar (and equivalent for other filling pressures).

Cylinders could be prepared as follows:

- any gas remaining in the cylinders should be removed by evacuating the container (at least to a remaining absolute pressure of 150 millibar);

or

- by blowing down each container, followed by purging using validated methods (partial pressurisation at least to 7 bar and then blowing down).

For cylinders equipped with residual (positive) pressure valves, one evacuation under vacuum at 150 millibar is sufficient if the pressure is positive. As an alternative, full analysis of the remaining gas should be carried out for each individual container.

5.3.8   There should be appropriate checks to ensure that containers have been filled. An indication that it is filling properly could be to ensure that the exterior of the cylinder is warm by touching it lightly during filling.

5.3.9   Each cylinder should be labelled and colour-coded. The batch number and/or filling date and expiry date may be on a separate label.

6   Quality Control

6.1   Water used for hydrostatic pressure testing should be at least of drinking water quality and monitored routinely for microbiological contamination.

6.2   Each medicinal gas should be tested and released according to its specifications. In addition, each medicinal gas should be tested to full relevant pharmacopoeial requirements at sufficient frequency to assure ongoing compliance.

6.3   The bulk gas supply should be released for filling. (see 5.2.12)

6.4   In the case of a single medicinal gas filled via a multi-cylinder manifold, at least one cylinder of product from each manifold filling should be tested for identity, assay and if necessary water content each time the cylinders are changed on the manifold.

6.5   In the case of a single medicinal gas filled into cylinders one at a time by individual filling operations, at least one cylinder of each uninterrupted filling cycle should be tested for identity and assay. An example of an uninterrupted filling operation cycle is one shift's production using the same personnel, equipment, and batch of bulk gas.

6.6   In the case of a medicinal gas produced by mixing two or more different gases in a cylinder from the same manifold, at least one cylinder from each manifold filling operation cycle should be tested for identity, assay and if necessary water content of all of the component gases and for identity of the balance gas in the mixture. When cylinders are filled individually, every cylinder should be tested for identity and assay of all of the component gases and at least one cylinder of each uninterrupted filling cycle should be tested for identity of the balance gas in the mixture.

6.7   When gases are mixed in-line before filling (e.g. nitrous oxide/oxygen mixture) continuous analysis of the mixture being filled is required.

6.8   When a cylinder is filled with more than one gas, the filling process must ensure that the gases are correctly mixed in every cylinder and are fully homogeneous.

6.9   Each filled cylinder should be tested for leaks using an appropriate method, prior to fitting the tamper evident seal. Where sampling and testing is carried out the leak test should be completed after testing.

6.10   In the case of cryogenic gas filled into cryogenic home vessels for delivery to users, each vessel should be tested for identity and assay.

6.11   Cryogenic vessels which are retained by customers and where the medicinal gas is refilled in place from dedicated mobile delivery tanks need not be sampled after filling provided the filling company delivers a certificate of analysis for a sample taken from the mobile delivery tank. Cryogenic vessels retained by customers should be periodically tested to confirm that the contents comply with pharmacopoeial requirements.

6.12   Retained samples are not required, unless otherwise specified.

7 Storage and Release

7.1   Filled cylinders should be held in quarantine until released by the qualified person.

7.2   Gas cylinders should be stored under cover and not be subjected to extremes of temperature. Storage areas should be clean, dry, well ventilated and free of combustible materials to ensure that cylinders remain clean up to the time of use.

7.3   Storage arrangements should permit segregation of different gases and of full/empty cylinders and permit rotation of stock on a first in – first out basis.

7.4   Gas cylinders should be protected from adverse weather conditions during transportation. Specific conditions for storage and transportation should be employed for gas mixtures for which phase separation occurs on freezing.

ANNEX 7   Manufacture of Herbal Medicinal Products

Principle

Because of their often complex and variable nature, and the number and small quantity of defined active ingredients, controls of starting materials, storage and processing assume particular importance in the manufacture of herbal medicinal products.

Premises

Storage areas

1   Crude (i.e. unprocessed) plants should be stored in separate areas. The storage area should be well ventilated and be equipped in such a way as to give protection against the entry of insects or other animals, especially rodents. Effective measures should be taken to prevent the spread of any such animals and microorganisms brought in with the crude plant and to prevent cross-contamination. Containers should be located in such a way as to allow free air circulation.

2   Special attention should be paid to the cleanliness and good maintenance of the storage areas particularly when dust is generated.

3   Storage of plants, extracts, tinctures and other preparations may require special conditions of humidity, temperature or light protection; these conditions should be provided and monitored.

Production area

4   Specific provisions should be taken during sampling, weighing, mixing and processing operations of crude plants whenever dust is generated, to facilitate cleaning and to avoid cross-contamination, as for example, dust extraction, dedicated premises etc.

Documentation

Specifications for starting materials

5   Apart from the data described in the Guide (Chapter 4, point 4.11), specifications for medicinal crude plants should include, as far as possible:

  • the botanical name (with, if appropriate, the name of the originator of the classification, e.g. Linnaeus);

- the details of the source of the plant (country or region of origin, and where applicable, cultivation, time of harvesting, collection procedures, possible pesticides used etc.);

- whether the whole plant or only a part is used;

- when a dried plant is purchased, the drying system should be specified;

- the description of the plant and its macro and microscopial examination;

- the suitable identification tests including, where appropriate, identification tests for known active ingredients, or markers. A reference authentic specimen should be available for identification purposes;

- the assay, where appropriate, of constituents of known therapeutic activity or of markers;

- the methods suitable to determine possible pesticide contamination and limits accepted;

- the tests to determine fungal and/or microbial contamination, including aflatoxins and pest-infestations, and limits accepted;

- the tests for toxic metals and for likely contaminants and adulterants;

- the tests for foreign materials.

Any treatment used to reduce fungal/microbial contamination or other infestation should be documented. Specifications for such procedures should be available and should include details of process, tests and limits for residues.

Processing instructions

6   The processing instructions should describe the different operations carried out upon the crude plant such as drying, crushing and sifting, and include drying time and temperatures, and methods used to control fragment or particle size. It should also describe security sieving or other methods of removing foreign materials.

For the production of a vegetable drug preparation, instructions should include details of base or solvent, time and temperatures of extraction, details of any concentration stages and methods used (see also the note for guidance, *Quality of herbal remedies*[(1)]).

Sampling

7   Due to the fact that crude drugs are an aggregate of individual plants and contain an element of heterogeneity, their sampling has to be

carried out with special care by personnel with particular expertise. Each batch should be identified by its own documentation.

Quality Control

8 Quality Control personnel should have particular expertise in herbal medicinal products in order to be able to carry out identification tests and recognise adulteration, the presence of fungal growth, infestations, non-uniformity within a delivery of crude plants etc.

9 The identity and quality of vegetable drug preparations and of finished product should be tested as described in the note for guidance, *Quality of herbal remedies*[1].

---

(1) In: COMMISSION OF THE EUROPEAN COMMUNITIES. *Rules governing medicinal products in the EC Vol III.* Luxembourg: Office for Official Publications of the EC.

ANNEX 8   Sampling of Starting and Packaging Materials

Principle

Sampling is an important operation in which only a small fraction of a batch is taken. Valid conclusions on the whole cannot be based on tests which have been carried out on non-representative samples. Correct sampling is thus an essential part of a system of Quality Assurance.

Note

Sampling is dealt with in Chapter 6 of the Guide, items 6.11 to 6.14. This annex gives additional guidance on the sampling of starting and packaging materials.

Personnel

1   Personnel who take samples should receive initial and on-going regular training in the disciplines relevant to correct sampling. This training should include:

- sampling plans;

- written sampling procedures;

- the techniques and equipment for sampling;

- the risks of cross-contamination;

- the precautions to be taken with regard to unstable and/or sterile substances;

- the importance of considering the visual appearance of materials, containers and labels;

- the importance of recording any unexpected or unusual circumstances.

Starting Materials

2   The identity of a complete batch of starting materials can normally only be ensured if individual samples are taken from all the containers and an identity test performed on each sample. It is permissible to sample only a proportion of the containers where a validated procedure has been established to ensure that no single container of starting material has been incorrectly labelled.

3   This validation should take account of at least the following aspects:

- the nature and status of the manufacturer and of the supplier and their understanding of the GMP requirements of the Pharmaceutical Industry;

- the Quality Assurance system of the manufacturer of the starting material;

- the manufacturing conditions under which the starting material is produced and controlled;

- the nature of the starting material and the medicinal products in which it will be used.

Under such a system, it is possible that a validated procedure exempting identity testing of each incoming container of starting material could be accepted for:

- starting materials coming from a single product manufacturer or plant;

- starting materials coming directly from a manufacturer or in the manufacturer's sealed container where there is a history of reliability and regular audits of the manufacturer's Quality Assurance system are conducted by the purchaser (the manufacturer of the medicinal product) or by an officially accredited body.

It is improbable that a procedure could be satisfactorily validated for:

- starting materials supplied by intermediaries such as brokers where the source of manufacture is unknown or not audited;

- starting materials for use in parenteral products.

4   The quality of a batch of starting materials may be assessed by taking and testing a representative sample. The samples taken for identity testing could be used for this purpose. The number of samples taken for the preparation of a representative sample should be determined statistically and specified in a sampling plan. The number of individual samples which may be blended to form a composite sample should also be defined, taking into account the nature of the material, knowledge of the supplier and the homogeneity of the composite sample.

Packaging Material

5   The sampling plan for packaging materials should take account of at least the following: the quantity received, the quality required, the nature of the material (e.g. primary packaging materials and/or printed packaging materials), the production methods, and what is known of the Quality Assurance system of the packaging materials manufacturer based on audits. The number of samples taken should be determined statistically and specified in a sampling plan.

Manufacture of Liquids, Creams and Ointments

Principle

Liquids, creams and ointments may be particularly susceptible to microbial and other contamination during manufacture. Therefore special measures must be taken to prevent any contamination.

Premises and Equipment

1 The use of closed systems for processing and transfer is recommended in order to protect the product from contamination. Production areas where the products or open clean containers are exposed should normally be effectively ventilated with filtered air.

2 Tanks, containers, pipework and pumps should be designed and installed so that they may be readily cleaned and if necessary sanitised. In particular, equipment design should include a minimum of dead-legs or sites where residues can accumulate and promote microbial proliferation.

3 The use of glass apparatus should be avoided wherever possible. High quality stainless steel is often the material of choice for parts coming into contact with the product.

Production

4 The chemical and microbiological quality of water used in production should be specified and monitored. Care should be taken in the maintenance of water systems in order to avoid the risk of microbial proliferation. After any chemical sanitisation of the water systems, a validated flushing procedure should be followed to ensure that the sanitising agent has been effectively removed.

5 The quality of materials received in bulk tankers should be checked before they are transferred to bulk storage tanks.

6 Care should be taken when transferring materials via pipelines to ensure that they are delivered to their correct destination.

7 Materials likely to shed fibres or other contaminants, like cardboard or wooden pallets, should not enter the areas where products or clean containers are exposed.

8 Care should be taken to maintain the homogeneity of mixtures, suspensions etc. during filling. Mixing and filling processes should be validated. Special care should be taken at the beginning of a filling process, after stoppages and at the end of the process to ensure that homogeneity is maintained.

9 When the finished product is not immediately packaged, the maximum period of storage and the storage conditions should be specified and adhered to.

Manufacture of Pressurised Metered Dose Aerosol Preparations for Inhalation

Principle

The manufacture of pressurised aerosol products for inhalation with metering valves requires special consideration because of the particular nature of this form of product. It should be done under conditions which minimise microbial and particulate contamination. Assurance of the quality of the valve components and, in the case of suspensions, of uniformity is also of particular importance.

General

1   There are presently two common manufacturing and filling methods as follows:

(a)   Two-shot system (pressure filling). The active ingredient is suspended in a high boiling point propellant, the dose is put into the container, the valve is crimped on and the lower boiling point propellant is injected through the valve stem to make up the finished product. The suspension of active ingredient in propellant is kept cool to reduce evaporation loss.

(b)   One-shot process (cold filling). The active ingredient is suspended in a mixture of propellants and held either under high pressure or at a low temperature, or both. The suspension is then filled directly into the container in one shot.

Premises and Equipment

2   Manufacture and filling should be carried out as far as possible in a closed system.

3   Where products or clean components are exposed, the area should be fed with filtered air, should comply with the requirements of at least a Grade D environment and should be entered through airlocks.

Production and Quality Control

4   Metering valves for aerosols are more complex pieces of engineering than most items used in pharmaceutical production. Their specifications, sampling and testing should recognise this. Auditing

the Quality Assurance system of the valve manufacturer is of particular importance.

5   All fluids (e.g. liquid or gaseous propellants) should be filtered to remove particles greater than 0.2 micron. An additional filtration where possible immediately before filling is desirable.

6   Containers and valves should be cleaned using a validated procedure appropriate to the use of the product to ensure the absence of any contaminants such as fabrication aids (e.g. lubricants) or undue microbiological contaminants. After cleaning, valves should be kept in clean, closed containers and precautions taken not to introduce contamination during subsequent handling, e.g. taking samples. Containers should be fed to the filling line in a clean condition or cleaned on line immediately before filling.

7   Precautions should be taken to ensure uniformity of suspensions at the point of fill throughout the filling process.

8   When a two-shot filling process is used, it is necessary to ensure that both shots are of the correct weight in order to achieve the correct composition. For this purpose, 100% weight checking at each stage is often desirable.

9   Controls after filling should ensure the absence of undue leakage. Any leakage test should be performed in a way which avoids microbial contamination or residual moisture.

Principle

The introduction of computerised systems into systems of manufacturing, including storage, distribution and quality control does not alter the need to observe the relevant principles given elsewhere in the Guide. Where a computerised system replaces a manual operation, there should be no resultant decrease in product quality or quality assurance. Consideration should be given to the risk of losing aspects of the previous system which could result from reducing the involvement of operators.

Personnel

1   It is essential that there is the closest cooperation between key personnel and those involved with computer systems. Persons in responsible positions should have the appropriate training for the management and use of systems within their field of responsibility which utilises computers. This should include ensuring that appropriate expertise is available and used to provide advice on aspects of design, validation, installation and operation of a computerised system.

Validation

2   The extent of validation necessary will depend on a number of factors including the use to which the system is to be put, whether the validation is to be prospective or retrospective and whether or not novel elements are incorporated. Validation should be considered as part of the complete life cycle of a computer system. This cycle includes the stages of planning, specification, programming, testing, commissioning, documentation, operation, monitoring and modifying.

System

3   Attention should be paid to the siting of equipment in suitable conditions where extraneous factors cannot interfere with the system.

4   A written detailed description of the system should be produced (including diagrams as appropriate) and kept up to date. It should describe the principles, objectives, security measures and scope of the system and the main features of the way in which the computer is used and how it interacts with other systems and procedures.

5   The software is a critical component of a computerised system. The user of such software should take all reasonable steps to ensure that it has been produced in accordance with a system of Quality Assurance.

6   The system should include, where appropriate, built-in checks of the correct entry and processing of data.

7   Before a system using a computer is brought into use, it should be thoroughly tested and confirmed as being capable of achieving the desired results. If a manual system is being replaced, the two should be run in parallel for a time, as part of this testing and validation.

8   Data should only be entered or amended by persons authorised to do so. Suitable methods of deterring unauthorised entry of data include the use of keys, pass cards, personal codes and restricted access to computer terminals. There should be a defined procedure for the issue, cancellation, and alteration of authorisation to enter and amend data, including the changing of personal passwords. Consideration should be given to systems allowing for recording of attempts to access by unauthorised persons.

9   When critical data are being entered manually (for example the weight and batch number of an ingredient during dispensing), there should be an additional check on the accuracy of the record which is made. This check may be done by a second operator or by validated electronic means.

10 The system should record the identity of operators entering or confirming critical data. Authority to amend entered data should be restricted to nominated persons. Any alteration to an entry of critical data should be authorised and recorded with the reason for the change. Consideration should be given to building into the system the creation of a complete record of all entries and amendments (an 'audit trail').

11 Alterations to a system or to a computer program should only be made in accordance with a defined procedure which should include provision for validating, checking, approving and implementing the change. Such an alteration should only be implemented with the agreement of the person responsible for the part of the system concerned, and the alteration should be recorded. Every significant modification should be validated.

12   For quality auditing purposes, it should be possible to obtain clear printed copies of electronically stored data.

13   Data should be secured by physical or electronic means against wilful or accidental damage, in accordance with item 4.9 of the Guide. Stored data should be checked for accessibility, durability and accuracy. If changes are proposed to the computer equipment or its programs, the above mentioned checks should be performed at a frequency appropriate to the storage medium being used.

14   Data should be protected by backing-up at regular intervals. Back-up data should be stored as long as necessary at a separate and secure location.

15   There should be available adequate alternative arrangements for systems which need to be operated in the event of a breakdown. The time required to bring the alternative arrangements into use should be related to the possible urgency of the need to use them. For example, information required to effect a recall must be available at short notice.

16   The procedures to be followed if the system fails or breaks down should be defined and validated. Any failures and remedial action taken should be recorded.

17   A procedure should be established to record and analyse errors and to enable corrective action to be taken.

18   When outside agencies are used to provide a computer service, there should be a formal agreement including a clear statement of the responsibilities of that outside agency (see Chapter 7).

19   When the release of batches for sale or supply is carried out using a computerised system, the system should allow for only a Qualified Person to release the batches and it should clearly identify and record the person releasing the batches.

ANNEX 12 Use of Ionising Radiation in the Manufacture of Medicinal Products

Note

The holder of, or applicant for, a marketing authorisation for a product which includes irradiation as part of its processing should also refer to the note produced by the Committee for Proprietary Medicinal Products giving guidance on ionising radiation in the manufacture of medicinal products[1].

Introduction

Ionising radiation may be used during the manufacturing process for various purposes including the reduction of bioburden and the sterilisation of starting materials, packaging components or products and the treatment of blood products.

There are two types of irradiation process: Gamma Irradiation from a radioactive source and high energy Electron Irradiation (Beta radiation) from an accelerator.

Gamma Irradiation: two different processing modes may be employed:

(i)   Batch mode: the product is arranged at fixed locations around the radiation source and cannot be loaded or unloaded while the radiation source is exposed.

(ii)   Continuous mode: an automatic system conveys the products into the radiation cell, past the exposed radiation source along a defined path and at an appropriate speed, and out of the cell.

Electron Irradiation: the product is conveyed past a continuous or pulsed beam of high energy electrons (Beta radiation) which is scanned back and forth across the product pathway.

Responsibilities

1   Treatment by irradiation may be carried out by the pharmaceutical manufacturer or by an operator of a radiation facility under contract (a 'contract manufacturer'), both of whom must hold an appropriate manufacturing authorisation.

2   The pharmaceutical manufacturer bears responsibility for the quality of the product including the attainment of the objective of irradiation. The contract operator of the radiation facility bears responsibility for ensuring that the dose of radiation required by the manufacturer is delivered to the irradiation container (i.e. the outermost container in which the products are irradiated).

3   The required dose including justified limits will be stated in the marketing authorisation for the product.

Dosimetry

4   Dosimetry is defined as the measurement of the absorbed dose by the use of dosimeters. Both understanding and correct use of the technique is essential for the validation, commissioning and control of the process.

5   The calibration of each batch of routine dosimeters should be traceable to a national or international standard. The period of validity of the calibration should be stated, justified and adhered to.

6   The same instrument should normally be used to establish the calibration curve of the routine dosimeters and to measure the change in their absorbance after irradiation. If a different instrument is used, the absolute absorbance of each instrument should be established.

7   Depending on the type of dosimeter used, due account should be taken of possible causes of inaccuracy including the change in moisture content, change in temperature, time elapsed between irradiation and measurement, and the dose rate.

8   The wavelength of the instrument used to measure the change in absorbance of dosimeters and the instrument used to measure their thickness should be subject to regular checks of calibration at intervals established on the basis of stability, purpose and usage.

Validation of the Process

9   Validation is the action of proving that the process, i.e. the delivery of the intended absorbed dose to the product, will achieve the expected results. The requirements for validation are given more fully in the note for guidance on the use of ionising radiation in the manufacture of medicinal products[1].

10   Validation should include dose mapping to establish the distribution of absorbed dose within the irradiation container when packed with product in a defined configuration.

11   An irradiation process specification should include at least the following:

(a)   details of the packaging of the product;

(b)   the loading pattern(s) of product within the irradiation container. Particular care needs to be taken, when a mixture of products is allowed in the irradiation container, that there is no underdosing of dense product or shadowing of other products by dense product. Each mixed product arrangement must be specified and validated;

(c)   the loading pattern of irradiation containers around the source (batch mode) or the pathway through the cell (continuous mode);

(d)   maximum and minimum limits of absorbed dose to the product (and associated routine dosimetry);

(e)   maximum and minimum limits of absorbed dose to the irradiation container and associated routine dosimetry to monitor this absorbed dose;

(f)   other process parameters, including dose rate, maximum time of exposure, number of exposures etc.

When irradiation is supplied under contract at least parts (d) and (e) of the irradiation process specification should form part of that contract.

Commissioning of the Plant

General

12   Commissioning is the exercise of obtaining and documenting evidence that the irradiation plant will perform consistently within predetermined limits when operated according to the process specification. In the context of this annex, predetermined limits are the maximum and minimum doses designed to be absorbed by the irradiation container. It must not be possible for variations to occur in the operation of the plant which give a dose to the container outside these limits without the knowledge of the operator.

13   Commissioning should include the following elements:

(a)   Design;

(b)   Dose mapping;

(c)   Documentation;

(d)   Requirement for re-commissioning.

Gamma Irradiators

14 *Design*

The absorbed dose received by a particular part of an irradiation container at any specific point in the irradiator depends primarily on the following factors:

(a)   the activity and geometry of the source;

(b)   the distance from source to container;

(c)   the duration of irradiation controlled by the timer setting or conveyor speed;

(d)   the composition and density of material, including other products, between the source and the particular part of the container.

15   The total absorbed dose will in addition depend on the path of containers through a continuous irradiator or the loading pattern in a batch irradiator, and on the number of exposure cycles.

16   For a continuous irradiator with a fixed path or a batch irradiator with fixed loading pattern, and with a given source strength and type of product, the key plant parameter controlled by the operator is conveyor speed or timer setting.

17 *Dose mapping*

For the dose mapping procedure, the irradiator should be filled with irradiation containers packed with dummy products or a representative product of uniform density. Dosimeters should be placed throughout a minimum of three loaded irradiation containers which are passed through the irradiator, surrounded by similar containers or dummy products. If the product is not uniformly packed, dosimeters should be placed in a larger number of containers.

18   The positioning of dosimeters will depend on the size of the irradiation container. For example, for containers up to 1 x 1 x 0.5 m, a three-dimensional 20 cm grid throughout the container including the outside surfaces might be suitable. If the expected positions of the minimum and maximum dose are known from a previous irradiator performance characterisation, some dosimeters could be removed from regions of average dose and replaced to form a 10 cm grid in the regions of extreme dose.

19   The results of this procedure will give minimum and maximum absorbed doses in the product and on the container surface for a given set of plant parameters, product density and loading pattern.

20 Ideally, reference dosimeters should be used for the dose mapping exercise because of their greater precision. Routine dosimeters are permissible but it is advisable to place reference dosimeters beside them at the expected positions of minimum and maximum dose and at the routine monitoring position in each of the replicate irradiation containers. The observed values of dose will have an associated random uncertainty which can be estimated from the variations in replicate measurements.

21 The minimum observed dose, as measured by the routine dosimeters, necessary to ensure that all irradiation containers receive the minimum required dose will be set in the knowledge of the random variability of the routine dosimeters used.

22 Irradiator parameters should be kept constant, monitored and recorded during dose mapping. The records, together with the dosimetry results and all other records generated, should be retained.

Electron Beam Irradiators

23 *Design*

The absorbed dose received by a particular portion of an irradiated product depends primarily on the following factors:

(a) the characteristics of the beam, which are: electron energy, average beam current, scan width and scan uniformity;

(b) the conveyor speed;

(c) the product composition and density;

(d) the composition, density and thickness of material between the output window and the particular portion of product;

(e) the output window to container distance.

24 Key parameters controlled by the operator are the characteristics of the beam and the conveyor speed.

25 *Dose mapping*

For the dose mapping procedure, dosimeters should be placed between layers of homogeneous absorber sheets making up a dummy product, or between layers of representative products of uniform density, such that at least ten measurements can be made within the maximum range of the electrons. Reference should also be made to sections 18 to 21.

26 Irradiator parameters should be kept constant, monitored and recorded during dose mapping. The records, together with the dosimetry results and all other records generated, should be retained.

Re-commissioning

27   Commissioning should be repeated if there is a change to the process or the irradiator which could affect the dose distribution to the irradiation container (e.g. change of source pencils). The extent to re-commissioning depends on the extent of the change in the irradiator or the load that has taken place. If in doubt, re-commission.

Premises

28   Premises should be designed and operated to segregate irradiated from non-irradiated containers to avoid their cross-contamination. Where materials are handled within closed irradiation containers, it may not be necessary to segregate pharmaceutical from non-pharmaceutical materials, provided there is no risk of the former being contaminated by the latter.

Any possibility of contamination of the products by radionuclide from the source must be excluded.

Processing

29   Irradiation containers should be packed in accordance with the specified loading pattern(s) established during validation.

30   During the process, the radiation dose to the irradiation containers should be monitored using validated dosimetry procedures. The relationship between this dose and the dose absorbed by the product inside the container must have been established during process validation and plant commissioning.

31   Radiation indicators should be used as an aid to differentiating irradiated from non-irradiated containers. They should not be used as the sole means of differentiation or as an indication of satisfactory processing.

32   Processing of mixed loads of containers within the irradiation cell should only be done when it is known from commissioning trials or other evidence that the radiation dose received by individual containers remains within the limits specified.

33   When the required radiation dose is by design given during more than one exposure or passage through the plant, this should be with the agreement of the holder of the marketing authorisation and occur within a predetermined time period. Unplanned interruptions during irradiation should be notified to the holder of the marketing authorisation if this extends the irradiation process beyond a previously agreed period.

34   Non-irradiated products must be segregated from irradiated products at all times. Methods of doing this include the use of radiation indicators (31.) and appropriate design of premises (28.).

Gamma Irradiators

35   For continuous processing modes, dosimeters should be placed so that at least two are exposed in the irradiation at all times.

36   For batch modes, at least two dosimeters should be exposed in positions related to the minimum dose position.

37   For continuous process modes, there should be a positive indication of the correct position of the source and an interlock between source position and conveyor movement. Conveyor speed should be monitored continuously and recorded.

38   For batch process modes source movement and exposure times for each batch should be monitored and recorded.

39   For a given desired dose, the timer setting or conveyor speed requires adjustment for source decay and source additions. The period of validity of the setting or speed should be recorded and adhered to.

Electron Beam Irradiators

40   A dosimeter should be placed on every container.

41   There should be continuous recording of average beam current, electron energy, scan-width and conveyor speed. These variables, other than conveyor speed, need to be controlled within the defined limits established during commissioning since they are liable to instantaneous change.

Documentation

42   The numbers of containers received, irradiated and dispatched should be reconciled with each other and with the associated documentation. Any discrepancy should be reported and resolved.

43   The irradiation plant operator should certify in writing the range of doses received by each irradiated container within a batch or delivery.

44   Process and control records for each irradiation batch should be checked and signed by a nominated responsible person and retained. The method and place of retention should be agreed between the plant operator and the holder of the marketing authorisation.

45   The documentation associated with the validation and commissioning of the plant should be retained for one year after the expiry date or at least five years after the release of the last product processed by the plant, whichever is the longer.

Microbiological Monitoring

46   Microbiological monitoring is the responsibility of the pharmaceutical manufacturer. It may include environmental monitoring where product is manufactured and pre-irradiation monitoring of the product as specified in the marketing authorisation.

---

(1)   In: COMMISSION OF THE EUROPEAN COMMUNITIES. *Rules governing medicinal products in the EC. Vol III. Addendum 2.* Luxembourg: Office for Official Publications of the EC, 1992. ISBN 92-826-4550-9.

ANNEX 13 Manufacture of Investigational Medicinal Products

Editor's note

The European Commission consulted on an extensive revision to this annex early in 2002. This is to meet the requirements of the Clinical Trials Directive 2001/20/EC, to be implemented by May 2004. At the time of printing the results of this consultation are not known.

Introduction

Medicinal products intended for research and development trials are not at present subject either to marketing or manufacturing Community legislation.

However, when adopting Directive 91/356/EEC on GMP for medicinal products for human use, it was agreed to include a 'whereas' stating that Member States may require compliance with the principles of GMP during the manufacture of products intended for use in clinical trials. It was also suggested in a EC Discussion Paper (III/3044/91) in January 1991 that it is illogical for experimental products not to be subject to the controls which would apply to the formulations of which they are the prototypes and most of the comments received from interested parties were in line with this suggestion.

Therefore it was agreed to prepare this annex to the Community Guide to Good Manufacturing Practice so that both those Member States instituting controls voluntarily and manufacturers of investigational products would have a reference point to enable common standards to evolve in all Member States.

The Commission is currently preparing a draft directive on clinical trials and this first revision of the annex will be reviewed when necessary.

Although veterinary investigational medicinal products should also be prepared under appropriate GMP conditions, most aspects of this annex derive from human GCP[(1)] and are thus specific to investigational medicinal products for human use.

Note

The principles and many of the detailed guidelines of Good Manufacturing Practice for Medicinal Products as well as some other guidelines published by the European Commission (e.g. validation of virus inactivation/removal) are relevant to the preparation of products for use in clinical trials.

This annex specifically addresses those practices which may be different for investigational products, which are usually not manufactured under a set routine, and with possibly incomplete characterisation of the product at initial stages of clinical development. It also includes guidance on ordering, shipping, and returning clinical supplies, which is at the interface with the Guideline on Good Clinical Practice (revised 1 January 1997[2]).

Quality Management

1. Some of the production processes of investigational medicinal products which have no marketing authorisation may not be validated to the extent necessary for a routine production. For sterile products, the validation of sterilising processes should be of the same standard as for products authorised for marketing. The product specifications and manufacturing instructions may vary during development. This increased complexity in manufacturing operations requires a highly effective system of Quality Assurance.

2. The Quality Assurance System, designed, set up and verified by the manufacturer, should be described in written procedures maintained by the sponsor, taking into account the GMP principles applied to investigational medicinal products.

3. Packaging and labelling operations are often performed after the release of the bulk product and in accordance with specific requirements of different trials. These operations are of paramount importance for the integrity of clinical trials. In this respect, self inspection or independent audits, as referred to in the Community Guideline on Good Clinical Practice[2] and in 9.2. of the Guide to GMP are an integral part of the Quality Assurance system.

Personnel

4. Although it is likely that the number of staff involved will be small, there should be separate people responsible for production and quality control. All production operations should be carried out under control of a clearly identified responsible person. Personnel involved in release of investigational medicinal products should be appropriately trained in quality systems, GMP and regulatory requirements specific to these types of products. They must be independent of the staff responsible for production.

Premises and Equipment

5   During manufacture of investigational medicinal products, it may be that different products are handled in the same premises and at the same time, and this reinforces the need to minimise all risks of contamination, including cross-contamination and product mix up, by using appropriate procedures.

6   For the production of the particular products referred to in paragraph 3.6 of the Guide to GMP, campaign working may be acceptable in place of dedicated and self-contained facilities. Because the toxicity of the materials may not be fully known, cleaning is of particular importance; account should be taken of the solubility of the product and of excipients in various cleaning solvents.

7   Validation of aseptic processes presents special problems when the batch size is small; in these cases the number of units filled may be the maximum number filled in production. Filling and sealing is often a hand operation presenting great challenges to sterility so enhanced attention should be given to environmental monitoring.

Documentation

8   Specifications (for starting materials, primary packaging materials, intermediate and bulk products and finished products), manufacturing formulae and processing and packaging instructions may be changed as development of the product progresses. Each new version should take into account the latest data, current technology used and the regulatory and pharmacopoeial requirements, and should refer to the previous version to allow traceability to the previous document. Rationales for changes should be recorded.

9   It may not be necessary to produce Master Formula and Processing Instructions, but for every manufacturing operation or supply there should be clear and adequate written instructions and written records. Records are particularly important for the preparation of the final version of the documents to be used in routine manufacture.

10   Batch manufacturing records should be retained for at least two years after completion of the clinical trial or at least two years after formal discontinuation or in conformance with the applicable regulatory requirement(s).

Order

11   The order may request the processing and/or packaging of a certain number or units and/or their shipping. It may only be given by the sponsor to the manufacturer of an investigational medicinal product. It should be in writing (though it may be transmitted by electronic

means), and precise enough to avoid any ambiguity. It should be formally authorised and it should refer to the approved Product Specification File.

Product Specification File

12   All the information necessary to draft the detailed written instructions on processing, packaging, quality control testing, batch release, storage conditions and/or shipping should be referenced in a Product Specification File. This Product Specification File should be continually updated, ensuring appropriate traceability to the previous versions.

Manufacturing Formulae and Processing Instructions

13   Any changes should be carried out according to a written procedure which should address any implications for stability and bioequivalence. Changes should be authorised by a responsible person and be clearly recorded.

Packaging Instructions

14   Packaging and labelling of investigational medicinal products are likely to be more complex and more liable to errors (which are also harder to detect) than of marketed products when 'blinded' labels are used. Supervision procedures such as label reconciliation, line clearance etc. and the independent checks by quality control staff should accordingly be intensified.

15   Investigational medicinal products must be packed in an individual way for each patient included in the clinical trial. Packaging instructions are based on the order. Contrary to what happens with large-scale manufacturing of licensed medicinal products, batches of investigational medicinal products may be subdivided into different packaging batches and packaged in several operations over a period of time.

16   The number of units to package should be specified prior to the start of the packaging operations, considering also the number of units necessary for carrying out quality controls and the number of samples to be kept. A reconciliation should take place at the end of the packaging and labelling process.

Labelling instructions

17   Labels should include:
   (a)   name of the sponsor;
   (b)   pharmaceutical dosage form, route of administration, quantity of dosage units (and name/identifier of the product and strength/potency in case of open trial);

(c)　　the batch and/or code number to identify the contents and packaging operation;

(d)　　the trial subject identification number, where applicable;

(e)　　directions for use;

(f)　　'for clinical trial use only';

(g)　　the name of the investigator (if not included as a code in the trial reference code);

(h)　　a trial reference code allowing identification of the trial site and investigator;

(i)　　the storage conditions;

(j)　　the period of use (use-by date, expiry date or re-test date as applicable) in month/year;

(k)　　'keep out of reach of children' except when the product is for use only in hospital.

The outer packaging may include symbols or pictograms to clarify certain information mentioned above and the request 'return empty packaging and unused products'. Additional information, for example any warnings and handling instructions, where applicable may be displayed according to the order. A copy of each type of label should be kept in the batch record.

18　　On the immediate packaging when the outer packaging carries the particulars mentioned in paragraph 17, a–k, the particulars mentioned in paragraph 17, a–f, shall be given.

19　　When the outer packaging carries the particulars mentioned in paragraph 17, a–k and the immediate packaging takes the form of blisterpacks or small immediate packaging units such as ampoules on which the particulars mentioned in paragraph 17, a–f cannot be displayed, the particulars mentioned in paragraph 17, a,c and d as well as route of administration in case of ampoules, shall at least appear on the immediate packaging.

20　　In case of use date extension, an additional label should be affixed to the investigational medicinal product. This additional label should include the new use date and repeat the batch number. It may be superimposed on the old use date, but, for quality control reasons, not on the original batch number. This operation may be performed on site by the clinical trial monitor(s) or the clinical trial site pharmacist, in accordance with specific and standard operating procedures and under contract if applicable. The operation should be checked by a second person. Documented evidence of this additional labelling should be available in the trial documentation and in the batch records.

Manufacturing and packaging batch records

21   Manufacturing and packaging batch records should be kept in sufficient detail for the sequence of operations to be accurately traced back. These records should contain any relevant remarks which enhance existing knowledge of the product and allow improvements of the manufacturing operations and justify the procedures used.

Production

Starting materials

22   The consistency of production may be influenced by quality of the starting materials. Their physical and chemical properties should therefore be defined, documented in their specifications and controlled. Specifications for active starting materials should be as comprehensive as possible, given the current state of knowledge. Specifications for both active and non-active starting materials (excipients) should be periodically re-assessed during development and updated as necessary.

23   Detailed information on the quality of active and non-active starting materials should be available in order to recognise and, as necessary, allow for variation of the production.

Manufacturing operations

24   During the development phase, validated procedures may not always be available, which makes it difficult to know in advance the critical parameters and the in-process controls that would help to control these parameters. In these cases, provisional production parameters and in-process controls may usually be deduced from experience with analogues. Careful consideration by key personnel is called for in order to formulate the necessary instructions and to adapt them continually to the experience gained in production.

25   Reconciliation is an essential part of the control of the manufacturing operations. Actual and theoretical yields should be reconciled and any abnormal discrepancy investigated.

26   Where applicable virus inactivation/removal and/or other impurities of biological origin should be no less than for products authorised for marketing. Cleaning procedures should be very stringent and designed in the light of the incomplete knowledge of the toxicity of the investigational product. Where processes such as mixing have not been validated, additional quality control testing may be necessary.

Principles applicable to comparator product

27   In studies whereby an investigational medicinal product is compared with a marketed product, attention should be paid to ensure the

integrity and quality of the comparator product (final dosage form, packaging materials, storage conditions, etc.). If significant changes are to be made to the product, data should be available (e.g. stability, comparative dissolution, bioavailability) to prove that these changes do not significantly alter the original quality characteristics of the product.

28   Because the expiry date stated on the original package has been determined for the medicinal product in that particular package and may not be applicable to the product where it has been repackaged in a different container, it is the responsibility of the sponsor, taking into account the nature of the product, the characteristics of the container and the storage conditions to which the article may be subjected, to determine a suitable use-by date to be placed on the label. Such a date is not later than the expiry date of the original package. In the absence of stability data or if stability is not followed during the clinical trial such date should not exceed 25% of the remaining time between the date of repackaging and the expiry date on the original manufacturer's bulk container or a six month period from the date the drug is repackaged, whichever is earlier.

Randomisation code

29   Procedures should describe the generation, distribution, handling and retention of any randomisation code used for packaging investigational products.

Blinding operations

30   A system should be implemented to allow for a proper identification of the 'blinded' products. The system, together with the randomisation code and randomisation list must allow proper identification of the product, including any necessary traceability to the codes and batch number of the product before the blinding operation.

31   Samples of blinded investigational medicinal products should be retained.

Quality Control

32   As processes may not be standardised or fully validated, end product testing takes on more importance to ensure that each batch meets its specification.

33   Quality Control should especially pay attention to the compliance with specifications which bear on the efficacy of medicinal products, namely:

- accuracy of the therapeutic or unitary dose: homogeneity, content uniformity;

- release of active substances: solubility, dissolution time etc;

- estimation of stability, if necessary in accelerated and stress conditions, determination of the preliminary storage conditions and shelf-life of the product.

When necessary, Quality Control should also verify the similarity in appearance, smell and taste of 'blinded' medicinal products.

34   Samples of each batch of product should be retained under the responsibility of either the manufacturer or of the importer which released the batch for use in the EEA. They should be kept in the primary container used for the study or in a suitable bulk container for at least one year beyond the final shelf-life or two years after completion of the clinical trial whichever is the longest. If the sample is not stored in the pack used for the study, stability data should be available to justify the shelf-life in the pack used.

Release of Batches

35   Product release is often carried out in two stages, before and after final packaging:

- bulk product assessment: it should cover all relevant factors, including production conditions, results of in-process testing, a review of manufacturing documentation and compliance with the Product Specification File and the Order;

- finished product assessment: it should cover, in addition to the bulk product assessment, all relevant factors, including packaging conditions, results of in-process testing, a review of packaging documentation and compliance with the Product Specification File and the Order.

Free Movement

36   Since investigational products are released ('technical green light') by appropriately qualified staff, subsequent analysis after shipping to other Member States is not justified as long as documented evidence is available that appropriate control analysis and product release have taken place in the EEA.

Contract Manufacture and Contract Analysis

37   The contract must clearly state, among other provisions, that the medicinal products are to be used in clinical trials. Co-operation between the contracting parties should be very close.

Complaints

38   The conclusions of any investigation carried out in relation to a complaint should be discussed between the manufacturer and the sponsor (if different) or between the responsible person of the manufacturer and those responsible for the relevant clinical trial in order to assess any potential impact on the trial and on the product development.

Recalls and Returns

39   Procedures for retrieving investigational medicinal products and documenting this retrieval (e.g. for defective products recall, returns after trial completion, expired product return) should be in place. They should be understood by the sponsor, investigator and monitor in addition to the person(s) responsible for recalls.

Shipping – Returns – Destruction

40   Shipping, return and destruction of unused products should be carried out according to written procedures.

Shipping

41   Shipping of investigational products is conducted according to orders given by the sponsor in the shipping order.

42   Investigational medicinal products are sent to an investigator only after a two step release procedure: the release of the product after quality control ('technical green light') and the authorisation to use the product, given by the sponsor ('regulatory green light'). Both releases should be recorded and retained.

43   The packaging must ensure that the medicinal product remains in good condition during transport and storage at intermediate destinations. Any opening or tampering of the outer packaging during transport should be readily discernible.

44   The sponsor should ensure that the shipment is to be received in the required conditions and acknowledged by the right addressee.

45   A detailed inventory of the shipments made by the manufacturer should be maintained. It should particularly mention the addressees' identification.

46   Transfers of investigational medicinal products from one trial site to another should remain the exception and only be allowed in case of very expensive product, limited quantity available for clinical trials or

in case of emergency. Such transfers should be covered by standard operating procedures which differentiate between the storage location of the product to be transferred (from warehouse under control of the sponsor, from the pharmacy of a trial site, or from the investigator). Should the transferred product have been stored by the investigator, not at the pharmacy, sufficient precautions and controls have to be considered prior to use at another trial site. In most cases, the product will need to be returned to the sponsor for re-labelling and full finished product specification retesting to ensure that it is still suitable for its intended use and new release.

Returns

47   Investigational medicinal products should be returned on agreed conditions defined by the sponsor, specified in written procedures, and approved by authorised staff members.

48   Returned investigational medicinal products should be clearly identified and stored in a dedicated area. Inventory records of the returned medicinal products should be kept.

Destruction

49   The Sponsor is responsible for the destruction of unused investigational medicinal products. Investigational medicinal products should therefore not be destroyed by the manufacturer without prior written authorisation by the Sponsor.

50   Recording of destruction operations should be carried out in such a manner that all operations may be accounted for. The records should be kept by the Sponsor. This destruction should be done only after the finalisation of the clinical trial and the compilation of the final report.

51   If the manufacturer is requested to destroy the products, he should deliver a certificate of destruction or a receipt for destruction to the Sponsor. These documents should clearly identify the batches and/or patient numbers involved and the actual quantities destroyed.

---

(1) GCP – Good Clinical Practice.

(2) Note for guidance on Good Clinical Practice. (CPMP/ICH/135/95). Implemented January 1997. Available from the MCA EuroDirect Publication Service. Market Towers, 1 Nine Elms Lane, Vauxhall, London SW8 5NQ. Telephone 0207-273 0352.

ANNEX 14 Manufacture of Medicinal[1] Products derived from human blood or human plasma

Principle

In accordance with Directive 75/318/EEC [2], for biological medicinal products derived from human blood or plasma, starting materials include the source materials such as cells or fluids including blood or plasma. Medicinal products derived from human blood or plasma have certain special features arising from the biological nature of the source material. For example, disease-transmitting agents, especially viruses, may contaminate the source material. The safety of these products relies therefore on the control of source materials and their origin as well as on the subsequent manufacturing procedures, including virus removal and inactivation.

The general chapters of the guide to GMP apply to medicinal products derived from human blood or plasma, unless otherwise stated. Some of the Annexes may also apply, e.g. manufacture of sterile medicinal products, use of ionising radiation in the manufacture of medicinal products, manufacture of biological medicinal products and computerised systems.

Since the quality of the final products is affected by all the steps in their manufacture, including the collection of blood or plasma, all operations should therefore be done in accordance with an appropriate system of Quality Assurance and current Good Manufacturing Practice.

By virtue of Directive 89/381/EEC, the necessary measures shall be taken to prevent the transmission of infectious diseases and the requirements and standards of the European Pharmacopoeia monographs regarding plasma for fractionation and medicinal products derived from human blood or plasma shall be applicable. These measures shall also comprise the Council Recommendation of 29 June 1998 *On the suitability of blood and plasma donors and the screening of donated blood in the European Community*[3] (98/463/EC), the recommendations of the Council of Europe (see *Guide to the preparation, use and quality assurance of blood components*, Council of Europe Press) and the World Health Organisation (see report by the WHO Expert Committee on Biological Standardisation, WHO Technical Report Series 840, 1994).

This annex should also be read in conjunction with the guidelines adopted by the CPMP, in particular *Note for guidance on plasma-derived medicinal products* (CPMP/BWP/269/95 rev.2), *Virus validation studies: the design, contribution and interpretation of studies validating the inactivation and removal of viruses* published in Volume 3A of the series *The rules governing medicinal products in the European Community* and *Contribution to part II of the structure of the dossier for applications for marketing authorisation – control of starting materials for the production of blood derivatives* (III/5272/94).

These documents are regularly revised and reference should be made to the latest revisions for current guidance.

The provisions of this annex apply to medicinal products derived from human blood and plasma. They do not cover blood components used in transfusion medicine, since these are presently not covered by EC directives. However many of these provisions may be applicable to such components and competent authorities may require compliance with them.

Quality Management

1   Quality Assurance should cover all stages leading to the finished product, from collection (including donor selection, blood bags, anticoagulant solutions and test kits) to storage, transport, processing, quality control and delivery of the finished product, all in accordance with the texts referred to under *Principle* at the beginning of this Annex.

2   Blood or plasma used as a source material for the manufacture of medicinal products should be collected by establishments and be tested in laboratories which are subject to inspection and approved by a competent authority.

3   Procedures to determine the suitability of individuals to donate blood and plasma, used as a source material for the manufacture of medicinal products, and the results of the testing of their donations should be documented by the collection establishment and should be available to the manufacturer of the medicinal product.

4   Monitoring of the quality of medicinal products derived from human blood or plasma should be carried out in such a way that any deviations from the quality specifications can be detected.

5   Medicinal products derived from human blood or plasma which have been returned unused should normally not be re-issued; (see also point 5.65 of the main GMP guide).

Premises and Equipment

6   The premises used for the collection of blood or plasma should be of suitable size, construction and location to facilitate their proper operation, cleaning and maintenance. Collection, processing and

testing of blood and plasma should not be performed in the same area. There should be suitable donor interview facilities so that these interviews are carried out in private.

7   Manufacturing, collection and testing equipment should be designed, qualified and maintained to suit its intended purpose and should not present any hazard. Regular maintenance and calibration should be carried out and documented according to established procedures.

8   In the preparation of plasma-derived medicinal products, viral inactivation or removal procedures are used and steps should be taken to prevent cross contamination of treated with untreated products; dedicated and distinct premises and equipment should be used for treated products.

Blood and Plasma Collection

9   A standard contract is required between the manufacturer of the medicinal product derived from human blood or plasma and the blood/plasma collection establishment or organisation responsible for collection. Guidance on the content of the standard contract is provided in *Contribution to part II of the structure of the dossier for applications for marketing authorisation – control of starting materials for the production of blood derivatives* (III/5272/94).

10   Each donor must be positively identified at reception and again before venepuncture; see also Council Recommendation of 29 June 1998 on the suitability of blood and plasma donors and the screening of donated blood in the European Community[(4)] (98/463/EC).

11   The method used to disinfect the skin of the donor should be clearly defined and shown to be effective. Adherence to that method should then be maintained.

12   Donation number labels must be re-checked independently to ensure that those on blood packs, sample tubes and donation records are identical.

13   Blood bag and apheresis systems should be inspected for damage or contamination before being used to collect blood or plasma. In order to ensure traceability, the batch number of blood bags and apheresis systems should be recorded.

Traceability and Post-Collection Measures

14   While fully respecting confidentiality, there must be a system in place which enables the path taken by each donation to be traced, both forward from the donor and back from the finished medicinal product, including the customer (hospital or health care professional).

It is normally the responsibility of this customer to identify the recipient.

15   Post-collection measures: A standard operating procedure describing the mutual information system between the blood/plasma collection establishment and the manufacturing/fractionation facility should be set up so that they can inform each other if, following donation:

- it is found that the donor did not meet the relevant donor health criteria;

- a subsequent donation from a donor previously found negative for viral markers is found positive for any of the viral markers;

- it is discovered that testing for viral markers has not been carried out according to agreed procedures;

- the donor has developed an infectious disease caused by an agent potentially transmissible by plasma-derived products (HBV, HCV, HAV and other non-A, non-B, non-C hepatitis viruses, HIV 1 and 2 and other agents in the light of current knowledge);

- the donor develops Creutzfeldt-Jakob disease (CJD or vCJD);

- the recipient of blood or a blood component develops post-transfusion/infusion infection which implicates or can be traced back to the donor.

The procedures to be followed in the event of any of the above should be documented in the standard operating procedure. Look-back should consist of tracing back of previous donations for at least six months prior to the last negative donation. In the event of any of the above, a re-assessment of the batch documentation should always be carried out. The need for withdrawal of the given batch should be carefully considered, taking into account criteria such as the transmissible agent involved, the size of the pool, the time period between donation and seroconversion, the nature of the product and its manufacturing method. Where there are indications that a donation contributing to a plasma pool was infected with HIV or hepatitis A, B or C, the case should be referred to the relevant competent authority(ies) responsible for the authorisation of the medicinal product and the company's view regarding continued manufacture from the implicated pool or of the possibility of withdrawal of the product(s) should be given. More specific guidance is given in the current version of the CPMP Note for Guidance on plasma-derived medicinal products.

Production and Quality Control

16   Before any blood and plasma donations, or any product derived therefrom, are released for issue and/or fractionation, they should be tested, using a validated test method of suitable sensitivity and specificity, for the following markers of specific disease-transmitting agents:

- HBsAg;
- antibodies to HIV 1 and HIV 2;
- antibodies to HCV.

If a repeat-reactive result is found in any of these tests, the donation is not acceptable. (Additional tests may form part of national requirements.)

17 The specified storage temperatures of blood, plasma and intermediate products when stored and during transportation from collection establishments to manufacturers, or between different manufacturing sites, should be checked and validated. The same applies to delivery of these products.

18 The first homogeneous plasma pool (e.g. after separation of the cryoprecipitate) should be tested using a validated test method, of suitable sensitivity and specificity, and found non-reactive for the following markers of specific disease-transmitting agents:

- HBsAg;
- antibodies to HIV 1 and HIV 2;
- antibodies to HCV.

Confirmed positive pools must be rejected.

19 Only batches derived from plasma pools tested and found non-reactive for HCV RNA by nucleic acid amplification technology (NAT), using a validated test method of suitable sensitivity and specificity, should be released.

20 Testing requirements for viruses, or other infectious agents, should be considered in the light of knowledge emerging as to infectious agents and the availability of appropriate test methods.

21 The labels on single units of plasma stored for pooling and fractionation must comply with the provisions of the European Pharmacopoeia monograph *Human plasma for fractionation* and bear at least the identification number of the donation, the name and address of the collection establishment or the references of the blood transfusion service responsible for preparation, the batch number of the container, the storage temperature, the total volume or weight of plasma, the type of anticoagulant used and the date of collection and/or separation.

22 In order to minimise the microbiological contamination of plasma for fractionation or the introduction of foreign material, the thawing and pooling should be performed at least in a grade D clean area,

wearing the appropriate clothing and in addition face masks and gloves should be worn. Methods used for opening bags, pooling and thawing should be regularly monitored, e.g. by testing for bioburden. The cleanroom requirements for all other open manipulations should conform to the requirements of Annex 1 of the EU guide to GMP.

23   Methods for clearly distinguishing between products or intermediates which have undergone a process of virus removal or inactivation, from those which have not, should be in place.

24   Validation of methods used for virus removal or virus inactivation should not be conducted in the production facilities in order not to put the routine manufacture at any risk of contamination with the viruses used for validation.

Retention of Samples

25   Where possible, samples of individual donations should be stored to facilitate any necessary look-back procedure. This would normally be the responsibility of the collection establishment. Samples of each pool of plasma should be stored under suitable conditions for at least one year after the expiry date of the finished product with the longest shelf-life.

Disposal of Rejected Blood, Plasma or Intermediates

26   There should be a standard operating procedure for the safe and effective disposal of blood, plasma or intermediates.

---

(1)   Council Directive 89/381/EEC of 14 June 1989 extending the scope of Directives 65/65/EEC and 75/319/EEC on the approximation of provisions laid down by law, regulation or administrative action relating to proprietary medicinal products and laying down special provisions for medicinal products derived from human blood or human plasma (OJ No L 181 of 28.6.1989).

(2)   Council Directive 75/318/EEC, of 20 May 1975, on the approximation of the laws of Member States relating to analytical, pharmacotoxicological and clinical standards and protocols in respect of the testing of medicinal products (OJ No L 147 of 9.6.1975, p. 1) as last amended by Council Directive 93/39/EEC (OJ No L 214 of 24.8.1993, p. 22).

(3)   O.J. L 20321.7.1998 p. 14.

(4)   O.J. L 20321.7.1998 p. 14.

ANNEX 15 Qualification and Validation

Principle

1   This Annex describes the principles of qualification and validation which are applicable to the manufacture of medicinal products. It is a requirement of GMP that manufacturers identify what validation work is needed to prove control of the critical aspects of their particular operations. Significant changes to the facilities, the equipment and the processes, which may affect the quality of the product, should be validated. A risk assessment approach should be used to determine the scope and extent of validation.

Planning for Validation

2   All validation activities should be planned. The key elements of a validation programme should be clearly defined and documented in a validation master plan (VMP) or equivalent documents.

3   The VMP should be a summary document which is brief, concise and clear.

4   The VMP should contain data on at least the following:

(a)   validation policy;

(b)   organisational structure of validation activities;

(c)   summary of facilities, systems, equipment and processes to be validated;

(d)   documentation format: the format to be used for protocols and reports;

(e)   planning and scheduling;

(f)   change control;

(g)   reference to existing documents.

5   In case of large projects, it may be necessary to create separate validation master plans.

Documentation

6   A written protocol should be established that specifies how qualification and validation will be conducted. The protocol should be reviewed and approved. The protocol should specify critical steps and acceptance criteria.

7   A report that cross-references the qualification and/or validation protocol should be prepared, summarising the results obtained, commenting on any deviations observed, and drawing the necessary conclusions, including recommending changes necessary to correct deficiencies. Any changes to the plan as defined in the protocol should be documented with appropriate justification.

8   After completion of a satisfactory qualification, a formal release for the next step in qualification and validation should be made as a written authorisation.

Qualification

Design qualification

9   The first element of the validation of new facilities, systems or equipment could be design qualification (DQ).

10   The compliance of the design with GMP should be demonstrated and documented.

Installation qualification

11   Installation qualification (IQ) should be performed on new or modified facilities, systems and equipment.

12   IQ should include, but not be limited to the following:

(a)   installation of equipment, piping, services and instrumentation checked to current engineering drawings and specifications;

(b)   collection and collation of supplier operating and working instructions and maintenance requirements;

(c)   calibration requirements;

(d)   verification of materials of construction.

Operational qualification

13   Operational qualification (OQ) should follow Installation qualification.

14   OQ should include, but not be limited to the following:

(a)   tests that have been developed from knowledge of processes, systems and equipment;

(b)   tests to include a condition or a set of conditions encompassing upper and lower operating limits, sometimes referred to as 'worst case' conditions.

15   The completion of a successful Operational qualification should allow the finalisation of calibration, operating and cleaning procedures, operator training and preventative maintenance requirements. It should permit a formal 'release' of the facilities, systems and equipment.

Performance qualification

16   Performance qualification (PQ) should follow successful completion of Installation qualification and Operational qualification.

17   PQ should include, but not be limited to the following:

(a)   tests, using production materials, qualified substitutes or simulated product, that have been developed from knowledge of the process and the facilities, systems or equipment;

(b)   tests to include a condition or set of conditions encompassing upper and lower operating limits.

18   Although PQ is described as a separate activity, it may in some cases be appropriate to perform it in conjunction with OQ.

Qualification of established (in-use) facilities, systems and equipment

19   Evidence should be available to support and verify the operating parameters and limits for the critical variables of the operating equipment. Additionally, the calibration, cleaning, preventative maintenance, operating procedures and operator training procedures and records should be documented.

Process Validation

General

20   The requirements and principles outlined in this chapter are applicable to the manufacture of pharmaceutical dosage forms. They cover the initial validation of new processes, subsequent validation of modified processes and revalidation.

21   Process validation should normally be completed prior to the distribution and sale of the medicinal product (prospective

validation). In exceptional circumstances, where this is not possible, it may be necessary to validate processes during routine production (concurrent validation). Processes in use for some time should also be validated (retrospective validation).

22   Facilities, systems and equipment to be used should have been qualified and analytical testing methods should be validated. Staff taking part in the validation work should have been appropriately trained.

23   Facilities, systems, equipment and processes should be periodically evaluated to verify that they are still operating in a valid manner.

Prospective validation

24   Prospective validation should include, but not be limited to the following:

(a)   short description of the process;

(b)   summary of the critical processing steps to be investigated;

(c)   list of the equipment/facilities to be used (including measuring/ monitoring/recording equipment) together with its calibration status;

(d)   finished product specifications for release;

(e)   list of analytical methods, as appropriate;

(f)   proposed in-process controls with acceptance criteria;

(g)   additional testing to be carried out, with acceptance criteria and analytical validation, as appropriate;

(h)   sampling plan;

(i)   methods for recording and evaluating results;

(j)   functions and responsibilities;

(k)   proposed timetable.

25   Using this defined process (including specified components) a series of batches of the final product may be produced under routine conditions. In theory the number of process runs carried out and observations made should be sufficient to allow the normal extent of variation and trends to be established and to provide sufficient data for evaluation. It is generally considered acceptable that three consecutive batches/runs within the finally agreed parameters, would constitute a validation of the process.

26   Batches made for process validation should be the same size as the intended industrial scale batches.

27   If it is intended that validation batches be sold or supplied, the conditions under which they are produced should comply fully with the requirements of Good Manufacturing Practice, including the

satisfactory outcome of the validation exercise, and with the marketing authorisation.

Concurrent validation

28   In exceptional circumstances it may be acceptable not to complete a validation programme before routine production starts.

29   The decision to carry out concurrent validation must be justified, documented and approved by authorised personnel.

30   Documentation requirements for concurrent validation are the same as specified for prospective validation.

Retrospective validation

31   Retrospective validation is only acceptable for well-established processes and will be inappropriate where there have been recent changes in the composition of the product, operating procedures or equipment.

32   Validation of such processes should be based on historical data. The steps involved require the preparation of a specific protocol and the reporting of the results of the data review, leading to a conclusion and a recommendation.

33   The source of data for this validation should include, but not be limited to batch processing and packaging records, process control charts, maintenance log books, records of personnel changes, process capability studies, finished product data, including trend cards and storage stability results.

34   Batches selected for retrospective validation should be representative of all batches made during the review period, including any batches that failed to meet specifications, and should be sufficient in number to demonstrate process consistency. Additional testing of retained samples may be needed to obtain the necessary amount or type of data to retrospectively validate the process.

35   For retrospective validation, generally data from ten to thirty consecutive batches should be examined to assess process consistency, but fewer batches may be examined if justified.

Cleaning Validation

36   Cleaning validation should be performed in order to confirm the effectiveness of a cleaning procedure. The rationale for selecting limits of carry over of product residues, cleaning agents and microbial contamination should be logically based on the materials involved. The limits should be achievable and verifiable.

37   Validated analytical methods having sensitivity to detect residues or contaminants should be used. The detection limit for each analytical method should be sufficiently sensitive to detect the established acceptable level of the residue or contaminant.

38   Normally only cleaning procedures for product contact surfaces of the equipment need to be validated. Consideration should be given to non-contact parts. The intervals between use and cleaning as well as cleaning and reuse should be validated. Cleaning intervals and methods should be determined.

39   For cleaning procedures for products and processes which are similar, it is considered acceptable to select a representative range of similar products and processes. A single validation study utilising a 'worst case' approach can be carried out which takes account of the critical issues.

40   Typically three consecutive applications of the cleaning procedure should be performed and shown to be successful in order to prove that the method is validated.

41   'Test until clean' is not considered an appropriate alternative to cleaning validation.

42   Products which simulate the physicochemical properties of the substances to be removed may exceptionally be used instead of the substances themselves, where such substances are either toxic or hazardous.

Change Control

43   Written procedures should be in place to describe the actions to be taken if a change is proposed to a starting material, product component, process equipment, process environment (or site), method of production or testing or any other change that may affect product quality or reproducibility of the process. Change control procedures should ensure that sufficient supporting data are generated to demonstrate that the revised process will result in a product of the desired quality, consistent with the approved specifications.

44   All changes that may affect product quality or reproducibility of the process should be formally requested, documented and accepted. The likely impact of the change of facilities, systems and equipment on the product should be evaluated, including risk analysis. The need for, and the extent of, requalification and revalidation should be determined.

Revalidation

45   Facilities, systems, equipment and processes, including cleaning, should be periodically evaluated to confirm that they remain valid. Where no significant changes have been made to the validated status, a review with evidence that facilities, systems, equipment and processes meet the prescribed requirements fulfils the need for revalidation.

ANNEX 16 Certification by a Qualified Person and Batch Release

1 Scope

1.1 This annex to the Guide to Good Manufacturing Practice for Medicinal Products ('the Guide') gives guidance on the certification by a Qualified Person (QP) and batch release within the European Community (EC) or European Economic Area (EEA) of medicinal products holding a marketing authorisation or made for export. The relevant legislative requirements are contained in Article 22 of Council Directive 75/319/EEC or Article 30 of Council Directive 81/851/EEC.

1.2 The annex covers in particular those cases where a batch has had different stages of production or testing conducted at different locations or by different manufacturers, and where an intermediate or bulk production batch is divided into more than one finished product batch. It also covers the release of batches which have been imported to the EC/EEA both when there is and is not a mutual recognition agreement between the Community and the third country. The guidance may also be applied to investigational medicinal products, subject to any difference in the legal provisions and more specific guidance in Annex 13 to the Guide.

1.3 This annex does not, of course, describe all possible arrangements which are legally acceptable. Neither does it address the official control authority batch release which may be specified for certain blood and immunological products in accordance with Article 3 of Directives 89/342/EEC and 89/381/EEC.

1.4 The basic arrangements for batch release for a product are defined by its Marketing Authorisation. Nothing in this annex should be taken as overriding those arrangements.

2 Principle

2.1 Each batch of finished product must be certified by a QP within the EC/EEA before being released for sale or supply in the EC/EEA or for export.

2.2 The purpose of controlling batch release in this way is:

- to ensure that the batch has been manufactured and checked in accordance with the requirements of its marketing authorisation, the principles and guidelines of EC Good Manufacturing Practice or the good manufacturing practice of a third country recognised as equivalent under a mutual recognition agreement and any other relevant legal requirement before it is placed on the market; and

- in the event that a defect needs to be investigated or a batch recalled, to ensure that the QP who certified the batch and the relevant records are readily identifiable.

3 Introduction

3.1 Manufacture, including quality control testing, of a batch of medicinal products takes place in stages which may be conducted at different sites and by different manufacturers. Each stage should be conducted in accordance with the relevant marketing authorisation, Good Manufacturing Practice and the laws of the Member State concerned and should be taken into account by the QP who certifies the finished product batch before release to the market.

3.2 However in an industrial situation it is usually not possible for a single QP to be closely involved with every stage of manufacture. The QP who certifies a finished product batch may need therefore to rely in part on the advice and decisions of others. Before doing so he should ensure that this reliance is well founded, either from personal knowledge or from the confirmation by other QPs within a quality system which he has accepted.

3.3 When some stages of manufacture occur in a third country it is still a requirement that production and testing are in accordance with the marketing authorisation, that the manufacturer is authorised according to the laws of the country concerned and that manufacture follows good manufacturing practices at least equivalent to those of the EC.

3.4 Certain words used in this annex have particular meanings attributed to them, as defined in the glossary.

4 General

4.1 One batch of finished product may have different stages of manufacture, importation, testing and storage before release conducted at different sites. Each site should be approved under one or more manufacturing authorisations and should have at its disposal the services of at least one QP. However the correct manufacture of a particular batch of product, regardless of how many sites are involved, should be the overall concern of the QP who certifies that finished product batch before release.

4.2   Different batches of a product may be manufactured or imported and released at different sites in the EC/EEA. For example a Community marketing authorisation may name batch release sites in more than one member state, and a national authorisation may also name more than one release site. In this situation the holder of the marketing authorisation and each site authorised to release batches of the product should be able to identify the site at which any particular batch has been released and the QP who was responsible for certifying that batch.

4.3   The QP who certifies a finished product batch before release may do so based on his personal knowledge of all the facilities and procedures employed, the expertise of the persons concerned and of the quality system within which they operate. Alternatively he may rely on the confirmation by one or more other QPs of the compliance of intermediate stages of manufacture within a quality system which he has accepted.

This confirmation by other QPs should be documented and should identify clearly the matters which have been confirmed. The systematic arrangements to achieve this should be defined in a written agreement.

4.4   The agreement mentioned above is required whenever a QP wishes to rely on the confirmation by another QP. The agreement should be in general accordance with Chapter 7 of the Guide. The QP who certifies the finished product batch should ensure the arrangements in the agreement are verified. The form of such an agreement should be appropriate to the relationship between the parties; for example a standard operating procedure within a company or a formal contract between different companies even if within the same group.

4.5   The agreement should include an obligation on the part of the provider of a bulk or intermediate product to notify the recipient(s) of any deviations, out-of-specification results, non-compliance with GMP, investigations, complaints or other matters which should be taken into account by the QP who is responsible for certifying the finished product batch.

4.6   When a computerised system is used for recording certification and batch release, particular note should be taken of the guidance in Annex 11 to this Guide.

4.7   Certification of a finished product batch against a relevant marketing authorisation by a QP in the EC/EEA need not be repeated on the same batch provided the batch has remained within the EC/EEA.

4.8   Whatever particular arrangements are made for certification and release of batches, it should always be possible to identify and recall without delay all products which could be rendered hazardous by a quality defect in the batch.

5   Batch Testing and Release of Products Manufactured in EC/EEA

5.1   *When all manufacture occurs at a single authorised site*

When all production and control stages are carried out at a single site, the conduct of certain checks and controls may be delegated to others but the QP at this site who certifies the finished product batch normally retains personal responsibility for these within a defined quality system. However he may, alternatively, take account of the confirmation of the intermediate stages by other QPs on the site who are responsible for those stages.

5.2   *Different stages of manufacture are conducted at different sites within the same company*

When different stages of the manufacture of a batch are carried out at different sites within the same company (which may or may not be covered by the same manufacturing authorisation) a QP should be responsible for each stage. Certification of the finished product batch should be performed by a QP of the manufacturing authorisation holder responsible for releasing the batch to the market, who may take personal responsibility for all stages or may take account of the confirmation of the earlier stages by the relevant QPs responsible for those stages.

5.3   *Some intermediate stages of manufacture are contracted to a different company*

One or more intermediate production and control stages may be contracted to a holder of a manufacturing authorisation in another company. A QP of the contract giver may take account of the confirmation of the relevant stage by a QP of the contract acceptor but is responsible for ensuring that this work is conducted within the terms of a written agreement. The finished product batch should be certified by a QP of the manufacturing authorisation holder responsible for releasing the batch to the market.

5.4   *A bulk production batch is assembled at different sites into several finished product batches which are released under a single marketing authorisation. This could occur, for example, under a national marketing authorisation when the assembly sites are all within one member state or under a Community marketing authorisation when the sites are in more than one member state.*

5.4.1   One alternative is for a QP of the manufacturing authorisation holder making the bulk production batch to certify all the finished product batches before release to the market. In doing so he may either take personal responsibility for all manufacturing stages or take account of the confirmation of assembly by the QPs of the assembly sites.

5.4.2   Another alternative is for the certification of each finished product batch before release to the market to be performed by a QP of the manufacturer who has conducted the final assembly operation. In doing so he may either take personal responsibility for all manufacturing stages or take account of the confirmation of the bulk production batch by a QP of the manufacturer of the bulk batch.

5.4.3   In all cases of assembly at different sites under a single marketing authorisation, there should be one person, normally a QP of the manufacturer of the bulk production batch, who has an overall responsibility for all released finished product batches which are derived from one bulk production batch. The duty of this person is to be aware of any quality problems reported on any of the finished product batches and to co-ordinate any necessary action arising from a problem with the bulk batch.

While the batch numbers of the bulk and finished product batches are not necessarily the same, there should be a documented link between the two numbers so that an audit trail can be established.

5.5   *A bulk production batch is assembled at different sites into several finished product batches which are released under different marketing authorisations. This could occur, for example, when a multi-national organisation holds national marketing authorisations for a product in several member states or when a generic manufacturer purchases bulk products and assembles and releases them for sale under his own marketing authorisation.*

5.5.1   A QP of the manufacturer doing the assembly who certifies the finished product batch may either take personal responsibility for all manufacturing stages or may take account of the confirmation of the bulk production batch by a QP of the bulk product manufacturer.

5.5.2   Any problem identified in any of the finished product batches which may have arisen in the bulk production batch should be communicated to the QP responsible for confirming the bulk production batch, who should then take any necessary action in respect of *all* finished product batches produced from the suspected bulk production batch. This arrangement should be defined in a written agreement.

5.6   *A finished product batch is purchased and released to the market by a manufacturing authorisation holder in accordance with his own marketing authorisation. This could occur, for example, when a company supplying generic products holds a marketing authorisation for products made by another company, purchases finished products which have not been certified against his marketing authorisation and releases them under his own manufacturing authorisation in accordance with his own marketing authorisation. In this situation a QP of the purchaser should certify the finished product batch before release. In doing so he may either take personal responsibility for all manufacturing stages or may take account of the confirmation of the batch by a QP of the vendor manufacturer.*

5.7 *The quality control laboratory and the production site are authorised under different manufacturing authorisations.*

A QP certifying a finished product batch may either take personal responsibility for the laboratory testing or may take account of the confirmation by another QP of the testing and results. The other laboratory and QP need not be in the same member state as the manufacturing authorisation holder releasing the batch. In the absence of such confirmation the QP should himself have personal knowledge of the laboratory and its procedures relevant to the finished product to be certified.

6 Batch Testing and Release of Products Imported from a Third Country

6.1 *General:*

6.1.1 Importation of finished products should be conducted by an importer as defined in the glossary to this annex.

6.1.2 Each batch of imported finished product should be certified by a QP of the importer before release for sale in the EC/EEA.

6.1.3 Unless a mutual recognition agreement is in operation between the Community and the third country (see Section 7), samples from each batch should be tested in the EC/EEA before certification of the finished product batch by a QP. Importation and testing need not necessarily be performed in the same member state.

6.1.4 The guidance in this section should also be applied as appropriate to the importation of partially manufactured products.

6.2 *A complete batch or the first part of a batch of a medicinal product is imported.*

The batch or part batch should be certified by a QP of the importer before release. This QP may take account of the confirmation of the checking, sampling or testing of the imported batch by a QP of another manufacturing authorisation holder (i.e. within EC/EEA).

6.3   *Part of a finished product batch is imported after another part of the same batch has previously been imported to the same or a different site.*

6.3.1   A QP of the importer receiving a subsequent part of the batch may take account of the testing and certification by a QP of the first part of the batch. If this is done, the QP should ensure, based on evidence, that the two parts do indeed come from the same batch, that the subsequent part has been transported under the same conditions as the first part and that the samples that were tested are representative of the whole batch.

6.3.2   The conditions in paragraph 6.3.1 are most likely to be met when the manufacturer in the third country and the importer(s) in the EC/EEA belong to the same organisation operating under a corporate system of quality assurance. If the QP cannot ensure that the conditions in paragraph 6.3.1 are met, each part of the batch should be treated as a separate batch.

6.3.3   When different parts of the batch are released under the same marketing authorisation, one person, normally a QP of the importer of the first part of a batch, should take overall responsibility for ensuring that records are kept of the importation of all parts of the batch and that the distribution of all parts of the batch is traceable within the EC/EEA. He should be made aware of any quality problems reported on any part of the batch and should co-ordinate any necessary action concerning these problems and their resolution. This should be ensured by a written agreement between all the importers concerned.

6.4   *Location of sampling for testing in EC/EEA*

6.4.1   Samples should be representative of the batch and be tested in the EC/EEA. In order to represent the batch it may be preferable to take some samples during processing in the third country. For example, samples for sterility testing may best be taken throughout the filling operation. However in order to represent the batch after storage and transportation some samples should also be taken after receipt of the batch in the EC/EEA.

6.4.2   When any samples are taken in a third country, they should either be shipped with and under the same conditions as the batch which they represent, or if sent separately it should be demonstrated that the samples are still representative of the batch, for example by defining and monitoring the conditions of storage and shipment. When the QP wishes to rely on testing of samples taken in a third country, this should be justified on technical grounds.

7 Batch Testing and Release of Products Imported from a Third Country with which the EC has a Mutual Recognition Agreement (MRA)

7.1 Unless otherwise specified in the agreement, an MRA does not remove the requirement for a QP within the EC/EEA to certify a batch before it is released for sale or supply within the EC/EEA. However, subject to details of the particular agreement, the QP of the importer may rely on the manufacturer's confirmation that the batch has been made and tested in accordance with its marketing authorisation and the GMP of the third country and need not repeat the full testing. The QP may certify the batch for release when he is satisfied with this confirmation and that the batch has been transported under the required conditions and has been received and stored in the EC/EEA by an importer as defined in section 8.

7.2 Other procedures, including those for receipt and certification of part batches at different times and/or at different sites, should be the same as in Section 6.

8 Routine Duties of a Qualified Person

8.1 Before certifying a batch prior to release the QP doing so should ensure, with reference to the guidance above, that at least the following requirements have been met:

   a) the batch and its manufacture comply with the provisions of the marketing authorisation (including the authorisation required for importation where relevant);

   b) manufacture has been carried out in accordance with Good Manufacturing Practice or, in the case of a batch imported from a third country, in accordance with good manufacturing practice standards at least equivalent to EC GMP;

   c) the principal manufacturing and testing processes have been validated; account has been taken of the actual production conditions and manufacturing records;

   d) any deviations or planned changes in production or quality control have been authorised by the persons responsible in accordance with a defined system. Any changes requiring variation to the marketing or manufacturing authorisation have been notified to and authorised by the relevant authority;

   e) all the necessary checks and tests have been performed, including any additional sampling, inspection, tests or checks initiated because of deviations or planned changes;

f) all necessary production and quality control documentation has been completed and endorsed by the staff authorised to do so;

g) all audits have been carried out as required by the quality assurance system;

h) the QP should in addition take into account any other factors of which he is aware which are relevant to the quality of the batch.

A QP may have additional duties in accordance with national legislation or administrative procedures.

8.2 A QP who confirms the compliance of an intermediate stage of manufacture, as described in paragraph 4.3, has the same obligations as above in relation to that stage unless specified otherwise in the agreement between the QPs.

8.3 A QP should maintain his knowledge and experience up to date in the light of technical and scientific progress and changes in quality management relevant to the products which he is required to certify.

8.4 If a QP is called upon to certify a batch of a product type with which he is unfamiliar, for example because the manufacturer for whom he works introduces a new product range or because he starts to work for a different manufacturer, he should first ensure that he has gained the relevant knowledge and experience necessary to fulfil this duty. In accordance with national requirements the QP may be required to notify the authorities of such a change and may be subject to renewed authorisation.

Note that this Annex should be read in conjunction with CPMP/QWP/3015/99 which was adopted by the Committee on Proprietary Medicinal Products (CPMP) in February 2001. See http://www.emea.eu.int/htms/human/qwp/qwpfin.htm

1 Principle

1.1 The definition of Parametric Release used in this Annex is based on that proposed by the European Organization for Quality: 'A system of release that gives the assurance that the product is of the intended quality based on information collected during the manufacturing process and on the compliance with specific GMP requirements related to Parametric Release.'

1.2 Parametric Release should comply with the basic requirements of GMP, with applicable annexes and the following guidelines.

2 Parametric Release

2.1 It is recognised that a comprehensive set of in-process tests and controls may provide greater assurance of the finished product meeting specification than finished product testing.

2.2 Parametric Release may be authorised for certain specific parameters as an alternative to routine testing of finished products. Authorisation for parametric release should be given, refused or withdrawn jointly by those responsible for assessing products together with the GMP inspectors.

3 Parametric Release for sterile products

3.1 This section is only concerned with that part of Parametric Release which deals with the routine release of finished products without carrying out a sterility test. Elimination of the sterility test is only valid on the basis of successful demonstration that predetermined, validated sterilising conditions have been achieved.

3.2 A sterility test only provides an opportunity to detect a major failure of the sterility assurance system due to statistical limitations of the method.

3.3   Parametric Release can be authorised if the data demonstrating correct processing of the batch provides sufficient assurance, on its own, that the process designed and validated to ensure the sterility of the product has been delivered.

3.4   At present Parametric Release can only be approved for products terminally sterilised in their final container.

3.5   Sterilisation methods according to European Pharmacopeia requirements using steam, dry heat and ionising radiation may be considered for Parametric Release.

3.6   It is unlikely that a completely new product would be considered as suitable for Parametric Release because a period of satisfactory sterility test results will form part of the acceptance criteria. There may be cases when a new product is only a minor variation, from the sterility assurance point of view, and existing sterility test data from other products could be considered as relevant.

3.7   A risk analysis of the sterility assurance system focused on an evaluation of releasing non-sterilised products should be performed.

3.8   The manufacturer should have a history of good compliance with GMP.

3.9   The history of non sterility of products and of results of sterility tests carried out on the product in question together with products processed through the same or a similar sterility assurance system should be taken into consideration when evaluating GMP compliance.

3.10   A qualified experienced sterility assurance engineer and a qualified microbiologist should normally be present on the site of production and sterilisation.

3.11   The design and original validation of the product should ensure that integrity can be maintained under all relevant conditions.

3.12   The change control system should require review of change by sterility assurance personnel.

3.13   There should be a system to control microbiological contamination in the product before sterilisation.

3.14   There should be no possibility for mix ups between sterilised and non-sterilised products. Physical barriers or validated electronic systems may provide such assurance.

3.15   The sterilisation records should be checked for compliance to specification by at least two independent systems. These systems may consist of two people or a validated computer system plus a person.

3.16   The following additional items should be confirmed prior to release of each batch of product:

- all planned maintenance and routine checks have been completed in the steriliser used;
- all repairs and modifications have been approved by the sterility assurance engineer and microbiologist;
- all instrumentation was in calibration;
- the steriliser had a current validation for the product load processed.

3.17   Once Parametric Release has been granted, decisions for release or rejection of a batch should be based on the approved specifications. Non-compliance with the specification for Parametric Release cannot be overruled by a pass of a sterility test.

ANNEX 18   Good Manufacturing Practice for Active
Pharmaceutical Ingredients

Note

*On 18th July 2001, the Commission adopted a new legislative proposal
which introduces a requirement for pharmaceutical manufacturers to use
only active substances which have been manufactured according to GMP
in the manufacture of medicinal products. Until this comes into force
requirements for GMP for active substances and hence the applicability
of this guideline will not be mandatory in the EU. However when there
are causes for concern, or when required by certain Member States, GMP
inspections of active ingredient manufacturers may be carried out by the
competent authorities of Member States. In these cases, and in particular
when these are performed in the context of an application for a
centralised authorisation, it has been agreed that the inspectors of the
competent authorities in the EU will inspect against the requirements in
this guideline.*

Table of Contents

1 Introduction

1.1 *Objective*

This document (Guide) is intended to provide guidance regarding good manufacturing practice (GMP) for the manufacturing of active pharmaceutical ingredients (APIs) under an appropriate system for managing quality. It is also intended to help ensure that APIs meet the requirements for quality and purity that they purport or are represented to possess.

In this Guide 'manufacturing' is defined to include all operations of receipt of materials, production, packaging, repackaging, labelling, relabelling, quality control, release, storage and distribution of APIs and the related controls. In this Guide the term 'should' indicates recommendations that are expected to apply unless shown to be inapplicable or replaced by an alternative demonstrated to provide at least an equivalent level of quality assurance. For the purposes of this Guide, the terms 'current good manufacturing practices' and 'good manufacturing practices' are equivalent.

The Guide as a whole does not cover safety aspects for the personnel engaged in the manufacture, nor aspects of protection of the environment. These controls are inherent responsibilities of the manufacturer and are governed by national laws.

This Guide is not intended to define registration/filing requirements or modify pharmacopoeial requirements. This Guide does not affect the ability of the responsible regulatory agency to establish specific registration/filing requirements regarding APIs within the context of marketing/manufacturing authorisations or drug applications. All commitments in registration/filing documents must be met.

1.2 *Regulatory Applicability*

Within the world community, materials may vary as to the legal classification as an API. When a material is classified as an API in the region or country in which it is manufactured or used in a drug product, it should be manufactured according to this Guide.

1.3 *Scope*

This Guide applies to the manufacture of APIs for use in human drug (medicinal) products. It applies to the manufacture of sterile APIs only up to the point immediately prior to the APIs being rendered sterile. The sterilisation and aseptic processing of sterile APIs are not covered by this guidance, but should be performed in accordance with GMP guidelines for drug (medicinal) products as defined by local authorities.

This Guide covers APIs that are manufactured by chemical synthesis, extraction, cell culture/fermentation, by recovery from natural sources, or by any combination of these processes. Specific guidance for APIs manufactured by cell culture/fermentation is described in Section 18.

This Guide excludes all vaccines, whole cells, whole blood and plasma, blood and plasma derivatives (plasma fractionation), and gene therapy APIs. However, it does include APIs that are produced using blood or plasma as raw materials. Note that cell substrates (mammalian, plant, insect or microbial cells, tissue or animal sources including transgenic animals) and early process steps may be subject to GMP but are not covered by this Guide. In addition, the Guide does not apply to medical gases, bulk-packaged drug (medicinal) products, and manufacturing/control aspects specific to radiopharmaceuticals.

Section 19 contains guidance that only applies to the manufacture of APIs used in the production of drug (medicinal) products specifically for clinical trials (investigational medicinal products).

An 'API Starting Material' is a raw material, intermediate, or an API that is used in the production of an API and that is incorporated as a significant structural fragment into the structure of the API. An API Starting Material can be an article of commerce, a material purchased from one or more suppliers under contract or commercial agreement, or produced in-house. API Starting Materials normally have defined chemical properties and structure.

The company should designate and document the rationale for the point at which production of the API begins. For synthetic processes, this is known as the point at which 'API Starting Materials' are entered into the process. For other processes (e.g. fermentation, extraction, purification, etc), this rationale should be established on a case-by-case basis. Table 1 gives guidance on the point at which the API Starting Material is normally introduced into the process.

From this point on, appropriate GMP as defined in this Guide should be applied to these intermediate and/or API manufacturing steps. This would include the validation of critical process steps determined to impact the quality of the API. However, it should be noted that the fact that a company chooses to validate a process step does not necessarily define that step as critical.

The guidance in this document would normally be applied to the steps shown in gray in Table 1. It does not imply that all steps shown should be completed. The stringency of GMP in API manufacturing should increase as the process proceeds from early API steps to final steps, purification, and packaging. Physical processing of APIs, such as granulation, coating or physical manipulation of particle size (e.g. milling, micronising), should be conducted at least to the standards of this Guide.

This GMP Guide does not apply to steps prior to the introduction of the defined 'API Starting Material'.

Table 1: Application of this Guide to API Manufacturing

Type of manufacturing	Application of this Guide to steps (shown in grey) used in this type of manufacturing				
Chemical Manufacturing	Production of the API Starting Material	Introduction of the API Starting Material into process	Production of Intermediate(s)	Isolation and purification	Physical processing, and packaging
API derived from animal sources	Collection of organ, fluid, or tissue	Cutting, mixing, and/or initial processing	Introduction of the API Starting Material into process	Isolation and purification	Physical processing, and packaging
API extracted from plant sources	Collection of plant	Cutting and initial extraction(s)	Introduction of the API Starting Material into process	Isolation and purification	Physical processing, and packaging
Herbal extracts used as API	Collection of plants	Cutting and initial extraction		Further extraction	Physical processing, and packaging
API consisting of comminuted or powdered herbs	Collection of plants and/or cultivation and harvesting	Cutting/ comminuting			Physical processing, and packaging
Biotechnology: fermentation/ cell culture	Establishment of master cell bank and working cell bank	Maintenance of working cell bank	Cell culture and/or fermentation	Isolation and purification	Physical processing, and packaging
'Classical' Fermentation to produce an API	Establishment of cell bank	Maintenance of the cell bank	Introduction of the cells into fermentation	Isolation and purification	Physical processing, and packaging

Increasing GMP requirements ⟶

2   Quality Management

2.1   *Principles*

2.10   Quality should be the responsibility of all persons involved in manufacturing.

2.11   Each manufacturer should establish, document, and implement an effective system for managing quality that involves the active participation of management and appropriate manufacturing personnel.

2.12   The system for managing quality should encompass the organisational structure, procedures, processes and resources, as well as activities necessary to ensure confidence that the API will meet its intended specifications for quality and purity. All quality related activities should be defined and documented.

2.13   There should be a quality unit(s) that is independent of production and that fulfills both quality assurance (QA) and quality control (QC) responsibilities. This can be in the form of separate QA and QC units or a single individual or group, depending upon the size and structure of the organisation.

2.14   The persons authorised to release intermediates and APIs should be specified.

2.15   All quality related activities should be recorded at the time they are performed.

2.16   Any deviation from established procedures should be documented and explained. Critical deviations should be investigated, and the investigation and its conclusions should be documented.

2.17   No materials should be released or used before the satisfactory completion of evaluation by the quality unit(s) unless there are appropriate systems in place to allow for such use (e.g. release under quarantine as described in Section 10.20 or the use of raw materials or intermediates pending completion of evaluation).

2.18   Procedures should exist for notifying responsible management in a timely manner of regulatory inspections, serious GMP deficiencies, product defects and related actions (e.g. quality related complaints, recalls, regulatory actions, etc.).

2.2   *Responsibilities of the Quality Unit(s)*

2.20   The quality unit(s) should be involved in all quality-related matters.

2.21   The quality unit(s) should review and approve all appropriate quality-related documents.

2.22   The main responsibilities of the independent quality unit(s) should not be delegated. These responsibilities should be described in writing and should include but not necessarily be limited to:

1.   Releasing or rejecting all APIs. Releasing or rejecting intermediates for use outside the control of the manufacturing company;

2.   Establishing a system to release or reject raw materials, intermediates, packaging and labelling materials;

3.   Reviewing completed batch production and laboratory control records of critical process steps before release of the API for distribution;

4.   Making sure that critical deviations are investigated and resolved;

5. Approving all specifications and master production instructions;

6. Approving all procedures impacting the quality of intermediates or APIs;

7. Making sure that internal audits (self-inspections) are performed;

8. Approving intermediate and API contract manufacturers;

9. Approving changes that potentially impact intermediate or API quality;

10. Reviewing and approving validation protocols and reports;

11. Making sure that quality related complaints are investigated and resolved;

12. Making sure that effective systems are used for maintaining and calibrating critical equipment;

13. Making sure that materials are appropriately tested and the results are reported;

14. Making sure that there is stability data to support retest or expiry dates and storage conditions on APIs and/or intermediates where appropriate; and

15. Performing product quality reviews (as defined in Section 2.5)

2.3 *Responsibility for Production Activities*

The responsibility for production activities should be described in writing, and should include but not necessarily be limited to:

1. Preparing, reviewing, approving and distributing the instructions for the production of intermediates or APIs according to written procedures;

2. Producing APIs and, when appropriate, intermediates according to pre-approved instructions;

3. Reviewing all production batch records and ensuring that these are completed and signed;

4. Making sure that all production deviations are reported and evaluated and that critical deviations are investigated and the conclusions are recorded;

5. Making sure that production facilities are clean and when appropriate disinfected;

6. Making sure that the necessary calibrations are performed and records kept;

7. Making sure that the premises and equipment are maintained and records kept;

8. Making sure that validation protocols and reports are reviewed and approved;

9. Evaluating proposed changes in product, process or equipment; and

10. Making sure that new and, when appropriate, modified facilities and equipment are qualified.

2.4 *Internal Audits (Self Inspection)*

2.40 In order to verify compliance with the principles of GMP for APIs, regular internal audits should be performed in accordance with an approved schedule.

2.41 Audit findings and corrective actions should be documented and brought to the attention of responsible management of the firm. Agreed corrective actions should be completed in a timely and effective manner.

2.5 *Product Quality Review*

2.50 Regular quality reviews of APIs should be conducted with the objective of verifying the consistency of the process. Such reviews should normally be conducted and documented annually and should include at least:

- A review of critical in-process control and critical API test results;

- A review of all batches that failed to meet established specification(s);

- A review of all critical deviations or non-conformances and related investigations;

- A review of any changes carried out to the processes or analytical methods;

- A review of results of the stability monitoring program;

- A review of all quality-related returns, complaints and recalls; and

- A review of adequacy of corrective actions.

2.51 The results of this review should be evaluated and an assessment made of whether corrective action or any revalidation should be undertaken. Reasons for such corrective action should be documented. Agreed corrective actions should be completed in a timely and effective manner.

3 Personnel

3.1 *Personnel Qualifications*

3.10 There should be an adequate number of personnel qualified by appropriate education, training and/or experience to perform and supervise the manufacture of intermediates and APIs.

3.11 The responsibilities of all personnel engaged in the manufacture of intermediates and APIs should be specified in writing.

3.12 Training should be regularly conducted by qualified individuals and should cover, at a minimum, the particular operations that the employee performs and GMP as it relates to the employee's functions. Records of training should be maintained. Training should be periodically assessed.

3.2 *Personnel Hygiene*

3.20 Personnel should practice good sanitation and health habits.

3.21 Personnel should wear clean clothing suitable for the manufacturing activity with which they are involved and this clothing should be changed when appropriate. Additional protective apparel, such as head, face, hand, and arm coverings, should be worn when necessary, to protect intermediates and APIs from contamination.

3.22 Personnel should avoid direct contact with intermediates or APIs.

3.23 Smoking, eating, drinking, chewing and the storage of food should be restricted to certain designated areas separate from the manufacturing areas.

3.24 Personnel suffering from an infectious disease or having open lesions on the exposed surface of the body should not engage in activities that could result in compromising the quality of APIs. Any person shown at any time (either by medical examination or supervisory observation) to have an apparent illness or open lesions should be excluded from activities where the health condition could adversely affect the quality of the APIs until the condition is corrected or qualified medical personnel determine that the person's inclusion would not jeopardise the safety or quality of the APIs.

3.3 *Consultants*

3.30 Consultants advising on the manufacture and control of intermediates or APIs should have sufficient education, training, and experience, or any combination thereof, to advise on the subject for which they are retained.

3.31 Records should be maintained stating the name, address, qualifications, and type of service provided by these consultants.

4 Buildings and Facilities

4.1 *Design and Construction*

4.10   Buildings and facilities used in the manufacture of intermediates and APIs should be located, designed, and constructed to facilitate cleaning, maintenance, and operations as appropriate to the type and stage of manufacture. Facilities should also be designed to minimise potential contamination. Where microbiological specifications have been established for the intermediate or API, facilities should also be designed to limit exposure to objectionable microbiological contaminants as appropriate.

4.11   Buildings and facilities should have adequate space for the orderly placement of equipment and materials to prevent mix-ups and contamination.

4.12   Where the equipment itself (e.g., closed or contained systems) provides adequate protection of the material, such equipment can be located outdoors.

4.13   The flow of materials and personnel through the building or facilities should be designed to prevent mix-ups or contamination.

4.14   There should be defined areas or other control systems for the following activities:

- Receipt, identification, sampling, and quarantine of incoming materials, pending release or rejection;

- Quarantine before release or rejection of intermediates and APIs;

- Sampling of intermediates and APIs;

- Holding rejected materials before further disposition (e.g., return, reprocessing or destruction);

- Storage of released materials;

- Production operations;

- Packaging and labelling operations; and

- Laboratory operations.

4.15   Adequate, clean washing and toilet facilities should be provided for personnel. These washing facilities should be equipped with hot and cold water as appropriate, soap or detergent, air driers or single service towels. The washing and toilet facilities should be separate from, but easily accessible to, manufacturing areas. Adequate facilities for showering and/or changing clothes should be provided, when appropriate.

4.16 Laboratory areas/operations should normally be separated from production areas. Some laboratory areas, in particular those used for in-process controls, can be located in production areas, provided the operations of the production process do not adversely affect the accuracy of the laboratory measurements, and the laboratory and its operations do not adversely affect the production process or intermediate or API.

4.2 *Utilities*

4.20 All utilities that could impact on product quality (e.g. steam, gases, compressed air, and heating, ventilation and air conditioning) should be qualified and appropriately monitored and action should be taken when limits are exceeded. Drawings for these utility systems should be available.

4.21 Adequate ventilation, air filtration and exhaust systems should be provided, where appropriate. These systems should be designed and constructed to minimise risks of contamination and cross-contamination and should include equipment for control of air pressure, microorganisms (if appropriate), dust, humidity, and temperature, as appropriate to the stage of manufacture. Particular attention should be given to areas where APIs are exposed to the environment.

4.22 If air is recirculated to production areas, appropriate measures should be taken to control risks of contamination and cross-contamination.

4.23 Permanently installed pipework should be appropriately identified. This can be accomplished by identifying individual lines, documentation, computer control systems, or alternative means. Pipework should be located to avoid risks of contamination of the intermediate or API.

4.24 Drains should be of adequate size and should be provided with an air break or a suitable device to prevent back-siphonage, when appropriate.

4.3 *Water*

4.30 Water used in the manufacture of APIs should be demonstrated to be suitable for its intended use.

4.31 Unless otherwise justified, process water should, at a minimum, meet World Health Organization (WHO) guidelines for drinking (potable) water quality.

4.32 If drinking (potable) water is insufficient to assure API quality, and tighter chemical and/or microbiological water quality specifications are called for, appropriate specifications for physical/chemical attributes, total microbial counts, objectionable organisms and/or endotoxins should be established.

4.33 Where water used in the process is treated by the manufacturer to achieve a defined quality, the treatment process should be validated and monitored with appropriate action limits.

4.34 Where the manufacturer of a non-sterile API either intends or claims that it is suitable for use in further processing to produce a sterile drug (medicinal) product, water used in the final isolation and purification steps should be monitored and controlled for total microbial counts, objectionable organisms, and endotoxins.

4.4 *Containment*

4.40 Dedicated production areas, which can include facilities, air handling equipment and/or process equipment, should be employed in the production of highly sensitising materials, such as penicillins or cephalosporins.

4.41 Dedicated production areas should also be considered when material of an infectious nature or high pharmacological activity or toxicity is involved (e.g., certain steroids or cytotoxic anti-cancer agents) unless validated inactivation and/or cleaning procedures are established and maintained.

4.42 Appropriate measures should be established and implemented to prevent cross-contamination from personnel, materials, etc. moving from one dedicated area to another.

4.43 Any production activities (including weighing, milling, or packaging) of highly toxic non-pharmaceutical materials such as herbicides and pesticides should not be conducted using the buildings and/or equipment being used for the production of APIs. Handling and storage of these highly toxic non-pharmaceutical materials should be separate from APIs.

4.5 *Lighting*

4.50 Adequate lighting should be provided in all areas to facilitate cleaning, maintenance, and proper operations.

4.6 *Sewage and Refuse*

4.60 Sewage, refuse, and other waste (e.g., solids, liquids, or gaseous by-products from manufacturing) in and from buildings and the immediate surrounding area should be disposed of in a safe, timely, and sanitary manner. Containers and/or pipes for waste material should be clearly identified.

4.7 *Sanitation and Maintenance*

4.70 Buildings used in the manufacture of intermediates and APIs should be properly maintained and repaired and kept in a clean condition.

4.71 Written procedures should be established assigning responsibility for sanitation and describing the cleaning schedules, methods, equipment, and materials to be used in cleaning buildings and facilities.

4.72 When necessary, written procedures should also be established for the use of suitable rodenticides, insecticides, fungicides, fumigating agents, and cleaning and sanitising agents to prevent the contamination of equipment, raw materials, packaging/labelling materials, intermediates, and APIs.

5 Process Equipment

5.1 *Design and Construction*

5.10 Equipment used in the manufacture of intermediates and APIs should be of appropriate design and adequate size, and suitably located for its intended use, cleaning, sanitisation (where appropriate), and maintenance.

5.11 Equipment should be constructed so that surfaces that contact raw materials, intermediates, or APIs do not alter the quality of the intermediates and APIs beyond the official or other established specifications.

5.12 Production equipment should only be used within its qualified operating range.

5.13 Major equipment (e.g., reactors, storage containers) and permanently installed processing lines used during the production of an intermediate or API should be appropriately identified.

5.14 Any substances associated with the operation of equipment, such as lubricants, heating fluids or coolants, should not contact intermediates or APIs so as to alter their quality beyond the official or other established specifications. Any deviations from this should be evaluated to ensure that there are no detrimental effects upon the fitness for purpose of the material. Wherever possible, food grade lubricants and oils should be used.

5.15 Closed or contained equipment should be used whenever appropriate. Where open equipment is used, or equipment is opened, appropriate precautions should be taken to minimise the risk of contamination.

5.16   A set of current drawings should be maintained for equipment and critical installations (e.g., instrumentation and utility systems).

5.2   *Equipment Maintenance and Cleaning*

5.20   Schedules and procedures (including assignment of responsibility) should be established for the preventative maintenance of equipment.

5.21   Written procedures should be established for cleaning of equipment and its subsequent release for use in the manufacture of intermediates and APIs. Cleaning procedures should contain sufficient details to enable operators to clean each type of equipment in a reproducible and effective manner. These procedures should include:

- assignment of responsibility for cleaning of equipment;

- cleaning schedules, including, where appropriate, sanitising schedules;

- a complete description of the methods and materials, including dilution of cleaning agents used to clean equipment;

- when appropriate, instructions for disassembling and reassembling each article of equipment to ensure proper cleaning;

- instructions for the removal or obliteration of previous batch identification;

- instructions for the protection of clean equipment from contamination prior to use;

- inspection of equipment for cleanliness immediately before use, if practical; and

- establishing the maximum time that may elapse between the completion of processing and equipment cleaning, when appropriate.

5.22   Equipment and utensils should be cleaned, stored, and, where appropriate, sanitised or sterilised to prevent contamination or carry-over of a material that would alter the quality of the intermediate or API beyond the official or other established specifications.

5.23   Where equipment is assigned to continuous production or campaign production of successive batches of the same intermediate or API, equipment should be cleaned at appropriate intervals to prevent build-up and carry-over of contaminants (e.g. degradants or objectionable levels of micro-organisms).

5.24   Non-dedicated equipment should be cleaned between production of different materials to prevent cross-contamination.

5.25   Acceptance criteria for residues and the choice of cleaning procedures and cleaning agents should be defined and justified.

5.26   Equipment should be identified as to its contents and its cleanliness status by appropriate means.

5.3   *Calibration*

5.30   Control, weighing, measuring, monitoring and test equipment that is critical for assuring the quality of intermediates or APIs should be calibrated according to written procedures and an established schedule.

5.31   Equipment calibrations should be performed using standards traceable to certified standards, if existing.

5.32   Records of these calibrations should be maintained.

5.33   The current calibration status of critical equipment should be known and verifiable.

5.34   Instruments that do not meet calibration criteria should not be used.

5.35   Deviations from approved standards of calibration on critical instruments should be investigated to determine if these could have had an impact on the quality of the intermediate(s) or API(s) manufactured using this equipment since the last successful calibration.

5.4   *Computerised Systems*

5.40   GMP related computerised systems should be validated. The depth and scope of validation depends on the diversity, complexity and criticality of the computerised application.

5.41   Appropriate installation qualification and operational qualification should demonstrate the suitability of computer hardware and software to perform assigned tasks.

5.42   Commercially available software that has been qualified does not require the same level of testing. If an existing system was not validated at time of installation, a retrospective validation could be conducted if appropriate documentation is available.

5.43   Computerised systems should have sufficient controls to prevent unauthorised access or changes to data. There should be controls to prevent omissions in data (e.g. system turned off and data not captured). There should be a record of any data change made, the previous entry, who made the change, and when the change was made.

5.44 Written procedures should be available for the operation and maintenance of computerised systems.

5.45 Where critical data are being entered manually, there should be an additional check on the accuracy of the entry. This can be done by a second operator or by the system itself.

5.46 Incidents related to computerised systems that could affect the quality of intermediates or APIs or the reliability of records or test results should be recorded and investigated.

5.47 Changes to the computerised system should be made according to a change procedure and should be formally authorised, documented and tested. Records should be kept of all changes, including modifications and enhancements made to the hardware, software and any other critical component of the system. These records should demonstrate that the system is maintained in a validated state.

5.48 If system breakdowns or failures would result in the permanent loss of records, a back-up system should be provided. A means of ensuring data protection should be established for all computerised systems.

5.49 Data can be recorded by a second means in addition to the computer system.

6   Documentation and Records

6.1   *Documentation System and Specifications*

6.10 All documents related to the manufacture of intermediates or APIs should be prepared, reviewed, approved and distributed according to written procedures. Such documents can be in paper or electronic form.

6.11 The issuance, revision, superseding and withdrawal of all documents should be controlled with maintenance of revision histories.

6.12 A procedure should be established for retaining all appropriate documents (e.g., development history reports, scale-up reports, technical transfer reports, process validation reports, training records, production records, control records, and distribution records). The retention periods for these documents should be specified.

6.13 All production, control, and distribution records should be retained for at least 1 year after the expiry date of the batch. For APIs with retest dates, records should be retained for at least 3 years after the batch is completely distributed.

6.14   When entries are made in records, these should be made indelibly in spaces provided for such entries, directly after performing the activities, and should identify the person making the entry. Corrections to entries should be dated and signed and leave the original entry still readable.

6.15   During the retention period, originals or copies of records should be readily available at the establishment where the activities described in such records occurred. Records that can be promptly retrieved from another location by electronic or other means are acceptable.

6.16   Specifications, instructions, procedures, and records can be retained either as originals or as true copies such as photocopies, microfilm, microfiche, or other accurate reproductions of the original records. Where reduction techniques such as microfilming or electronic records are used, suitable retrieval equipment and a means to produce a hard copy should be readily available.

6.17   Specifications should be established and documented for raw materials, intermediates where necessary, APIs, and labelling and packaging materials. In addition, specifications may be appropriate for certain other materials, such as process aids, gaskets, or other materials used during the production of intermediates or APIs that could critically impact on quality. Acceptance criteria should be established and documented for in-process controls.

6.18   If electronic signatures are used on documents, they should be authenticated and secure.

6.2   *Equipment Cleaning and Use Record*

6.20   Records of major equipment use, cleaning, sanitisation and/or sterilisation and maintenance should show the date, time (if appropriate), product, and batch number of each batch processed in the equipment, and the person who performed the cleaning and maintenance.

6.21   If equipment is dedicated to manufacturing one intermediate or API, then individual equipment records are not necessary if batches of the intermediate or API follow in traceable sequence. In cases where dedicated equipment is employed, the records of cleaning, maintenance, and use can be part of the batch record or maintained separately.

6.3   *Records of Raw Materials, Intermediates, API Labelling and Packaging Materials*

6.30   Records should be maintained including:

- the name of the manufacturer, identity and quantity of each shipment of each batch of raw materials, intermediates or labelling and packaging materials for APIs; the name of the supplier; the supplier's control number(s), if known, or other identification number; the number allocated on receipt; and the date of receipt;

- the results of any test or examination performed and the conclusions derived from this;

- records tracing the use of materials;

- documentation of the examination and review of API labelling and packaging materials for conformity with established specifications; and

- the final decision regarding rejected raw materials, intermediates or API labelling and packaging materials.

6.31   Master (approved) labels should be maintained for comparison to issued labels.

6.4   *Master Production Instructions (Master Production and Control Records)*

6.40   To ensure uniformity from batch to batch, master production instructions for each intermediate and API should be prepared, dated, and signed by one person and independently checked, dated, and signed by a person in the quality unit(s).

6.41   Master production instructions should include:

- the name of the intermediate or API being manufactured and an identifying document reference code, if applicable;

- a complete list of raw materials and intermediates designated by names or codes sufficiently specific to identify any special quality characteristics;

- an accurate statement of the quantity or ratio of each raw material or intermediate to be used, including the unit of measure. Where the quantity is not fixed, the calculation for each batch size or rate of production should be included. Variations to quantities should be included where they are justified;

- the production location and major production equipment to be used;

- detailed production instructions, including the:

    - sequences to be followed;

    - ranges of process parameters to be used;

    - sampling instructions and in-process controls with their acceptance criteria, where appropriate;

- time limits for completion of individual processing steps and/or the total process, where appropriate; and

- expected yield ranges at appropriate phases of processing or time;

• where appropriate, special notations and precautions to be followed, or cross-references to these; and

• the instructions for storage of the intermediate or API to assure its suitability for use, including the labelling and packaging materials and special storage conditions with time limits, where appropriate.

6.5 *Batch Production Records (Batch Production and Control Records)*

6.50 Batch production records should be prepared for each intermediate and API and should include complete information relating to the production and control of each batch. The batch production record should be checked before issuance to assure that it is the correct version and a legible accurate reproduction of the appropriate master production instruction. If the batch production record is produced from a separate part of the master document, that document should include a reference to the current master production instruction being used.

6.51 These records should be numbered with a unique batch or identification number, dated and signed when issued. In continuous production, the product code together with the date and time can serve as the unique identifier until the final number is allocated.

6.52 Documentation of completion of each significant step in the batch production records (batch production and control records) should include:

• dates and, when appropriate, times;

• identity of major equipment (e.g., reactors, driers, mills, etc.) used;

• specific identification of each batch, including weights, measures, and batch numbers of raw materials, intermediates, or any reprocessed materials used during manufacturing;

• actual results recorded for critical process parameters;

• any sampling performed;

• signatures of the persons performing and directly supervising or checking each critical step in the operation;

• in-process and laboratory test results;

- actual yield at appropriate phases or times;

- description of packaging and label for intermediate or API;

- representative label of API or intermediate if made commercially available;

- any deviation noted, its evaluation, investigation conducted (if appropriate) or reference to that investigation if stored separately; and

- results of release testing.

6.53 Written procedures should be established and followed for investigating critical deviations or the failure of a batch of intermediate or API to meet specifications. The investigation should extend to other batches that may have been associated with the specific failure or deviation.

6.6 *Laboratory Control Records*

6.60 Laboratory control records should include complete data derived from all tests conducted to ensure compliance with established specifications and standards, including examinations and assays, as follows:

- a description of samples received for testing, including the material name or source, batch number or other distinctive code, date sample was taken, and, where appropriate, the quantity and date the sample was received for testing;

- a statement of or reference to each test method used;

- a statement of the weight or measure of sample used for each test as described by the method; data on or cross-reference to the preparation and testing of reference standards, reagents and standard solutions;

- a complete record of all raw data generated during each test, in addition to graphs, charts, and spectra from laboratory instrumentation, properly identified to show the specific material and batch tested;

- a record of all calculations performed in connection with the test, including, for example, units of measure, conversion factors, and equivalency factors;

- a statement of the test results and how they compare with established acceptance criteria;

- the signature of the person who performed each test and the date(s) the tests were performed; and

- the date and signature of a second person showing that the original records have been reviewed for accuracy, completeness, and compliance with established standards.

6.61   Complete records should also be maintained for:

- any modifications to an established analytical method;

- periodic calibration of laboratory instruments, apparatus, gauges, and recording devices;

- all stability testing performed on APIs; and

- out-of-specification (OOS) investigations.

6.7   *Batch Production Record Review*

6.70   Written procedures should be established and followed for the review and approval of batch production and laboratory control records, including packaging and labelling, to determine compliance of the intermediate or API with established specifications before a batch is released or distributed.

6.71   Batch production and laboratory control records of critical process steps should be reviewed and approved by the quality unit(s) before an API batch is released or distributed. Production and laboratory control records of non-critical process steps can be reviewed by qualified production personnel or other units following procedures approved by the quality unit(s).

6.72   All deviation, investigation, and OOS reports should be reviewed as part of the batch record review before the batch is released.

6.73   The quality unit(s) can delegate to the production unit the responsibility and authority for release of intermediates, except for those shipped outside the control of the manufacturing company.

7   Materials Management

7.1   *General Controls*

7.10   There should be written procedures describing the receipt, identification, quarantine, storage, handling, sampling, testing, and approval or rejection of materials.

7.11   Manufacturers of intermediates and/or APIs should have a system for evaluating the suppliers of critical materials.

7.12   Materials should be purchased against an agreed specification, from a supplier or suppliers approved by the quality unit(s).

7.13   If the supplier of a critical material is not the manufacturer of that material, the name and address of that manufacturer should be known by the intermediate and/or API manufacturer.

7.14 Changing the source of supply of critical raw materials should be treated according to Section 13, **Change Control**.

7.2 *Receipt and Quarantine*

7.20 Upon receipt and before acceptance, each container or grouping of containers of materials should be examined visually for correct labelling (including correlation between the name used by the supplier and the in-house name, if these are different), container damage, broken seals and evidence of tampering or contamination. Materials should be held under quarantine until they have been sampled, examined or tested as appropriate, and released for use.

7.21 Before incoming materials are mixed with existing stocks (e.g., solvents or stocks in silos), they should be identified as correct, tested, if appropriate, and released. Procedures should be available to prevent discharging incoming materials wrongly into the existing stock.

7.22 If bulk deliveries are made in non-dedicated tankers, there should be assurance of no cross-contamination from the tanker. Means of providing this assurance could include one or more of the following:

- certificate of cleaning;

- testing for trace impurities;

- audit of the supplier.

7.23 Large storage containers, and their attendant manifolds, filling and discharge lines should be appropriately identified.

7.24 Each container or grouping of containers (batches) of materials should be assigned and identified with a distinctive code, batch, or receipt number. This number should be used in recording the disposition of each batch. A system should be in place to identify the status of each batch.

7.3 *Sampling and Testing of Incoming Production Materials*

7.30 At least one test to verify the identity of each batch of material should be conducted, with the exception of the materials described below in 7.32. A supplier's Certificate of Analysis can be used in place of performing other tests, provided that the manufacturer has a system in place to evaluate suppliers.

7.31 Supplier approval should include an evaluation that provides adequate evidence (e.g., past quality history) that the manufacturer can consistently provide material meeting specifications. Full analyses should be conducted on at least three batches before reducing in-house testing. However, as a minimum, a full analysis should be performed at appropriate intervals and compared with the

Certificates of Analysis. Reliability of Certificates of Analysis should be checked at regular intervals.

7.32 Processing aids, hazardous or highly toxic raw materials, other special materials, or materials transferred to another unit within the company's control do not need to be tested if the manufacturer's Certificate of Analysis is obtained, showing that these raw materials conform to established specifications. Visual examination of containers, labels, and recording of batch numbers should help in establishing the identity of these materials. The lack of on-site testing for these materials should be justified and documented.

7.33 Samples should be representative of the batch of material from which they are taken. Sampling methods should specify the number of containers to be sampled, which part of the container to sample, and the amount of material to be taken from each container. The number of containers to sample and the sample size should be based upon a sampling plan that takes into consideration the criticality of the material, material variability, past quality history of the supplier, and the quantity needed for analysis.

7.34 Sampling should be conducted at defined locations and by procedures designed to prevent contamination of the material sampled and contamination of other materials.

7.35 Containers from which samples are withdrawn should be opened carefully and subsequently reclosed. They should be marked to indicate that a sample has been taken.

7.4 *Storage*

7.40 Materials should be handled and stored in a manner to prevent degradation, contamination, and cross-contamination.

7.41 Materials stored in fiber drums, bags, or boxes should be stored off the floor and, when appropriate, suitably spaced to permit cleaning and inspection.

7.42 Materials should be stored under conditions and for a period that have no adverse affect on their quality, and should normally be controlled so that the oldest stock is used first.

7.43 Certain materials in suitable containers can be stored outdoors, provided identifying labels remain legible and containers are appropriately cleaned before opening and use.

7.44 Rejected materials should be identified and controlled under a quarantine system designed to prevent their unauthorised use in manufacturing.

7.5 *Re-evaluation*

7.50 Materials should be re-evaluated as appropriate to determine their suitability for use (e.g., after prolonged storage or exposure to heat or humidity).

8 Production and In-Process Controls

8.1 *Production Operations*

8.10 Raw materials for intermediate and API manufacturing should be weighed or measured under appropriate conditions that do not affect their suitability for use. Weighing and measuring devices should be of suitable accuracy for the intended use.

8.11 If a material is subdivided for later use in production operations, the container receiving the material should be suitable and should be so identified that the following information is available:

- material name and/or item code;

- receiving or control number;

- weight or measure of material in the new container; and

- re-evaluation or retest date if appropriate.

8.12 Critical weighing, measuring, or subdividing operations should be witnessed or subjected to an equivalent control. Prior to use, production personnel should verify that the materials are those specified in the batch record for the intended intermediate or API.

8.13 Other critical activities should be witnessed or subjected to an equivalent control.

8.14 Actual yields should be compared with expected yields at designated steps in the production process. Expected yields with appropriate ranges should be established based on previous laboratory, pilot scale, or manufacturing data. Deviations in yield associated with critical process steps should be investigated to determine their impact or potential impact on the resulting quality of affected batches.

8.15 Any deviation should be documented and explained. Any critical deviation should be investigated.

8.16 The processing status of major units of equipment should be indicated either on the individual units of equipment or by appropriate documentation, computer control systems, or alternative means.

8.17 Materials to be reprocessed or reworked should be appropriately controlled to prevent unauthorised use.

8.2 *Time Limits*

8.20 If time limits are specified in the master production instruction (see 6.41), these time limits should be met to ensure the quality of intermediates and APIs. Deviations should be documented and evaluated. Time limits may be inappropriate when processing to a target value (e.g., pH adjustment, hydrogenation, drying to predetermined specification) because completion of reactions or processing steps are determined by in-process sampling and testing.

8.21 Intermediates held for further processing should be stored under appropriate conditions to ensure their suitability for use.

8.3 *In-process Sampling and Controls*

8.30 Written procedures should be established to monitor the progress and control the performance of processing steps that cause variability in the quality characteristics of intermediates and APIs. In-process controls and their acceptance criteria should be defined based on the information gained during the development stage or historical data.

8.31 The acceptance criteria and type and extent of testing can depend on the nature of the intermediate or API being manufactured, the reaction or process step being conducted, and the degree to which the process introduces variability in the product's quality. Less stringent in-process controls may be appropriate in early processing steps, whereas tighter controls may be appropriate for later processing steps (e.g., isolation and purification steps).

8.32 Critical in-process controls (and critical process monitoring), including the control points and methods, should be stated in writing and approved by the quality unit(s).

8.33 In-process controls can be performed by qualified production department personnel and the process adjusted without prior quality unit(s) approval if the adjustments are made within pre-established limits approved by the quality unit(s). All tests and results should be fully documented as part of the batch record.

8.34 Written procedures should describe the sampling methods for in-process materials, intermediates, and APIs. Sampling plans and procedures should be based on scientifically sound sampling practices.

8.35 In-process sampling should be conducted using procedures designed to prevent contamination of the sampled material and other intermediates or APIs. Procedures should be established to ensure the integrity of samples after collection.

8.36 Out-of-specification (OOS) investigations are not normally needed for in-process tests that are performed for the purpose of monitoring and/or adjusting the process.

8.4 *Blending Batches of Intermediates or APIs*

8.40   For the purpose of this document, blending is defined as the process of combining materials within the same specification to produce a homogeneous intermediate or API. In-process mixing of fractions from single batches (e.g., collecting several centrifuge loads from a single crystallisation batch) or combining fractions from several batches for further processing is considered to be part of the production process and is not considered to be blending.

8.41   Out-of-Specification batches should not be blended with other batches for the purpose of meeting specifications. Each batch incorporated into the blend should have been manufactured using an established process and should have been individually tested and found to meet appropriate specifications prior to blending.

8.42   Acceptable blending operations include but are not limited to:

- blending of small batches to increase batch size;
- blending of tailings (i.e., relatively small quantities of isolated material) from batches of the same intermediate or API to form a single batch.

8.43   Blending processes should be adequately controlled and documented and the blended batch should be tested for conformance to established specifications where appropriate.

8.44   The batch record of the blending process should allow traceability back to the individual batches that make up the blend.

8.45   Where physical attributes of the API are critical (e.g., APIs intended for use in solid oral dosage forms or suspensions), blending operations should be validated to show homogeneity of the combined batch. Validation should include testing of critical attributes (e.g., particle size distribution, bulk density, and tap density) that may be affected by the blending process.

8.46   If the blending could adversely affect stability, stability testing of the final blended batches should be performed.

8.47   The expiry or retest date of the blended batch should be based on the manufacturing date of the oldest tailings or batch in the blend.

8.5 *Contamination Control*

8.50   Residual materials can be carried over into successive batches of the same intermediate or API if there is adequate control. Examples include residue adhering to the wall of a microniser, residual layer of damp crystals remaining in a centrifuge bowl after discharge, and incomplete discharge of fluids or crystals from a processing vessel upon transfer of the material to the next step in the process. Such carryover should not result in the carryover of degradants or microbial contamination that may adversely alter the established API impurity profile.

8.51   Production operations should be conducted in a manner that will prevent contamination of intermediates or APIs by other materials.

8.52   Precautions to avoid contamination should be taken when APIs are handled after purification.

9   Packaging and Identification Labelling of APIs and Intermediates

9.1   *General*

9.10   There should be written procedures describing the receipt, identification, quarantine, sampling, examination and/or testing and release, and handling of packaging and labelling materials.

9.11   Packaging and labelling materials should conform to established specifications. Those that do not comply with such specifications should be rejected to prevent their use in operations for which they are unsuitable.

9.12   Records should be maintained for each shipment of labels and packaging materials showing receipt, examination, or testing, and whether accepted or rejected.

9.2   *Packaging Materials*

9.20   Containers should provide adequate protection against deterioration or contamination of the intermediate or API that may occur during transportation and recommended storage.

9.21   Containers should be clean and, where indicated by the nature of the intermediate or API, sanitised to ensure that they are suitable for their intended use. These containers should not be reactive, additive, or absorptive so as to alter the quality of the intermediate or API beyond the specified limits.

9.22   If containers are re-used, they should be cleaned in accordance with documented procedures and all previous labels should be removed or defaced.

9.3   *Label Issuance and Control*

9.30   Access to the label storage areas should be limited to authorised personnel.

9.31   Procedures should be used to reconcile the quantities of labels issued, used, and returned and to evaluate discrepancies found between the number of containers labelled and the number of labels issued. Such discrepancies should be investigated, and the investigation should be approved by the quality unit(s).

9.32   All excess labels bearing batch numbers or other batch-related printing should be destroyed. Returned labels should be maintained and stored in a manner that prevents mix-ups and provides proper identification.

9.33   Obsolete and out-dated labels should be destroyed.

9.34   Printing devices used to print labels for packaging operations should be controlled to ensure that all imprinting conforms to the print specified in the batch production record.

9.35   Printed labels issued for a batch should be carefully examined for proper identity and conformity to specifications in the master production record. The results of this examination should be documented.

9.36   A printed label representative of those used should be included in the batch production record.

9.4   *Packaging and Labelling Operations*

9.40   There should be documented procedures designed to ensure that correct packaging materials and labels are used.

9.41   Labelling operations should be designed to prevent mix-ups. There should be physical or spatial separation from operations involving other intermediates or APIs.

9.42   Labels used on containers of intermediates or APIs should indicate the name or identifying code, the batch number of the product, and storage conditions, when such information is critical to assure the quality of intermediate or API.

9.43   If the intermediate or API is intended to be transferred outside the control of the manufacturer's material management system, the name and address of the manufacturer, quantity of contents, and special transport conditions and any special legal requirements should also be included on the label. For intermediates or APIs with an expiry date, the expiry date should be indicated on the label and Certificate of Analysis. For intermediates or APIs with a retest date, the retest date should be indicated on the label and/or Certificate of Analysis.

9.44   Packaging and labelling facilities should be inspected immediately before use to ensure that all materials not needed for the next packaging operation have been removed. This examination should be documented in the batch production records, the facility log, or other documentation system.

9.45　Packaged and labelled intermediates or APIs should be examined to ensure that containers and packages in the batch have the correct label. This examination should be part of the packaging operation. Results of these examinations should be recorded in the batch production or control records.

9.46　Intermediate or API containers that are transported outside of the manufacturer's control should be sealed in a manner such that, if the seal is breached or missing, the recipient will be alerted to the possibility that the contents may have been altered.

10　Storage and Distribution

10.1　*Warehousing Procedures*

10.10　Facilities should be available for the storage of all materials under appropriate conditions (e.g. controlled temperature and humidity when necessary). Records should be maintained of these conditions if they are critical for the maintenance of material characteristics.

10.11　Unless there is an alternative system to prevent the unintentional or unauthorised use of quarantined, rejected, returned, or recalled materials, separate storage areas should be assigned for their temporary storage until the decision as to their future use has been taken.

10.2　*Distribution Procedures*

10.20　APIs and intermediates should only be released for distribution to third parties after they have been released by the quality unit(s). APIs and intermediates can be transferred under quarantine to another unit under the company's control when authorised by the quality unit(s) and if appropriate controls and documentation are in place.

10.21　APIs and intermediates should be transported in a manner that does not adversely affect their quality.

10.22　Special transport or storage conditions for an API or intermediate should be stated on the label.

10.23　The manufacturer should ensure that the contract acceptor (contractor) for transportation of the API or intermediate knows and follows the appropriate transport and storage conditions.

10.24　A system should be in place by which the distribution of each batch of intermediate and/or API can be readily determined to permit its recall.

11 Laboratory Controls

11.1 *General Controls*

11.10 The independent quality unit(s) should have at its disposal adequate laboratory facilities.

11.11 There should be documented procedures describing sampling, testing, approval or rejection of materials, and recording and storage of laboratory data. Laboratory records should be maintained in accordance with Section 6.6.

11.12 All specifications, sampling plans, and test procedures should be scientifically sound and appropriate to ensure that raw materials, intermediates, APIs, and labels and packaging materials conform to established standards of quality and/or purity. Specifications and test procedures should be consistent with those included in the registration/filing. There can be specifications in addition to those in the registration/filing. Specifications, sampling plans, and test procedures, including changes to them, should be drafted by the appropriate organisational unit and reviewed and approved by the quality unit(s).

11.13 Appropriate specifications should be established for APIs in accordance with accepted standards and consistent with the manufacturing process. The specifications should include a control of the impurities (e.g. organic impurities, inorganic impurities, and residual solvents). If the API has a specification for microbiological purity, appropriate action limits for total microbial counts and objectionable organisms should be established and met. If the API has a specification for endotoxins, appropriate action limits should be established and met.

11.14 Laboratory controls should be followed and documented at the time of performance. Any departures from the above described procedures should be documented and explained.

11.15 Any out-of-specification result obtained should be investigated and documented according to a procedure. This procedure should require analysis of the data, assessment of whether a significant problem exists, allocation of the tasks for corrective actions, and conclusions. Any resampling and/or retesting after OOS results should be performed according to a documented procedure.

11.16 Reagents and standard solutions should be prepared and labelled following written procedures. 'Use by' dates should be applied as appropriate for analytical reagents or standard solutions.

11.17   Primary reference standards should be obtained as appropriate for the manufacture of APIs. The source of each primary reference standard should be documented. Records should be maintained of each primary reference standard's storage and use in accordance with the supplier's recommendations. Primary reference standards obtained from an officially recognised source are normally used without testing if stored under conditions consistent with the supplier's recommendations.

11.18   Where a primary reference standard is not available from an officially recognised source, an 'in-house primary standard' should be established. Appropriate testing should be performed to establish fully the identity and purity of the primary reference standard. Appropriate documentation of this testing should be maintained.

11.19   Secondary reference standards should be appropriately prepared, identified, tested, approved, and stored. The suitability of each batch of secondary reference standard should be determined prior to first use by comparing against a primary reference standard. Each batch of secondary reference standard should be periodically requalified in accordance with a written protocol.

11.2   *Testing of Intermediates and APIs*

11.20   For each batch of intermediate and API, appropriate laboratory tests should be conducted to determine conformance to specifications.

11.21   An impurity profile describing the identified and unidentified impurities present in a typical batch produced by a specific controlled production process should normally be established for each API. The impurity profile should include the identity or some qualitative analytical designation (e.g. retention time), the range of each impurity observed, and classification of each identified impurity (e.g. inorganic, organic, solvent). The impurity profile is normally dependent upon the production process and origin of the API. Impurity profiles are normally not necessary for APIs from herbal or animal tissue origin. Biotechnology considerations are covered in ICH Guideline Q6B.

11.22   The impurity profile should be compared at appropriate intervals against the impurity profile in the regulatory submission or compared against historical data in order to detect changes to the API resulting from modifications in raw materials, equipment operating parameters, or the production process.

11.23   Appropriate microbiological tests should be conducted on each batch of intermediate and API where microbial quality is specified.

11.3 *Validation of Analytical Procedures* – see Section 12.

11.4 *Certificates of Analysis*

11.40 Authentic Certificates of Analysis should be issued for each batch of intermediate or API on request.

11.41 Information on the name of the intermediate or API including where appropriate its grade, the batch number, and the date of release should be provided on the Certificate of Analysis. For intermediates or APIs with an expiry date, the expiry date should be provided on the label and Certificate of Analysis. For intermediates or APIs with a retest date, the retest date should be indicated on the label and/or Certificate of Analysis.

11.42 The Certificate should list each test performed in accordance with compendial or customer requirements, including the acceptance limits, and the numerical results obtained (if test results are numerical).

11.43 Certificates should be dated and signed by authorised personnel of the quality unit(s) and should show the name, address and telephone number of the original manufacturer. Where the analysis has been carried out by a repacker or reprocessor, the Certificate of Analysis should show the name, address and telephone number of the repacker/reprocessor and a reference to the name of the original manufacturer.

11.44 If new Certificates are issued by or on behalf of repackers/reprocessors, agents or brokers, these Certificates should show the name, address and telephone number of the laboratory that performed the analysis. They should also contain a reference to the name and address of the original manufacturer and to the original batch Certificate, a copy of which should be attached.

11.5 *Stability Monitoring of APIs*

11.50 A documented, on-going testing program should be designed to monitor the stability characteristics of APIs, and the results should be used to confirm appropriate storage conditions and retest or expiry dates.

11.51 The test procedures used in stability testing should be validated and be stability indicating.

11.52 Stability samples should be stored in containers that simulate the market container. For example, if the API is marketed in bags within fiber drums, stability samples can be packaged in bags of the same material and in smaller-scale drums of similar or identical material composition to the market drums.

11.53   Normally the first three commercial production batches should be placed on the stability monitoring program to confirm the retest or expiry date. However, where data from previous studies show that the API is expected to remain stable for at least two years, fewer than three batches can be used.

11.54   Thereafter, at least one batch per year of API manufactured (unless none is produced that year) should be added to the stability monitoring program and tested at least annually to confirm the stability.

11.55   For APIs with short shelf-lives, testing should be done more frequently. For example, for those biotechnological/biologic and other APIs with shelf-lives of one year or less, stability samples should be obtained and should be tested monthly for the first three months, and at three month intervals after that. When data exist that confirm that the stability of the API is not compromised, elimination of specific test intervals (e.g. 9 month testing) can be considered.

11.56   Where appropriate, the stability storage conditions should be consistent with the ICH guidelines on stability.

11.6 *Expiry and Retest Dating*

11.60   When an intermediate is intended to be transferred outside the control of the manufacturer's material management system and an expiry or retest date is assigned, supporting stability information should be available (e.g. published data, test results).

11.61   An API expiry or retest date should be based on an evaluation of data derived from stability studies. Common practice is to use a retest date, not an expiration date.

11.62   Preliminary API expiry or retest dates can be based on pilot scale batches if (1) the pilot batches employ a method of manufacture and procedure that simulates the final process to be used on a commercial manufacturing scale; and (2) the quality of the API represents the material to be made on a commercial scale.

11.63   A representative sample should be taken for the purpose of performing a retest.

11.7 *Reserve/Retention Samples*

11.70   The packaging and holding of reserve samples is for the purpose of potential future evaluation of the quality of batches of API and not for future stability testing purposes.

11.71   Appropriately identified reserve samples of each API batch should be retained for one year after the expiry date of the batch assigned by the manufacturer, or for three years after distribution of the batch, whichever is the longer. For APIs with retest dates, similar reserve samples should be retained for three years after the batch is completely distributed by the manufacturer.

11.72   The reserve sample should be stored in the same packaging system in which the API is stored or in one that is equivalent to or more protective than the marketed packaging system. Sufficient quantities should be retained to conduct at least two full compendial analyses or, when there is no pharmacopoeial monograph, two full specification analyses.

12   Validation

12.1   *Validation Policy*

12.10   The company's overall policy, intentions, and approach to validation, including the validation of production processes, cleaning procedures, analytical methods, in-process control test procedures, computerised systems, and persons responsible for design, review, approval and documentation of each validation phase, should be documented.

12.11   The critical parameters/attributes should normally be identified during the development stage or from historical data, and the ranges necessary for the reproducible operation should be defined. This should include:

- defining the API in terms of its critical product attributes;

- identifying process parameters that could affect the critical quality attributes of the API;

- determining the range for each critical process parameter expected to be used during routine manufacturing and process control.

12.12   Validation should extend to those operations determined to be critical to the quality and purity of the API.

12.2   *Validation Documentation*

12.20   A written validation protocol should be established that specifies how validation of a particular process will be conducted. The protocol should be reviewed and approved by the quality unit(s) and other designated units.

12.21   The validation protocol should specify critical process steps and acceptance criteria as well as the type of validation to be conducted (e.g. retrospective, prospective, concurrent) and the number of process runs.

12.22   A validation report that cross-references the validation protocol should be prepared, summarising the results obtained, commenting on any deviations observed, and drawing the appropriate conclusions, including recommending changes to correct deficiencies.

12.23   Any variations from the validation protocol should be documented with appropriate justification.

12.3   *Qualification*

12.30   Before starting process validation activities, appropriate qualification of critical equipment and ancillary systems should be completed. Qualification is usually carried out by conducting the following activities, individually or combined:

- Design Qualification (DQ): documented verification that the proposed design of the facilities, equipment, or systems is suitable for the intended purpose;

- Installation Qualification (IQ): documented verification that the equipment or systems, as installed or modified, comply with the approved design, the manufacturer's recommendations and/or user requirements;

- Operational Qualification (OQ): documented verification that the equipment or systems, as installed or modified, perform as intended throughout the anticipated operating ranges;

- Performance Qualification (PQ): documented verification that the equipment and ancillary systems, as connected together, can perform effectively and reproducibly based on the approved process method and specifications.

12.4   *Approaches to Process Validation*

12.40   Process Validation (PV) is the documented evidence that the process, operated within established parameters, can perform effectively and reproducibly to produce an intermediate or API meeting its predetermined specifications and quality attributes.

12.41   There are three approaches to validation. Prospective validation is the preferred approach, but there are exceptions where the other approaches can be used. These approaches and their applicability are listed below.

12.42   Prospective validation should normally be performed for all API processes as defined in 12.12. Prospective validation performed on an API process should be completed before the commercial distribution of the final drug product manufactured from that API.

12.43   Concurrent validation can be conducted when data from replicate production runs are unavailable because only a limited number of API batches have been produced, API batches are produced infrequently, or API batches are produced by a validated process that has been modified. Prior to the completion of concurrent validation, batches can be released and used in final drug product for commercial distribution based on thorough monitoring and testing of the API batches.

12.44   An exception can be made for retrospective validation for well established processes that have been used without significant changes to API quality due to changes in raw materials, equipment, systems, facilities, or the production process. This validation approach may be used where:

(1)   critical quality attributes and critical process parameters have been identified;

(2)   appropriate in-process acceptance criteria and controls have been established;

(3)   there have not been significant process/product failures attributable to causes other than operator error or equipment failures unrelated to equipment suitability; and

(4)   impurity profiles have been established for the existing API.

12.45   Batches selected for retrospective validation should be representative of all batches made during the review period, including any batches that failed to meet specifications, and should be sufficient in number to demonstrate process consistency. Retained samples can be tested to obtain data to retrospectively validate the process.

12.5   *Process Validation Program*

12.50   The number of process runs for validation should depend on the complexity of the process or the magnitude of the process change being considered. For prospective and concurrent validation, three consecutive successful production batches should be used as a guide, but there may be situations where additional process runs are warranted to prove consistency of the process (e.g., complex API processes or API processes with prolonged completion times). For retrospective validation, generally data from ten to thirty consecutive batches should be examined to assess process consistency, but fewer batches can be examined if justified.

12.51 Critical process parameters should be controlled and monitored during process validation studies. Process parameters unrelated to quality, such as variables controlled to minimise energy consumption or equipment use, need not be included in the process validation.

12.52 Process validation should confirm that the impurity profile for each API is within the limits specified. The impurity profile should be comparable to or better than historical data and, where applicable, the profile determined during process development or for batches used for pivotal clinical and toxicological studies.

12.6 *Periodic Review of Validated Systems*

12.60 Systems and processes should be periodically evaluated to verify that they are still operating in a valid manner. Where no significant changes have been made to the system or process, and a quality review confirms that the system or process is consistently producing material meeting its specifications, there is normally no need for revalidation.

12.7 *Cleaning Validation*

12.70 Cleaning procedures should normally be validated. In general, cleaning validation should be directed to situations or process steps where contamination or carryover of materials poses the greatest risk to API quality. For example, in early production it may be unnecessary to validate equipment cleaning procedures where residues are removed by subsequent purification steps.

12.71 Validation of cleaning procedures should reflect actual equipment usage patterns. If various APIs or intermediates are manufactured in the same equipment and the equipment is cleaned by the same process, a representative intermediate or API can be selected for cleaning validation. This selection should be based on the solubility and difficulty of cleaning and the calculation of residue limits based on potency, toxicity, and stability.

12.72 The cleaning validation protocol should describe the equipment to be cleaned, procedures, materials, acceptable cleaning levels, parameters to be monitored and controlled, and analytical methods. The protocol should also indicate the type of samples to be obtained and how they are collected and labelled.

12.73 Sampling should include swabbing, rinsing, or alternative methods (e.g., direct extraction), as appropriate, to detect both insoluble and soluble residues. The sampling methods used should be capable of quantitatively measuring levels of residues remaining on the equipment surfaces after cleaning. Swab sampling may be impractical when product contact surfaces are not easily accessible due to equipment design and/or process limitations (e.g., inner surfaces of hoses, transfer pipes, reactor tanks with small ports or handling toxic materials, and small intricate equipment such as micronisers and microfluidisers).

12.74   Validated analytical methods having sensitivity to detect residues or contaminants should be used. The detection limit for each analytical method should be sufficiently sensitive to detect the established acceptable level of the residue or contaminant. The method's attainable recovery level should be established. Residue limits should be practical, achievable, verifiable and based on the most deleterious residue. Limits can be established based on the minimum known pharmacological, toxicological, or physiological activity of the API or its most deleterious component.

12.75   Equipment cleaning/sanitisation studies should address microbiological and endotoxin contamination for those processes where there is a need to reduce total microbiological count or endotoxins in the API, or other processes where such contamination could be of concern (e.g., non-sterile APIs used to manufacture sterile products).

12.76   Cleaning procedures should be monitored at appropriate intervals after validation to ensure that these procedures are effective when used during routine production. Equipment cleanliness can be monitored by analytical testing and visual examination, where feasible. Visual inspection can allow detection of gross contamination concentrated in small areas that could otherwise go undetected by sampling and/or analysis.

12.8   *Validation of Analytical Methods*

12.80   Analytical methods should be validated unless the method employed is included in the relevant pharmacopoeia or other recognised standard reference. The suitability of all testing methods used should nonetheless be verified under actual conditions of use and documented.

12.81   Methods should be validated to include consideration of characteristics included within the ICH guidelines on validation of analytical methods. The degree of analytical validation performed should reflect the purpose of the analysis and the stage of the API production process.

12.82   Appropriate qualification of analytical equipment should be considered before starting validation of analytical methods.

12.83   Complete records should be maintained of any modification of a validated analytical method. Such records should include the reason for the modification and appropriate data to verify that the modification produces results that are as accurate and reliable as the established method.

13   Change Control

13.10   A formal change control system should be established to evaluate all changes that may affect the production and control of the intermediate or API.

13.11   Written procedures should provide for the identification, documentation, appropriate review, and approval of changes in raw materials, specifications, analytical methods, facilities, support systems, equipment (including computer hardware), processing steps, labelling and packaging materials, and computer software.

13.12   Any proposals for GMP relevant changes should be drafted, reviewed, and approved by the appropriate organisational units, and reviewed and approved by the quality unit(s).

13.13   The potential impact of the proposed change on the quality of the intermediate or API should be evaluated. A classification procedure may help in determining the level of testing, validation, and documentation needed to justify changes to a validated process. Changes can be classified (e.g. as minor or major) depending on the nature and extent of the changes, and the effects these changes may impart on the process. Scientific judgement should determine what additional testing and validation studies are appropriate to justify a change in a validated process.

13.14   When implementing approved changes, measures should be taken to ensure that all documents affected by the changes are revised.

13.15   After the change has been implemented, there should be an evaluation of the first batches produced or tested under the change.

13.16   The potential for critical changes to affect established retest or expiry dates should be evaluated. If necessary, samples of the intermediate or API produced by the modified process can be placed on an accelerated stability program and/or can be added to the stability monitoring program.

13.17   Current dosage form manufacturers should be notified of changes from established production and process control procedures that can impact the quality of the API.

14   Rejection and Re-Use of Materials

14.1   *Rejection*

14.10   Intermediates and APIs failing to meet established specifications should be identified as such and quarantined. These intermediates or APIs can be reprocessed or reworked as described below. The final disposition of rejected materials should be recorded.

14.2   *Reprocessing*

14.20   Introducing an intermediate or API, including one that does not conform to standards or specifications, back into the process and reprocessing by repeating a crystallisation step or other appropriate chemical or physical manipulation steps (e.g., distillation, filtration, chromatography, milling) that are part of the established manufacturing process is generally considered acceptable. However, if such reprocessing is used for a majority of batches, such reprocessing should be included as part of the standard manufacturing process.

14.21   Continuation of a process step after an in-process control test has shown that the step is incomplete is considered to be part of the normal process. This is not considered to be reprocessing.

14.22   Introducing unreacted material back into a process and repeating a chemical reaction is considered to be reprocessing unless it is part of the established process. Such reprocessing should be preceded by careful evaluation to ensure that the quality of the intermediate or API is not adversely impacted due to the potential formation of by-products and over-reacted materials.

14.3   *Reworking*

14.30   Before a decision is taken to rework batches that do not conform to established standards or specifications, an investigation into the reason for non-conformance should be performed.

14.31   Batches that have been reworked should be subjected to appropriate evaluation, testing, stability testing if warranted, and documentation to show that the reworked product is of equivalent quality to that produced by the original process. Concurrent validation is often the appropriate validation approach for rework procedures. This allows a protocol to define the rework procedure, how it will be carried out, and the expected results. If there is only one batch to be reworked, then a report can be written and the batch released once it is found to be acceptable.

14.32   Procedures should provide for comparing the impurity profile of each reworked batch against batches manufactured by the established process. Where routine analytical methods are inadequate to characterise the reworked batch, additional methods should be used.

14.4   *Recovery of Materials and Solvents*

14.40   Recovery (e.g. from mother liquor or filtrates) of reactants, intermediates, or the API is considered acceptable, provided that approved procedures exist for the recovery and the recovered materials meet specifications suitable for their intended use.

14.41   Solvents can be recovered and reused in the same processes or in different processes, provided that the recovery procedures are controlled and monitored to ensure that solvents meet appropriate standards before reuse or co-mingling with other approved materials.

14.42   Fresh and recovered solvents and reagents can be combined if adequate testing has shown their suitability for all manufacturing processes in which they may be used.

14.43   The use of recovered solvents, mother liquors, and other recovered materials should be adequately documented.

14.5   *Returns*

14.50   Returned intermediates or APIs should be identified as such and quarantined.

14.51   If the conditions under which returned intermediates or APIs have been stored or shipped before or during their return or the condition of their containers casts doubt on their quality, the returned intermediates or APIs should be reprocessed, reworked, or destroyed, as appropriate.

14.52   Records of returned intermediates or APIs should be maintained. For each return, documentation should include:

- name and address of the consignee;

- intermediate or API, batch number, and quantity returned;

- reason for return; and

- use or disposal of the returned intermediate or API.

15   Complaints and Recalls

15.10   All quality related complaints, whether received orally or in writing, should be recorded and investigated according to a written procedure.

15.11   Complaint records should include:

- name and address of complainant;

- name (and, where appropriate, title) and phone number of person submitting the complaint;

- complaint nature (including name and batch number of the API);

- date complaint is received;

- action initially taken (including dates and identity of person taking the action);

- any follow-up action taken;

- response provided to the originator of complaint (including date response sent); and

- final decision on intermediate or API batch or lot.

15.12 Records of complaints should be retained in order to evaluate trends, product-related frequencies, and severity with a view to taking additional, and if appropriate, immediate corrective action.

15.13 There should be a written procedure that defines the circumstances under which a recall of an intermediate or API should be considered.

15.14 The recall procedure should designate who should be involved in evaluating the information, how a recall should be initiated, who should be informed about the recall, and how the recalled material should be treated.

15.15 In the event of a serious or potentially life-threatening situation, local, national, and/or international authorities should be informed and their advice sought.

16 Contract Manufacturers (including Laboratories)

16.10 All contract manufacturers (including laboratories) should comply with the GMP defined in this Guide. Special consideration should be given to the prevention of cross-contamination and to maintaining traceability.

16.11 Contract manufacturers (including laboratories) should be evaluated by the contract giver to ensure GMP compliance of the specific operations occurring at the contract sites.

16.12 There should be a written and approved contract or formal agreement between the contract giver and the contract acceptor that defines in detail the GMP responsibilities, including the quality measures, of each party.

16.13 The contract should permit the contract giver to audit the contract acceptor's facilities for compliance with GMP.

16.14 Where subcontracting is allowed, the contract acceptor should not pass to a third party any of the work entrusted to him under the contract without the contract giver's prior evaluation and approval of the arrangements.

16.15   Manufacturing and laboratory records should be kept at the site where the activity occurs and be readily available.

16.16   Changes in the process, equipment, test methods, specifications, or other contractual requirements should not be made unless the contract giver is informed and approves the changes.

17   Agents, Brokers, Traders, Distributors, Repackers, and Relabellers

17.1   *Applicability*

17.10   This section applies to any party other than the original manufacturer who may trade and/or take possession, repack, relabel, manipulate, distribute or store an API or intermediate.

17.11   All agents, brokers, traders, distributors, repackers, and relabellers should comply with GMP as defined in this Guide.

17.2   *Traceability of Distributed APIs and Intermediates*

17.20   Agents, brokers, traders, distributors, repackers, or relabellers should maintain complete traceability of APIs and intermediates that they distribute. Documents that should be retained and available include:

- identity of original manufacturer;
- address of original manufacturer;
- purchase orders;
- bills of lading (transportation documentation);
- receipt documents;
- name or designation of API or intermediate;
- manufacturer's batch number;
- transportation and distribution records;
- all authentic Certificates of Analysis, including those of the original manufacturer; and
- retest or expiry date.

17.3   *Quality Management*

17.30   Agents, brokers, traders, distributors, repackers, or relabellers should establish, document and implement an effective system of managing quality, as specified in Section 2.

17.4 *Repackaging, Relabelling and Holding of APIs and Intermediates*

17.40 Repackaging, relabelling and holding of APIs and intermediates should be performed under appropriate GMP controls, as stipulated in this Guide, to avoid mix-ups and loss of API or intermediate identity or purity.

17.41 Repackaging should be conducted under appropriate environmental conditions to avoid contamination and cross-contamination.

17.5 *Stability*

17.50 Stability studies to justify assigned expiration or retest dates should be conducted if the API or intermediate is repackaged in a different type of container than that used by the API or intermediate manufacturer.

17.6 *Transfer of Information*

17.60 Agents, brokers, distributors, repackers, or relabellers should transfer all quality or regulatory information received from an API or intermediate manufacturer to the customer, and from the customer to the API or intermediate manufacturer.

17.61 The agent, broker, trader, distributor, repacker, or relabeller who supplies the API or intermediate to the customer should provide the name of the original API or intermediate manufacturer and the batch number(s) supplied.

17.62 The agent should also provide the identity of the original API or intermediate manufacturer to regulatory authorities upon request. The original manufacturer can respond to the regulatory authority directly or through its authorised agents, depending on the legal relationship between the authorised agents and the original API or intermediate manufacturer. (In this context 'authorised' refers to authorised by the manufacturer.)

17.63 The specific guidance for Certificates of Analysis included in Section 11.4 should be met.

17.7 *Handling of Complaints and Recalls*

17.70 Agents, brokers, traders, distributors, repackers, or relabellers should maintain records of complaints and recalls, as specified in Section 15, for all complaints and recalls that come to their attention.

17.71 If the situation warrants, the agents, brokers, traders, distributors, repackers, or relabellers should review the complaint with the original API or intermediate manufacturer in order to determine whether any further action, either with other customers who may have received this API or intermediate or with the regulatory authority, or both, should be initiated. The investigation into the cause for the complaint or recall should be conducted and documented by the appropriate party.

17.72   Where a complaint is referred to the original API or intermediate manufacturer, the record maintained by the agents, brokers, traders, distributors, repackers, or relabellers should include any response received from the original API or intermediate manufacturer (including date and information provided).

17.8   *Handling of Returns*

17.80   Returns should be handled as specified in Section 14.52. The agents, brokers, traders, distributors, repackers, or relabellers should maintain documentation of returned APIs and intermediates.

18   Specific Guidance for APIs Manufactured by Cell Culture/Fermentation

18.1   *General*

18.10   Section 18 is intended to address specific controls for APIs or intermediates manufactured by cell culture or fermentation using natural or recombinant organisms and that have not been covered adequately in the previous sections. It is not intended to be a stand-alone Section. In general, the GMP principles in the other sections of this document apply. Note that the principles of fermentation for 'classical' processes for production of small molecules and for processes using recombinant and non-recombinant organisms for production of proteins and/or polypeptides are the same, although the degree of control will differ. Where practical, this section will address these differences. In general, the degree of control for biotechnological processes used to produce proteins and polypeptides is greater than that for classical fermentation processes.

18.11   The term 'biotechnological process' (biotech) refers to the use of cells or organisms that have been generated or modified by recombinant DNA, hybridoma or other technology to produce APIs. The APIs produced by biotechnological processes normally consist of high molecular weight substances, such as proteins and polypeptides, for which specific guidance is given in this section. Certain APIs of low molecular weight, such as antibiotics, amino acids, vitamins, and carbohydrates, can also be produced by recombinant DNA technology. The level of control for these types of APIs is similar to that employed for classical fermentation.

18.12   The term 'classical fermentation' refers to processes that use microorganisms existing in nature and/or modified by conventional methods (e.g. irradiation or chemical mutagenesis) to produce APIs.

APIs produced by 'classical fermentation' are normally low molecular weight products such as antibiotics, amino acids, vitamins, and carbohydrates.

18.13   Production of APIs or intermediates from cell culture or fermentation involves biological processes such as cultivation of cells or extraction and purification of material from living organisms. Note that there may be additional process steps, such as physicochemical modification, that are part of the manufacturing process. The raw materials used (media, buffer components) may provide the potential for growth of microbiological contaminants. Depending on the source, method of preparation, and the intended use of the API or intermediate, control of bioburden, viral contamination, and/or endotoxins during manufacturing and monitoring of the process at appropriate stages may be necessary.

18.14   Appropriate controls should be established at all stages of manufacturing to assure intermediate and/or API quality. While this Guide starts at the cell culture/fermentation step, prior steps (e.g. cell banking) should be performed under appropriate process controls. This Guide covers cell culture/fermentation from the point at which a vial of the cell bank is retrieved for use in manufacturing.

18.15   Appropriate equipment and environmental controls should be used to minimise the risk of contamination. The acceptance criteria for quality of the environment and the frequency of monitoring should depend on the step in production and the production conditions (open, closed, or contained systems).

18.16   In general, process controls should take into account:

- maintenance of the working cell bank (where appropriate);

- proper inoculation and expansion of the culture;

- control of the critical operating parameters during fermentation/ cell culture;

- monitoring of the process for cell growth, viability (for most cell culture processes) and productivity where appropriate;

- harvest and purification procedures that remove cells, cellular debris and media components while protecting the intermediate or API from contamination (particularly of a microbiological nature) and from loss of quality;

- monitoring of bioburden and, where needed, endotoxin levels at appropriate stages of production; and

- viral safety concerns as described in ICH Guideline Q5A *Quality of biotechnological products: viral safety evaluation of biotechnology products derived from cell lines of human or animal origin.*

18.17 Where appropriate, the removal of media components, host cell proteins, other process-related impurities, product-related impurities and contaminants should be demonstrated.

18.2 *Cell Bank Maintenance and Record Keeping*

18.20 Access to cell banks should be limited to authorised personnel.

18.21 Cell banks should be maintained under storage conditions designed to maintain viability and prevent contamination.

18.22 Records of the use of the vials from the cell banks and storage conditions should be maintained.

18.23 Where appropriate, cell banks should be periodically monitored to determine suitability for use.

18.24 See ICH Guideline Q5D *Quality of biotechnological products: derivation and characterisation of cell substrates used for production of biotechnological/biological products* for a more complete discussion of cell banking.

18.3 *Cell Culture/Fermentation*

18.30 Where aseptic addition of cell substrates, media, buffers, and gases is needed, closed or contained systems should be used where possible. If the inoculation of the initial vessel or subsequent transfers or additions (media, buffers) are performed in open vessels, there should be controls and procedures in place to minimise the risk of contamination.

18.31 Where the quality of the API can be affected by microbial contamination, manipulations using open vessels should be performed in a biosafety cabinet or similarly controlled environment.

18.32 Personnel should be appropriately gowned and take special precautions handling the cultures.

18.33 Critical operating parameters (for example temperature, pH, agitation rates, addition of gases, pressure) should be monitored to ensure consistency with the established process. Cell growth, viability (for most cell culture processes), and, where appropriate, productivity should also be monitored. Critical parameters will vary from one process to another, and for classical fermentation, certain parameters (cell viability, for example) may not need to be monitored.

18.34 Cell culture equipment should be cleaned and sterilised after use. As appropriate, fermentation equipment should be cleaned, and sanitised or sterilised.

18.35 Culture media should be sterilised before use when appropriate to protect the quality of the API.

18.36 There should be appropriate procedures in place to detect contamination and determine the course of action to be taken. This should include procedures to determine the impact of the contamination on the product and those to decontaminate the equipment and return it to a condition to be used in subsequent batches. Foreign organisms observed during fermentation processes should be identified as appropriate and the effect of their presence on product quality should be assessed, if necessary. The results of such assessments should be taken into consideration in the disposition of the material produced.

18.37 Records of contamination events should be maintained.

18.38 Shared (multi-product) equipment may warrant additional testing after cleaning between product campaigns, as appropriate, to minimise the risk of cross-contamination.

18.4 *Harvesting, Isolation and Purification*

18.40 Harvesting steps, either to remove cells or cellular components or to collect cellular components after disruption, should be performed in equipment and areas designed to minimise the risk of contamination.

18.41 Harvest and purification procedures that remove or inactivate the producing organism, cellular debris and media components (while minimising degradation, contamination, and loss of quality) should be adequate to ensure that the intermediate or API is recovered with consistent quality.

18.42 All equipment should be properly cleaned and, as appropriate, sanitised after use. Multiple successive batching without cleaning can be used if intermediate or API quality is not compromised.

18.43 If open systems are used, purification should be performed under environmental conditions appropriate for the preservation of product quality.

18. 44 Additional controls, such as the use of dedicated chromatography resins or additional testing, may be appropriate if equipment is to be used for multiple products.

18.5 *Viral Removal/Inactivation steps*

18.50 See the ICH Guideline Q5A *Quality of biotechnological products: viral safety evaluation of biotechnology products derived from cell lines of human or animal origin* for more specific information.

18.51　Viral removal and viral inactivation steps are critical processing steps for some processes and should be performed within their validated parameters.

18.52　Appropriate precautions should be taken to prevent potential viral contamination from pre-viral to post-viral removal/inactivation steps. Therefore, open processing should be performed in areas that are separate from other processing activities and have separate air handling units.

18.53　The same equipment is not normally used for different purification steps. However, if the same equipment is to be used, the equipment should be appropriately cleaned and sanitised before reuse. Appropriate precautions should be taken to prevent potential virus carry-over (e.g. through equipment or environment) from previous steps.

19　APIs for Use in Clinical Trials

19.1　*General*

19.10　Not all the controls in the previous sections of this Guide are appropriate for the manufacture of a new API for investigational use during its development. Section 19 provides specific guidance unique to these circumstances.

19.11　The controls used in the manufacture of APIs for use in clinical trials should be consistent with the stage of development of the drug product incorporating the API. Process and test procedures should be flexible to provide for changes as knowledge of the process increases and clinical testing of a drug product progresses from pre-clinical stages through clinical stages. Once drug development reaches the stage where the API is produced for use in drug products intended for clinical trials, manufacturers should ensure that APIs are manufactured in suitable facilities using appropriate production and control procedures to ensure the quality of the API.

19.2　*Quality*

19.20　Appropriate GMP concepts should be applied in the production of APIs for use in clinical trials with a suitable mechanism of approval of each batch.

19.21　A quality unit(s) independent from production should be established for the approval or rejection of each batch of API for use in clinical trials.

19.22　Some of the testing functions commonly performed by the quality unit(s) can be performed within other organisational units.

19.23   Quality measures should include a system for testing of raw materials, packaging materials, intermediates, and APIs.

19.24   Process and quality problems should be evaluated.

19.25   Labelling for APIs intended for use in clinical trials should be appropriately controlled and should identify the material as being for investigational use.

19.3   *Equipment and Facilities*

19.30   During all phases of clinical development, including the use of small-scale facilities or laboratories to manufacture batches of APIs for use in clinical trials, procedures should be in place to ensure that equipment is calibrated, clean and suitable for its intended use.

19.31   Procedures for the use of facilities should ensure that materials are handled in a manner that minimises the risk of contamination and cross-contamination.

19.4   *Control of Raw Materials*

19.40   Raw materials used in production of APIs for use in clinical trials should be evaluated by testing, or received with a supplier's analysis and subjected to identity testing. When a material is considered hazardous, a supplier's analysis should suffice.

19.41   In some instances, the suitability of a raw material can be determined before use based on acceptability in small-scale reactions (i.e., use testing) rather than on analytical testing alone.

19.5   *Production*

19.50   The production of APIs for use in clinical trials should be documented in laboratory notebooks, batch records, or by other appropriate means. These documents should include information on the use of production materials, equipment, processing, and scientific observations.

19.51   Expected yields can be more variable and less defined than the expected yields used in commercial processes. Investigations into yield variations are not expected.

19.6   *Validation*

19.60   Process validation for the production of APIs for use in clinical trials is normally inappropriate, where a single API batch is produced or where process changes during API development make batch replication difficult or inexact. The combination of controls, calibration, and, where appropriate, equipment qualification assures API quality during this development phase.

19.61 Process validation should be conducted in accordance with Section 12 when batches are produced for commercial use, even when such batches are produced on a pilot or small scale.

19.7 *Changes*

19.70 Changes are expected during development, as knowledge is gained and the production is scaled up. Every change in the production, specifications, or test procedures should be adequately recorded.

19.8 *Laboratory Controls*

19.80 While analytical methods performed to evaluate a batch of API for clinical trials may not yet be validated, they should be scientifically sound.

19.81 A system for retaining reserve samples of all batches should be in place. This system should ensure that a sufficient quantity of each reserve sample is retained for an appropriate length of time after approval, termination, or discontinuation of an application.

19.82 Expiry and retest dating as defined in Section 11.6 applies to existing APIs used in clinical trials. For new APIs, Section 11.6 does not normally apply in early stages of clinical trials.

19.9 *Documentation*

19.90 A system should be in place to ensure that information gained during the development and the manufacture of APIs for use in clinical trials is documented and available.

19.91 The development and implementation of the analytical methods used to support the release of a batch of API for use in clinical trials should be appropriately documented.

19.92 A system for retaining production and control records and documents should be used. This system should ensure that records and documents are retained for an appropriate length of time after the approval, termination, or discontinuation of an application.

Glossary of terms used in the EC Guide to GMP

Editor's note

Definitions given below apply to the words as used in the EC Guide, including all its annexes. They may have different or specific meanings in other contexts. In some cases a Glossary word is defined only in a specific annex, indicated here by 'A'. In other cases a word is defined differently in the main Guide and in an annex (e.g. 'Batch' in the main Guide and in Annex 18) in which case the main Guide definition comes first, followed by the annex definition indicated by 'A'.

Acceptance criteria

A 18   Numerical limits, ranges or other suitable measures for acceptance of test results.

Active Pharmaceutical Ingredient (API) (or Drug substance)

A 18   Any substance or mixture of substances to be used in the manufacture of a drug (medicinal) product and that, when used in the production of a drug, becomes an active ingredient of the drug product. Such substances are intended to furnish pharmacological activity or other direct effect in the diagnosis, cure, mitigation, treatment or prevention of disease, or to affect the structure and function of the body.

Air separation plant

A 6   Air separation plants take atmospheric air and, through processes of purification, cleaning, compression, cooling, liquefaction and distillation, separate the air into three gases – oxygen, nitrogen and argon.

Airlock

An enclosed space with two or more doors and which is interposed between two or more rooms, e.g. of differing class of cleanliness, for the purpose of controlling the air flow between those rooms when they need to be entered. An airlock is designed for and used by either people or goods.

API starting material

A 18   A raw material, intermediate, or an API that is used in the production of an API and that is incorporated as a significant structural fragment into the structure of the API. An API starting material can be an article of commerce, a material purchased from one or more suppliers under contract or commercial agreement, or produced in-house. API starting materials are normally of defined chemical properties and structure.

Area

A 6   Part of a premises that is specific to the manufacture of medicinal gases.

Batch (or Lot)

A defined quantity of starting material, packaging material or product processed in one process or series of processes so that it could be expected to be homogeneous.

Note

To complete certain stages of manufacture, it may be necessary to divide a batch into a number of sub-batches, which are later brought together to form a final homogeneous batch. In the case of continuous manufacture, the batch must correspond to a defined fraction of the production, characterised by its intended homogeneity.

For control of the finished product, the following definition has been given in Directive 75/318/EEC: 'For the control of the finished product, a batch of a proprietary medicinal product comprises all the units of a pharmaceutical form which are made from the same initial mass of material and have undergone a single series of manufacturing operations or a single sterilisation operation or, in the case of a continuous production process, all the units manufactured in a given period of time.'

A 18   A specific quantity of material produced in a process or series of processes so that it is expected to be homogeneous within specified limits. In the case of continuous production, a batch may correspond to a defined fraction of the production. The batch size can be defined either by a fixed quantity or by the amount produced in a fixed time interval.

Batch number (or Lot number)

A distinctive combination of numbers and/or letters which specifically identify a batch.

A 18   A unique combination of numbers, letters and/or symbols that identifies a batch (or lot) and from which the production and distribution history can be determined.

Bioburden

A 18   The level and type (e.g. objectionable or not) of micro-organisms that can be present in raw materials, API starting materials, intermediates or APIs. Bioburden should not be considered contamination unless the levels have been exceeded or defined objectionable organisms have been detected.

Biogenerator

A contained system, such as a fermenter, into which biological agents are introduced along with other materials so as to effect their multiplication or their production of other substances by reaction with the other materials. Biogenerators are generally fitted with devices for regulation, control, connection, material addition and material withdrawal.

Biological agents

Micro-organisms, including genetically engineered micro-organisms, cell cultures and endoparasites, whether pathogenic or not.

Blinding

A 13   A procedure in which one or more parties to the trial are kept unaware of the treatment assignment(s). Single-blinding usually refers to the subject(s) being unaware, and double-blinding usually refers to the subject(s), investigator(s), monitor and, in some cases, data analyst(s) being unaware of the treatment assignment(s).

Blood

A 14   Whole blood collected from a single donor and processed either for transfusion or further manufacturing.

Blood components

A 14   Therapeutic components of blood (red cells, white cells, plasma, platelets) that can be prepared by centrifugation, filtration and freezing using conventional blood bank methodology.

Blowing down

A 6   An action whereby pressure is blown down to atmospheric pressure.

Bulk gas

A 6   Any gas intended for medicinal use, which has completed all processing up to but not including final packaging.

Bulk product

Any product which has completed all processing stages up to, but not including, final packaging.

Bulk production batch

A 16   A batch of product, of a size described in the application for a marketing authorisation, either ready for assembly into final containers or in individual containers ready for assembly into final packs. (A bulk production batch may, for example, consist of a bulk quantity of liquid product, of solid dosage forms such as tablets or capsules, or of filled ampoules.)

Calibration

The set of operations which establish, under specified conditions, the relationship between values indicated by a measuring instrument or measuring system, or values represented by a material measure, and the corresponding known values of a reference standard.

A 18   The demonstration that a particular instrument or device produces results within specified limits by comparison with those produced by a reference or traceable standard over an appropriate range of measurements.

Cell bank

Cell bank system

A cell bank system is a system whereby successive batches of a product are manufactured by culture in cells derived from the same master cell bank (fully characterised for identity and absence of contamination). A number of containers from the master cell bank are used to prepare a working cell bank. The cell bank system is validated for a passage level or number of population doublings beyond that achieved during routine production.

Master cell bank

A culture of (fully characterised) cells distributed into containers in a single operation, processed together in such a manner as to ensure uniformity and stored in such a manner as to ensure stability. A master cell bank is usually stored at -70°C or lower.

Working cell bank

A culture of cells derived from the master cell bank and intended for use in the preparation of production cell cultures. The working cell bank is usually stored at -70°C or lower.

Cell culture

The result from the in vitro growth of cells isolated from multicellular organisms.

Certification of the finished product batch

A 16   The certification in a register or equivalent document by a QP, as defined in Article 22 of Directive 75/319/EEC and Article 30 of Directive 81/851/EEC, before a batch is released for sale or distribution.

Change control

A 15   A formal system by which qualified representatives of appropriate disciplines review proposed or actual changes that might affect the validated status of facilities, systems, equipment or processes. The intent is to determine the need for action which would ensure and document that the system is maintained in a validated state.

Clean area

An area with defined environmental control of particulate and microbial contamination, constructed and used in such a way as to reduce the introduction, generation and retention of contaminants within the area.

Note

The different degrees of environmental control are defined in the annex on the manufacture of sterile medicinal products (Annex 1).

Clean/contained area

An area constructed and operated in such a manner that will achieve the aims of both a clean area and a contained area at the same time.

Cleaning validation

A 15   Cleaning validation is documented evidence that an approved cleaning procedure will provide equipment, which is suitable for processing medicinal products.

Clinical trial

A 13   Any investigation in human subjects intended to discover or verify the clinical, pharmacological and/or other pharmacodynamic effects of an investigational product(s), and/or to identify any adverse reactions to an investigational product(s), and/or to study absorption, distribution, metabolism and excretion of an investigational product(s) with the object of ascertaining its safety and/or efficacy.

Comparator product

A 13   An investigational or marketed product (i.e. active control), or placebo, used as a reference in a clinical trial.

Compressed gas

A 6   A gas, which when packaged under pressure, is entirely gaseous at -50°C (ISO 10286).

Computer system

A 18   A group of hardware components and associated software designed and assembled to perform a specific function or group of functions.

Computerised system

A system including the input of data, electronic processing and the output of information to be used either for reporting or automatic control.

A 18   A process or operation integrated with a computer system.

Concurrent validation

A 15   The validation carried out during routine production of products intended for sale.

Confirmation

A 16   A signed statement that a process or test has been conducted in accordance with Good Manufacturing Practice (GMP) and the relevant marketing authorisation, as agreed in writing with the QP responsible for certifying the finished product batch before release. 'Confirm' and 'confirmed' have equivalent meanings.

Contained area

An area constructed and operated in such a manner (and equipped with appropriate air handling and filtration) so as to prevent contamination of the external environment by biological agents from within the area.

Container

A 6   A container is a cryogenic vessel, a tank, a tanker, a cylinder, a cylinder bundle or any other package that is in direct contact with the medicinal gas.

Containment

The action of confining a biological agent or other entity within a defined space.

Primary containment

A system of containment that prevents the escape of a biological agent into the immediate working environment. It involves the use of closed containers or safety biological cabinets along with secure operating procedures.

Secondary containment

A system of containment that prevents the escape of a biological agent into the external environment or into other working areas. It involves the use of rooms with specially designed air handling, the existence of airlocks and/or sterilisers for the exit of materials and secure operating procedures. In many cases it may add to the effectiveness of primary containment.

Contamination

A 18   The undesired introduction of impurities of a chemical or microbiological nature, or of foreign matter, into or onto a raw material, intermediate or API during production, sampling, packaging or repackaging, storage or transport.

Contract manufacturer

A 18   A company that performs some aspect of manufacturing on behalf of the original manufacturer.

Controlled area

An area constructed and operated in such a manner that some attempt is made to control the introduction of potential contamination (an air supply approximating to grade D may be appropriate) and the consequences of accidental release of living organisms. The level of control exercised should reflect the nature of the organism employed in the process. At a minimum, the area should be maintained at a pressure negative to the immediate external environment and allow for the efficient removal of small quantities of airborne contaminants.

Critical

A 18   Describes a process step, process condition, test requirement or other relevant parameter or item that must be controlled within predetermined criteria to ensure that the API meets its specification.

Cross-contamination

A 18   The contamination of a material or product with another material or product.

Crude plant (vegetable drug)

A fresh or dried medicinal plant or parts thereof.

Cryogenic gas

A 6   A gas that liquefies at 1.013 bar at a temperature below −150°C.

Cryogenic vessel

A container designed to contain liquefied gas at an extremely low temperature.

A 6   A static or mobile thermally insulated container designed to contain liquefied or cryogenic gases. The gas is removed in gaseous or liquid form.

Cylinder

A container designed to contain gas at a high pressure.

A 6   A transportable pressure container with a water capacity not exceeding 150 litres. In this document when using the term 'cylinder' it includes cylinder bundle (or cylinder pack) when appropriate.

Cylinder bundle

A 6   A set assembly of cylinders, which are fastened together in a frame and interconnected by a manifold, transported and used as a unit.

Design Qualification (DQ)

The documented verification that the proposed design of the facilities, systems and equipment is suitable for the intended purpose.

Deviation

A 18   A departure from an approved instruction or established standard.

Drug (medicinal) product

A 18   The dosage form in the final immediate packaging intended for marketing (Reference Q1A).

Drug substance

A 18   See Active Pharmaceutical Ingredient.

Evacuate

A 6   To remove the residual gas in a container by pulling a vacuum on it.

Exotic organism

A biological agent where either the corresponding disease does not exist in a given country or geographical area, or where the disease is the subject of prophylactic measures or an eradication programme undertaken in the given country or geographical area.

Expiry date (or Expiration date)

A 18   The date placed on the container/labels of an API designating the time during which the API is expected to remain within established shelf-life specifications, if stored under defined conditions, and after which it should not be used.

Finished product

A medicinal product that has undergone all stages of production, including packaging in its final container.

Finished product batch

A 16   With reference to the control of the finished product, a finished product batch is defined in Part 2 section E 1 of the annexes to Directives 75/318/EEC and 81/852/EEC. In the context of this annex **A 16** the term in particular denotes the batch of product in its final pack for release to the market.

Gas

A 6   A substance or a mixture of substances that is completely gaseous at 1,013 bar (101,325 kPa) and +15°C or has a vapour pressure exceeding 3 bar (300 kPa) at +50°C (ISO 10286).

Herbal medicinal product

A medicinal product containing, as active ingredients, exclusively plant material and/or vegetable drug preparations.

Hydrostatic pressure test

A 6   A test performed for safety reasons as required by national or international guidelines in order to make sure that cylinders or tanks can withhold high pressures.

Importer

A 16   The holder of the authorisation required by Article 16.3 of Directive 75/319/EEC or Article 24.3 of Directive 81/851/EEC for importing medicinal products from third countries.

Impurity

A 18   Any component present in the intermediate or API that is not the desired entity.

Impurity profile

A 18   A description of the identified and unidentified impurities present in an API.

Infected

Contaminated with extraneous biological agents and therefore capable of spreading infection.

In-process control (or Process control)

Checks performed during production in order to monitor and if necessary to adjust the process to ensure that the product conforms to its specification. The control of the environment or equipment may also be regarded as a part of in-process control.

A 18 Checks performed during production in order to monitor and, if appropriate, to adjust the process and/or to ensure that the intermediate or API conforms to its specifications.

Installation Qualification (IQ)

A 15 The documented verification that the facilities, systems and equipment, as installed or modified, comply with the approved design and the manufacturer's recommendations.

Intermediate

A 18 A material produced during steps of the processing of an API that undergoes further molecular change or purification before it becomes an API. Intermediates may or may not be isolated.

Note

This Guide only addresses those intermediates produced after the point that the company has defined as the point at which the production of the API begins.

Intermediate product

Partly processed material that must undergo further manufacturing steps before it becomes a bulk product.

Investigational medicinal product

A 13 A pharmaceutical form of an active ingredient or placebo being tested or used as a reference in a clinical trial – including a product with a marketing authorisation when used or assembled (formulated or packaged) in a way different from the approved form – or when used for an unapproved indication or to gain further information about an approved use.

Investigator

A 13 A person responsible for the conduct of the clinical trial at a trial site. If a trial is conducted by a team of individuals at a trial site, the investigator is the responsible leader of the team and may be called the principal investigator.

Liquefiable gases

Those gases which, at the normal filling temperature and pressure, remain liquid in the cylinder.

Liquefied gas

A 6 A gas which, when packaged under pressure, is partially liquid (gas over a liquid) at -50°C.

Lot

A 18   See Batch.

Lot number

A 18   See Batch number.

Manifold

Equipment or apparatus designed to enable one or more gas containers to be filled simultaneously from the same source.

A 6   Equipment or apparatus designed to enable one or more gas containers to be emptied and filled at a time.

Manufacture

All operations of purchase of materials and products, production, Quality Control, release, storage, distribution of medicinal products and the related controls.

A 18   All operations of receipt of materials, production, packaging, repackaging, labelling, relabelling, Quality Control, release, storage, and distribution of APIs and related controls.

Manufacturer

The holder of a manufacturing authorisation as described in Article 40 of Directive 2001/83/EC or Article 44 of Directive 2001/82/EC.

Material

A 18   A general term used to denote raw materials (starting materials, reagents, solvents), process aids, intermediates, APIs and packaging and labelling materials.

Maximum theoretical residual impurity

A 6   A gaseous impurity coming from a possible retropollution and remaining after a cylinder's pre-treatment before filling. The calculation of the maximum theoretical impurity is only relevant for compressed gases and supposes that these gases act as perfect gases.

Medicinal gas

A 6   Any gas or mixture of gases intended to be administered to patients for therapeutic, diagnostic or prophylactic purposes using pharmacological action and classified as a medicinal product.

Medicinal plant

A plant, the whole or part of which is used for a medicinal purpose.

Medicinal product

Any substance or combination of substances presented for treating or preventing disease in human beings or animals.

Any substance or combination of substances that may be administered to human beings or animals with a view to making a medical diagnosis or to restoring, correcting or modifying physiological functions in human beings or in animals is likewise considered a medicinal product.

Medicinal product derived from blood or plasma

A 14   The same definition as that given in Directive 89/381/EEC.

Minimum pressure retention valve

A 6   A valve equipped with a non-return system which maintains a definite pressure (about 3–5 bars over atmospheric pressure) in order to prevent contamination during use.

Mother liquor

A 18   The residual liquid that remains after the crystallisation or isolation processes. Mother liquor may contain unreacted materials, intermediates, levels of the API and/or impurities. It may be used for further processing.

Mutual Recognition Agreement (MRA)

A 16   The 'appropriate arrangement' between the European Community and an exporting third country mentioned in Article 22.1 of Directive 75/319/EEC and Article 30 of Directive 81/851/EEC.

Non-return valve

A 6   A valve that permits flow in one direction only.

Operational Qualification (OQ)

A 15   The documented verification that the facilities, systems and equipment, as installed or modified, perform as intended throughout the anticipated operating ranges.

Order

A 13   An instruction to process, package and/or ship a certain number of units of investigational product.

Packaging

All operations, including filling and labelling, which a bulk product has to undergo in order to become a finished product.

Note

Sterile filling would not normally be regarded as part of packaging; the bulk product would be the filled, but not finally packaged, primary containers.

Packaging material

Any material employed in the packaging of a medicinal product, excluding any outer packaging used for transportation or shipment. Packaging materials are referred to as primary or secondary according to whether or not they are intended to be in direct contact with the product.

A 18   Any material intended to protect an intermediate or API during storage and transport.

Parametric Release

A 17   A system of release that gives the assurance that the product is of the intended quality based on information collected during the manufacturing process and on compliance with specific Good Manufacturing Practice (GMP) requirements related to Parametric Release.

Performance Qualification (PQ)

A 15   The documented verification that the facilities, systems and equipment, as connected together, can perform effectively and be replicated, based on the approved process method and product specification.

Procedure

A description of the operations to be carried out, the precautions to be taken and measures to be applied directly or indirectly in relation to the manufacture of a medicinal product.

A 18   A documented description of the operations to be performed, the precautions to be taken and measures to be applied directly or indirectly in relation to the manufacture of an intermediate or API.

Process aids

A 18   Materials, excluding solvents, used as aids in the manufacture of an intermediate or API that do not themselves participate in a chemical or biological reaction (e.g. filter aid, activated carbon, etc.).

Process control

A 18   See In-process control.

Process validation

A 15 The documented evidence that the process, operated within established parameters, can perform effectively and reproducibly to produce a medicinal product meeting its predetermined specifications and quality attributes.

Product specification file

A 13 A reference file containing all the information necessary to draft detailed written instructions on processing, packaging, quality control testing, batch release and shipping.

Production

All operations involved in the preparation of a medicinal product, from receipt of materials through processing and packaging to completion as a finished product.

A 18 All operations involved in the preparation of an API from receipt of materials through processing and packaging of the API.

Prospective validation

A 15 The validation carried out before routine production of products intended for sale.

Purge

A 6 To empty and clean a cylinder

- by blowing down and evacuating or
- by blowing down, partial pressurisation with the gas in question and then blowing down again.

Qualification

An action proving that any equipment works correctly and actually leads to the expected results. The term 'validation' is sometimes widened to incorporate the concept of qualification.

A 18 An action proving and documenting that equipment or ancillary systems are properly installed, work correctly and actually lead to the expected results. Qualification is part of validation, but the individual qualification steps alone do not constitute process validation.

Qualified Person (QP)

A 16 The person defined in Article 48 of Directive 2001/83/EC or Article 52 of Directive 2001/82/EC.

Quality Assurance (QA)

A 18   The sum total of the organised arrangements made with the object of ensuring that all APIs are of the quality required for their intended use and that quality systems are maintained.

Quality Control (QC)

See Chapter 1.

A 18   Checking or testing that specifications are met.

Quality unit

A 18   An organisational unit independent of production that fulfils both quality assurance and quality control responsibilities. This can be in the form of separate QA and QC units or a single individual or group, depending upon the size and structure of the organisation.

Quarantine

The status of starting or packaging materials, intermediate, bulk or finished products isolated physically or by other effective means whilst awaiting a decision on their release or refusal.

A 18   The status of materials isolated physically or by other effective means pending a decision on their subsequent approval or rejection.

Radiopharmaceutical

Any medicinal product which, when ready for use, contains one or more radionuclides (radioactive isotopes) included for a medicinal purpose (Directive 89/343/EEC extending the scope of Directives 65/65/EEC and 75/319/EEC to radiopharmaceuticals and laying down additional provisions).

Raw material

A 18   A general term used to denote starting materials, reagents and solvents intended for use in the production of intermediates or APIs.

Reconciliation

A comparison, making due allowance for normal variation, between the amount of product or materials theoretically and actually produced or used.

Record

See Chapter 4.

Recovery

The introduction of all or part of previous batches of the required quality into another batch at a defined stage of manufacture.

Reference standard, primary

A 18   A substance that has been shown by an extensive set of analytical tests to be authentic material that should be of high purity. This standard can be:

1) obtained from an officially recognised source; or

2) prepared by independent synthesis; or

3) obtained from existing production material of high purity; or

4) prepared by further purification of existing production material.

Reference standard, secondary

A 18   A substance of established quality and purity, as shown by comparison to a primary reference standard, used as a reference standard for routine laboratory analysis.

Reprocessing

The reworking of all or part of a batch of product of an unacceptable quality from a defined stage of production so that its quality may be rendered acceptable by one or more additional operations.

A 18   Introducing an intermediate or API, including one that does not conform to standards or specifications, back into the process and repeating a crystallisation step or other appropriate chemical or physical manipulation steps (e.g. distillation, filtration, chromatography, milling) that are part of the established manufacturing process. Continuation of a process step after an in-process control test has shown that the step is incomplete is considered to be part of the normal process, not reprocessing.

Retest date

A 18   The date when a material should be re-examined to ensure that it is still suitable for use.

Retrospective validation

A 15   The validation of a process for a product that has been marketed based upon accumulated manufacturing, testing and control batch data.

Return

A medicinal product that has been sent back to the manufacturer or distributor, which may or may not present a quality defect.

Re-validation

A 15 A repeat process validation to provide an assurance that changes in the process/ equipment introduced in accordance with change control procedures do not adversely affect process characteristics and product quality.

Reworking

A 18 Subjecting an intermediate or API that does not conform to standards or specifications to one or more processing steps that are different from the established manufacturing process to obtain an acceptable quality intermediate or API (e.g. recrystallising with a different solvent).

Risk analysis

A 15 The method used to assess and characterise the critical parameters in the functionality of equipment or a process.

Seed lot

Master seed lot

A culture of a micro-organism distributed from a single bulk into containers in a single operation in such a manner as to ensure uniformity, to prevent contamination and to ensure stability. A master seed lot in liquid form is usually stored at or below -70°C. A freeze-dried master seed lot is stored at a temperature known to ensure stability.

Seed lot system

A system according to which successive batches of a product are derived from the same master seed lot at a given passage level. For routine production, a working seed lot is prepared from the master seed lot. The final product is derived from the working seed lot and will not have undergone more passages from the master seed lot than the vaccine shown in clinical studies to be satisfactory, with respect to safety and efficacy. The origin and the passage history of the master seed lot and the working seed lot are recorded.

Working seed lot

A culture of a micro-organism derived from the master seed lot and intended for use in production. Working seed lots are distributed into containers and stored as described above for master seed lots.

Shipping/dispatch

A 13 The operation of packaging for shipment and sending ordered medicinal products for clinical trials.

Signature

A 18 See Signed.

Signed (or Signature)

A 18 A record of the individual who performed a particular action or review. This record can be initials, a full handwritten signature, a personal seal or an authenticated and secure electronic signature.

Simulated product

A 15 A material that closely approximates the physical and, where practical, the chemical characteristics (e.g. viscosity, particle size, pH, etc.) of the product under validation. In many cases these characteristics may be satisfied by a placebo product batch.

Solvent

A 18 An inorganic or organic liquid used as a vehicle for the preparation of solutions or suspensions in the manufacture of an intermediate or API.

Specification

See Chapter 4.

A 18 A list of tests, references to analytical procedures, and appropriate acceptance criteria that are numerical limits, ranges or other criteria for the test described. It establishes the set of criteria to which a material should conform to be considered acceptable for its intended use. 'Conformance to specification' means that the material, when tested according to the listed analytical procedures, will meet the listed acceptance criteria.

Sponsor

A 13 An individual, company, institution or organisation which takes responsibility for the initiation, management and/or financing of a clinical trial.

Starting material

Any substance used in the production of a medicinal product but excluding packaging materials.

Sterility

Sterility is the absence of living organisms. The conditions of the sterility test are given in the *European Pharmacopoeia*.

Sterility Assurance System

A 17 The sum total of the arrangements made to assure the sterility of products. For terminally sterilised products these typically include the following stages:

a) product design;

b) knowledge of and, if possible, control of the microbiological condition of starting materials and process aids (e.g. gases and lubricants);

c) control of the contamination of the process of manufacture to avoid the ingress of micro-organisms and their multiplication in the product. This is usually accomplished by cleaning and sanitisation of product contact surfaces, prevention of aerial contamination by handling in clean rooms, use of process control time limits and, if applicable, filtration stages;

d) prevention of mix-up between sterile and non-sterile product streams;

e) maintenance of product integrity;

f) the sterilisation process;

g) the totality of the quality system which contains the Sterility Assurance System, e.g. change control, training, written procedures, release checks, planned preventative maintenance, failure mode analysis, prevention of human error, validation calibration, etc.

System

A regulated pattern of interacting activities and techniques that are united to form an organised whole.

A 15 Equipment with a common purpose.

Tank

A 6 A static container for the storage of liquefied or cryogenic gas.

Tanker

A 6 A container fixed on a vehicle for the transport of liquefied or cryogenic gas.

Validation

An action proving, in accordance with the principles of Good Manufacturing Practice (GMP), that any procedure, process, equipment, material, activity or system actually leads to the expected results. *See also* Qualification.

A 18 A documented programme that provides a high degree of assurance that a specific process, method or system will consistently produce a result meeting predetermined acceptance criteria.

Validation protocol

A 18   A written plan stating how validation will be conducted and defining acceptance criteria. For example, the protocol for a manufacturing process identifies processing equipment, critical process parameters/ operating ranges, product characteristics, sampling, test data to be collected, the number of validation runs and acceptable test results.

Valve

A 6   A device for opening and closing containers.

Worst case

A 15   A condition or set of conditions encompassing upper and lower processing limits and circumstances, within standard operating procedures, which pose the greatest chance of product or process failure when compared to ideal conditions. Such conditions do not necessarily induce product or process failure.

Yield, expected

A 18   The quantity of material or the percentage of theoretical yield anticipated at any appropriate phase of production based on previous laboratory, pilot scale or manufacturing data.

Yield, theoretical

A 18   The quantity that would be produced at any appropriate phase of production, based upon the quantity of material to be used, in the absence of any loss or error in actual production.

Index to the EC Guide to GMP

Locators indicate chapter and paragraph numbers.
A = annex; Ch. = chapter; Gls. = glossary.

Freeze Driers A5.27
Fumigation A1.39

Gamma Irradiation A12
    Design A12.14–A12.16
    Dose Mapping A12.17–A12.22
    Processing A12.35–A12.39
Garments, *See* Clothing
Gas(es) Gls.
    Cylinders, *See* Cylinders
    Liquefied A6.3.2.5, A6.5.2.10, Gls.
    Medicinal, *See* Medicinal Gases
Good Manufacturing Practice (GMP) 1.3

Hand-washing Facilities 2.19, A1.27
Harvesting, Cell Culture/Fermentation Systems A18.18.4
Heat Sterilisation A1.62–A1.65
HEPA Air Filters A1.3, A1.69, A5.11
Herbal Products A7, Gls.
    Documentation A7.5–A7.6
    Premises A7.1–A7.4
    Quality Control A7.8–A7.9
    Sampling A7.7
Holding, Active Pharmaceutical Ingredients A18.17.4
Hydrostatic Pressure Test A6.5.3.6, A6.6.1, Gls.
Hygiene 2.13–2.20, A1.16, A18.3.2

Immunological Veterinary Products A5
    Animals & Animal Houses A5.28–A5.31
    Disinfection/Waste Disposal A5.32
    Equipment A5.21–A5.27
    Personnel A5.1–A5.5, A5.45
    Premises A5.6–A5.20
    Production A5.33–A5.64
    Quality Control A5.35–A5.36, A5.65–A5.68
Imported Products 2.4
    Certification & Batch Release A16.6–A6.7
    Country with Mutual Recognition Agreement (MRA) A16.7
Importer Gls.
Impurity Gls.
    Maximum Theoretical Residual Gls.
    Profile A18.11.21–A18.11.22, Gls.
In-process Controls 3.17, 6.18, Gls.
    Active Pharmaceutical Ingredients A18.8
    Biological Medicinal Products A2.41
    Immunological Veterinary Products A5.65
    Medicinal Gases A6.5.2.4

Part II

Wholesale dealing

CHAPTER 5

UK LEGISLATION ON WHOLESALE DEALING

Standard provisions for wholesale dealer's licences

Extracts from:

The Medicines (Standard Provisions for Licences and Certificates) Regulations 1971 (SI 1971 No 972) as amended by Amendment Regulations 1972 (SI 1972 No 1226), 1977 (SI 1977 No 1053), 1983 (SI 1983 No 1730), 1992 (SI 1992 No 2846), 1993 (SI 1993 No 833), 1999 (SI 1999 No 4) and 2002 (SI 2002 No 236).

Editor's Note

These extracts from the Regulations are presented for the reader's convenience and incorporate amendments up to March 2002. For any definitive information, reference must be made to the original Regulations. They include provisions for a wholesale dealer's import licence required for importing products from a country outside the European Union or the European Economic Area.

Schedule 3 of the regulations

1   The licence holder shall provide and maintain such staff, premises, equipment and facilities for the handling, storage and distribution of the medicinal products which he handles, stores or distributes under his licence, as are necessary to avoid deterioration of the medicinal products and he shall not use for such purposes premises other than those specified in the licence or which may be approved from time to time by the licensing authority.

2   The licence holder shall provide such information as may be requested by the licensing authority concerning the type and quantity of any medicinal product which he currently handles, stores or distributes.

3   The licence holder shall inform the licensing authority of any proposed structural alterations to, or discontinuance of use of, premises to which the licence relates or premises which have been approved from time to time by the licensing authority.

4   The licence holder shall keep such documents relating to his transactions by way of the sale of medicinal products to which the licence relates as will facilitate the withdrawal or recall from sale or exportation of such products.

4A   Where the licence relates to products to which the provisions of the 2001 Directive apply, the licence holder shall institute an emergency plan which ensures effective implementation of any recall from the market which is either –

(a)   ordered by the licensing authority or the competent authority of a Member State other than the United Kingdom; or

(b)   carried out in co-operation with the manufacturer or the holder of the product licence or of the marketing authorisation granted by the competent authority of a Member State other than the United Kingdom in respect of the products.

4B   (1)   Where the licence relates to products to which the provisions of the 2001 Directive apply, the licence holder shall keep records, which may be in the form of invoices or on computer or in any other form, giving the following information in respect of such products which have been received or dispatched –

(a)   the date of receipt and of dispatch;

(b)   the name of the products;

(c)   the quantity of the products received or dispatched;

(d)   the name and address of the person from whom or to whom the products are sold or supplied, as appropriate.

(2)   The records referred to in sub-paragraph (1) above shall be made available for inspection by any person duly authorised in writing by the licensing authority for a period of five years after the date of receipt or dispatch.

5   Where the licence holder has been informed by the licensing authority or by the holder of the product licence that any batch of any medicinal product to which the wholesale dealer's licence relates has been found not to conform as regards strength, quality or purity with the specification of that product or with the provisions of the Act or of any such regulations under the Act that are applicable to the medicinal product, he shall, if so directed, withhold such batch from sale or exportation, so far as may be reasonably practicable, for such a period not exceeding six weeks as may be specified by the licensing authority.

6   (1)   Subject to the provisions of sub-paragraph (2) of this paragraph, no medicinal product to which the wholesale dealer's licence relates shall be sold or offered for sale by way of wholesale dealing as by virtue of that licence unless there has

been granted in respect of that medicinal product a product licence which is for the time being in force and any sale or offer for sale shall be in conformity with the provisions of such product licence.

(2) The provisions of the preceding sub-paragraph of this paragraph shall not apply where –

    (i) by virtue of any provisions of the Act or of any order made thereunder, the sale (other than sale by way of wholesale dealing) of the medicinal product to which the wholesale dealer's licence relates is not subject to the restrictions imposed by section 7(2) of the Act, or

    (ii) the sale or offer for sale by way of wholesale dealing is of a medicinal product the dealings in which, at the time of its acquisition by the licence holder, were not subject to the said restrictions imposed by section 7 (2) of the Act or

    (iii) at the time of such sale or offer for sale, the licence holder does not know, or could not by reasonable diligence and care have known, that such sale or offer for sale is of a medicinal product, or believes, on reasonable grounds, that the provisions of sub-paragraphs 2(i) or 2(ii) of this paragraph apply in relation to such sale or offer for sale.

7 The licence holder, for the purpose of enabling the licensing authority to ascertain whether there are any grounds for suspending, revoking or varying any licence or certificates granted or issued under Part II of the Act, shall permit, and provide all necessary facilities to enable any person duly authorised in writing by the licensing authority, on production if required of his credentials, to carry out such inspection or to take samples or copies, in relation to things belonging to, or any business carried on by, the licence holder, as such person would have the right to carry out or take under the Act for the purpose of verifying any statement contained in an application for a licence or certificate.

7A (1) Where the licence relates to products to which the provisions of the 2001 Directive apply, the licence holder shall at all times have at his disposal the services of a person (in this paragraph called a 'responsible person') who possesses, in the opinion of the licensing authority –

    (a) knowledge of the activities to be carried out and of the procedures to be performed under the licence which is adequate for performing the functions of the responsible person, and

    (b) experience in those activities and procedures which is adequate for those purposes.

(2)   The functions of the responsible person shall be to ensure that the conditions under which the licence has been granted have been, and are being, complied with and that the quality of the products is being maintained in accordance with the requirements of the appropriate product licences.

(3)   The provisions of sub-paragraphs (5) and (6) of paragraph 8 of this Schedule shall apply in relation to a responsible person as they apply in relation to a qualified person within the meaning of that paragraph, but as though the references to –

(a)   the provisions of Articles 49 and 50 of the 2001 Directive as respects qualifications and experience were to the provisions of sub-paragraphs (1) and (2) of this paragraph, and

(b)   to sub-paragraph (3) of paragraph 8 were to sub-paragraph (2) of this paragraph.

7B   Where the licence relates to products to which the provisions of the 2001 Directive apply, the licence holder shall obtain supplies of such products only from –

(a)   any person who is the holder of a manufacturer's licence or a wholesale dealer's licence which relates to those products; or

(b)   any person who holds an authorisation granted by a competent authority of a Member State other than the United Kingdom authorising the manufacture of such products or the distribution by way of wholesale dealing of such products.

7C   (1)   Where the licence relates to products to which the provisions of the 2001 Directive apply, the licence holder shall distribute them by way of wholesale dealing only to:–

(a)   the holder of a wholesale dealer's licence which relates to those products; or

(b)   the holder of an authorisation granted by the competent authority of a Member State other than the United Kingdom authorising the supply of those products by way of wholesale distribution; or

(c)   any person who may lawfully sell those products by retail or may lawfully supply them in circumstances corresponding to retail sale; or

(d)   any person who may lawfully administer those products.

(2)   Where supply is made pursuant to paragraph (1) (c) above, the licence holder shall enclose with the products a document which makes it possible to ascertain –

(a) the date on which the transaction took place;

(b) the name and pharmaceutical form of the products;

(c) the quantity of products supplied;

(d) the names and addresses of the persons from whom the products were supplied.

8 (1) Subject to sub-paragraphs (7), (7A) and (8) below, where the licence relates to imported proprietary products the licence holder shall at all times have at his disposal the services of a person who as respects qualifications and experience satisfies the provisions of Articles 49 and 50 of the 2001 Directive to carry out the functions specified in sub-paragraph (3) below ('qualified person'). For the purposes of this paragraph, but without prejudice to sub-paragraph (6) below, the licence holder may regard a person as satisfying the provisions of the said Article 50 as respects formal qualifications if he produces evidence that he is a member of the Pharmaceutical Society or of the Royal Institute of Chemistry or of such other body as may appear to the licensing authority to be an appropriate body for the purpose, and that he is regarded by the body of which he is a member as so satisfying those provisions.

(2) The licence holder shall at all times provide and maintain such staff, premises, equipment and facilities as will enable the qualified person who is at his disposal to carry out the said functions.

(3) The functions to be carried out by the qualified person shall be as follows:–

(a) to ensure that each production batch of any imported proprietary product to which the licence relates has undergone a full qualitative analysis, a quantitative analysis of at least all the active ingredients and all other tests or checks necessary to ensure that the quality of the product imported satisfies the requirements of the product licence which relates to the product;

(b) to certify in a register, or other record appropriate for the purpose, whether each batch of the imported proprietary product to which the licence relates satisfies the requirements set out in (a) above and to ensure that such register or other record is regularly maintained.

Provided that the above functions shall be deemed to be carried out in respect of a batch which had entered the territory of another Member State prior to its importation if there is available evidence in writing, signed by a person carrying out the functions of a qualified person in that Member State, that the batch in question satisfies the requirements set out in (a) above.

(4)   The licence holder shall keep the said register or other record readily available for inspection by a person authorised by the licensing authority and such register or other record shall not be destroyed for a period of five years from the date of the certification referred to in sub-paragraph (3) (b) above.

(5)   The licence holder shall notify the licensing authority of the name and address and degrees, diplomas or qualifications and experience of the person who will carry out the functions of a qualified person and shall notify the licensing authority of any change as to the qualified person and shall not permit any person to act as a qualified person except the person named in his licence as the qualified person for the purposes of this paragraph or, subject to the provisions of paragraph (6) below, any other such person whose name is notified to the licensing authority.

(6)   Where, after giving the licence holder and the person acting as a qualified person the opportunity of making representations to them (orally or in writing), the licensing authority are of the opinion that the person so acting does not satisfy the provisions of the said Articles 49 and 50 of the 2001 Directive as respects qualifications and experiences, or that he is failing to carry out the functions specified in sub-paragraph (3) above, and have notified the licence holder accordingly in writing, the licence holder shall not permit that person to act as a qualified person so long as the said notification has not been withdrawn by the licensing authority.

(7)   The provisions of this paragraph shall not apply where the imported proprietary product that is to be sold or offered for sale or in any other way distributed has been in the possession of a person in the course of his business who is the holder of a wholesale dealer's licence which relates to imported proprietary products of the same description in circumstances by virtue of which that licence holder is required to comply with the provisions of this paragraph.

(7A) The provisions of this paragraph shall also not apply where the imported proprietary product is an exempt imported product.

(8)   The provisions of this paragraph shall also not apply where the licence holder handles the imported proprietary product –

    (a) in the course of the provision of facilities solely for the transport of the medicinal product, or

    (b) in the course of a business carried on by him as an import agent where he imports the medicinal product solely to the order of another person who intends, in the course of a business carried on by him, to sell, or offer for sale the medicinal product by way of wholesale dealing or in any other way intends to distribute the medicinal product.

(9)   The provisions of this paragraph shall not have effect until 22nd November 1977 in relation to a licence which has been granted before the coming into operation of these regulations.

8A   Where the licence relates to imported proprietary products, the licence holder shall in relation to medicinal products for human use –

(a)   ensure that all manufacture and assembly operations have been carried out by a duly authorised manufacturer or assembler and that the products have been manufactured and assembled in accordance with the principles and guidelines of good manufacturing practice;

(b)   keep readily available for examination by a person authorised by the licensing authority samples of each batch of finished products for at least one year after their expiry date except where the licence holder is authorised by the licensing authority to destroy such samples earlier;

(c)   implement a system for recording and reviewing complaints relating to the medicinal products to which his licence relates, together with an effective system for recalling promptly and at any time any such medicinal product in the distribution network; and

(d)   record and investigate all such complaints and immediately inform the licensing authority of any defect which could result in a recall from sale, supply or exportation or in an abnormal restriction on such sale, supply or exportation.

8B   (1)   Where the licence relates to exempt imported products, the licence holder shall only sell or supply such products in response to a bona fide unsolicited order to fulfil special needs, formulated in accordance with the specification of a doctor or dentist and for use by his individual patients on his direct personal responsibility and where the provisions set out in sub-paragraphs (2) to (9) are complied with.

(2)   No later than 28 days prior to each importation of an exempt imported product, the licence holder shall give written notice to the licensing authority stating his intention to import that medicinal product and stating the following particulars –

(a)   the name of the medicinal product, being the brand name or the common name, or the scientific name, and any name, if different, under which the medicinal product is to be sold or supplied in the United Kingdom;

(b)   any trademark or name of the manufacturer of the medicinal product;

(c)   in respect of each active constituent of the medicinal product, any international non-proprietary name or the

British approved name or the monograph name or, where that constituent does not have an international non-proprietary name, a British approved name or a monograph name, the accepted scientific name or any other name descriptive of the true nature of that constituent;

(d) the quantity of medicinal product which is to be imported which shall not exceed the quantity specified in sub-paragraph (6); and

(e) the name and address of the manufacturer or assembler of that medicinal product in the form in which it is to be imported and, if the person who will supply that medicinal product for importation is not the manufacturer or assembler, the name and address of such supplier.

(3) Subject to sub-paragraph (4), the licence holder shall not import the exempt imported product if, before the end of 28 days from the date on which the licensing authority sends or gives the licence holder an acknowledgement in writing by the licensing authority that they have received the notice referred to in sub-paragraph (2) above, the licensing authority have notified him in writing that the product should not be imported.

(4) The licence holder may import the exempt imported product referred to in the notice where he has been notified in writing by the licensing authority, before the end of the 28-day period referred to in sub-paragraph (3), that the exempt imported product may be imported.

(5) Where the licence holder sells or supplies exempt imported products, he shall, in addition to those records mentioned in paragraph 4B of this Schedule make and maintain written records relating to –

(a) the batch number of the batch of the product from which the sale or supply was made; and

(b) details of any adverse reaction to the product so sold or supplied of which he becomes aware.

(6) The licence holder shall import no more on any one occasion than such amount as is sufficient for 25 single administrations, or for 25 courses of treatment where the amount imported is sufficient for a maximum of three months' treatment and on any such occasion shall not import more than the quantity notified to the licensing authority under sub-paragraph (2)(d).

(7) The licence holder shall inform the licensing authority forthwith of any matter coming to his attention which might reasonably cause the licensing authority to believe that the

medicinal product can no longer be regarded either as a product which can safely be administered to human beings or as a product which is of satisfactory quality for such administration.

(8) The licence holder shall not issue any advertisement, catalogue, price list or circular relating to the exempt imported product or make any representations in respect of that product.

(9) The licence holder shall cease importing or supplying an exempt imported product if he has received a notice in writing from the licensing authority directing that, as from a date specified in that notice, a particular product or class of products shall no longer be imported or supplied.

(10) In this paragraph –
'British approved name' means the name which appears in the current edition of the list prepared by the appropriate body in accordance with section 100 of the Act and published by the Ministers on the recommendation of the Medicines Commission and 'current' in this definition means current at the time the notice is sent to the licensing authority; 'common name' means the international non-proprietary name or, if one does not exist, the usual common name; 'international non-proprietary name' means a name which has been selected by the World Health Organization as a recommended international non-proprietary name and in respect of which the Director-General of the World Health Organization has given notice to that effect in the *World Health Organization Chronicle*; and 'monograph name' means the name or approved synonym which appears at the head of a monograph in the current edition of the *British Pharmacopoeia*, the *British Pharmaceutical Codex*, the *European Pharmacopoeia* or a foreign or international compendium of standards and 'current' in this definition means current at the time the notice is sent to the licensing authority.

9 (1) Subject to sub-paragraphs (7) and (8) below, where licence relates to an imported proprietary veterinary drug or any imported ready-made veterinary drug the licence holder shall at all times have at his disposal the services of a person who as respects qualifications and experience satisfies the provisions of Articles 31 and 32 of the Council Directive to carry out the functions specified in sub-paragraph (3) below ('qualified person'). For the purposes of this paragraph, but without prejudice to sub-paragraph (6) below, the licence holder may regard a person as satisfying the provisions of the said Article 32 as respects formal qualifications if he produces evidence that he is a member of the Pharmaceutical Society or of the Royal Society of Chemistry or of such other body as may

appear to the licensing authority to be an appropriate body for the purpose, and that he is regarded by the body of which he is a member as so satisfying those provisions.

(2)   The licence holder shall at all times provide and maintain such staff, premises, equipment and facilities as will enable the qualified person who is at his disposal to carry out the said functions.

(3)   The functions to be carried out by the qualified person shall be as follows:–

(a)   to ensure that each production batch of any imported proprietary veterinary drug or imported ready-made veterinary drug to which the licence relates has undergone a full qualitative analysis, a quantitative analysis of at least all the active ingredients and all other tests or checks necessary to ensure that the quality of the drug imported satisfies the requirements of the product licence which relates to the drug;

(b)   to certify in a register, or other record appropriate for the purpose, whether each batch of the imported proprietary veterinary drug or imported ready-made veterinary drug to which the licence relates satisfies the requirements set out in (a) above and to ensure that such a register or other record is regularly maintained; except that the above functions shall be deemed to be carried out in respect of a batch which had entered the territory of another Member State prior to its importation if there is available evidence in writing, signed by a person carrying out the functions of a qualified person in that Member State, that the batch in question satisfies the requirements set out in (a) above.

(4)   The licence holder shall keep the said register or other record readily available for inspection by a person authorised by the licensing authority and such register or other record shall not be destroyed for a period of five years from the date of the certification referred to in sub-paragraph (3) (b) above.

(5)   The licence holder shall notify the licensing authority of the name and address and degrees, diplomas or qualifications and experience of the person who will carry out the functions of a qualified person and shall notify the licensing authority of any change as to the qualified person and shall not permit any person to act as a qualified person except the person named in his licence as the qualified person for the purposes of this paragraph or, subject to the provisions of paragraph (6) below, any other such person whose name is notified to the licensing authority.

(6)   Where, after giving the licence holder and the person acting as

a qualified person the opportunity of making representations to them (orally or in writing), the licensing authority are of the opinion that the person so acting does not satisfy the provisions of the said Articles 31 and 32 of the Council Directive as respects qualifications and experience or that he is failing to carry out the functions specified in sub-paragraph (3) above, and have notified the licence holder accordingly in writing, the licence holder shall not permit that person to act as a qualified person so long as the said notification has not been withdrawn by the licensing authority.

(7) The provisions of this paragraph shall not apply where the imported proprietary veterinary drug or imported ready-made veterinary drug that is to be sold or offered for sale or in any other way distributed has been in the possession of a person in the course of his business who is the holder of a wholesale dealer's licence which relates to imported proprietary veterinary drugs or imported ready-made veterinary drugs of the same description in circumstances by virtue of which that licence holder is required to comply with the provisions of this paragraph.

(8) The provisions of this paragraph shall also not apply where the licence holder handles the imported proprietary veterinary drug or imported ready-made veterinary drug –

(a) in the course of the provision of facilities solely for the transport of the drug; or

(b) in the course of a business carried on by him as an import agent where he imports the drug solely to the order of another person who intends, in the course of a business carried on by him, to sell, or offer for sale the drug by way of wholesale dealing or in any other way intends to distribute the drug.

(9) For the purposes of this paragraph –

(a) 'imported' means imported other than from a Member State;

(b) 'proprietary medicinal products' and 'ready-made veterinary drug' have the same meaning as in sections 7 (7) and 8 (4) of the Act (a); and

(c) 'proprietary veterinary drug' means a veterinary drug which is a proprietary medical product.

(10) The provisions of this paragraph shall not have effect until 9th October 1984 in relation to a licence which has been granted before the coming into operation of these regulations.

Guidance on the appointment and duties of the Responsible Person

1   Title VII of the Directive on the Community code relating to medicinal products for human use (Directive 2001/83/EC) obliges holders of a distribution authorisation to have a 'Qualified Person designated as responsible'. The *Standard Provisions for wholesale dealer's licences*, Schedule 3, paragraph 7A state the requirement for a Responsible Person (RP) within the UK.[1] The RP is responsible for safeguarding product users against potential hazards arising from poor distribution practices – as a result, for example, of purchasing suspect products, poor storage or failure to establish the bona fides of purchasers.

2   The RP should ensure that the conditions of the wholesale dealer's licence (WL) are met and that the guidelines on Good Distribution Practice (GDP) are complied with. Although the Licensing Authority holds the licence holder accountable for breaches of the licence, the RP may also incur a liability under civil law for breaches of the licence. If the RP is not adequately carrying out his duties, the Licensing Authority may consider the suspension of the licence, withdrawal of acceptance of the RP on that licence and his acceptability on any other licence.

3   The RP does not have to be an employee of the licence holder but he must be at his disposal. Where the RP is not an employee there should be a written contract which specifies his responsibilities, duties, authority and so on. In the case of small companies the Licensing Authority may accept the licence holder as the nominated RP. In larger companies, however, this is not desirable.

4   There is no statutory requirement for the RP to be a pharmacist, although this is desirable. However, he should have access to pharmaceutical knowledge and advice when it is required, and have personal knowledge of:

(a)   The relevant provisions of the Medicines Act 1968 and the Medicines for Human Use (Marketing Authorisations, Etc.) Regulations 1994 (SI 1994/3144).

(b) Directive 2001/83/EC on the wholesale distribution of medicinal products for human use.

(c) Guidelines on GDP of medicinal products for human use (94/C 63/03).

(d) The conditions of the WL for which he is nominated.

(e) The products traded under the licence and the conditions necessary for their safe storage and distribution.

(f) The categories of persons to whom products may be distributed.

5 Where the RP is not a pharmacist or eligible to act as a Qualified Person (QP) (as defined in Directive 2001/83/EC), he should have at least one year's practical experience in both or either of the following areas:

(a) Handling, storage and distribution of medicinal products.

(b) Transactions in or selling or procuring medicinal products.

In addition, the RP should have at least one year's managerial experience in controlling and directing the wholesale distribution of medicinal products on a scale, and of a kind, appropriate to the licence for which he is nominated.

6 To carry out his responsibilities the RP should:

(a) Have a clear reporting line to either the licence holder or the Managing Director.

(b) Have access to all areas, sites, stores and records which relate to the licensable activities being carried out.

(c) Regularly review and monitor all such areas, sites, etc. or have delegated arrangements whereby he receives written reports that such actions have been carried out on his behalf. Where arrangements are delegated the RP remains responsible and he should personally carry out the delegated functions at least once a year.

(d) Focus on the management of licensable activities, the accuracy and quality of records, compliance with established standard operating procedures, the quality of handling and storage equipment and facilities, and the standards achieved.

(e) Keep appropriate records relating to the discharge of his responsibilities.

7 Where the licence covers a number of sites, the RP may have a nominated deputy with appropriate reporting and delegating arrangements. However, the RP should assure himself and the Licensing Authority that the necessary controls and checks are in place.

8   For his part, the licence holder should ensure that there is a written standard operating procedure for receiving advice and comment from the RP and recording the consequent action taken.

9   Should it prove impossible to resolve a disagreement between the licence holder and the RP, the Licensing Authority should be consulted. Whilst a joint referral is clearly to be preferred, either party may approach the Licensing Authority independently. If an RP finds that he is in difficulty over his statutory responsibilities and the activities being carried out under the licence he should, in strict confidence, consult the Licensing Authority.

This guidance was first issued by the Inspection and Enforcement Division of the Medicines Control Agency in 1996, revised 2002.

---

(1) Refer to SI 1971 No 972 as amended.

Control and monitoring of storage and transportation temperatures

Editor's note

Following discussions between the MCA and representatives of UK organisations who distribute medicinal products on how the EU recommendations on the control and monitoring of storage and transportation temperatures of medicinal products may be met, the MCA developed guidance in consultation with those representatives. This was published in The Pharmaceutical Journal *in July 2001[1] and summarised in the MCA's newsletter* MAIL[2].

A summary of this guidance is given below.

Introduction

EU requirements and guidelines on Good Distribution Practice (GDP) (see Chapters 7 and 8) require distributors to 'ensure that storage conditions are observed at all times, including during transportation'.

What follows gives guidance on how this may be achieved.

Cold Storage

Many medicinal products require storage at controlled low temperature. Some of these such as vaccines, insulins and products of biotechnology can be denatured by freezing and thus must be maintained within a narrow temperature range above freezing point.

The temperature in small refrigerators used to store medicines should be measured continuously and the maximum and minimum temperatures recorded daily. Sufficient space should be maintained to permit adequate air circulation. If the refrigerator is filled to capacity the effect on temperature distribution should be investigated. Refrigerators used for vaccines and other sensitive products should be capable of maintaining the temperature between 2°C and 8°C with the minimum of intervention. Temperature monitoring of these should be by electronic max/min thermometer, with an accuracy of $\pm 0.5°C$, which should be readable from outside the unit. Refrigerators should not be sited in an environment where extremes of temperature (i.e. <10°C or >32°C) will affect their performance.

Large commercial refrigerators and walk-in cold rooms should be monitored with an electronic temperature-recording device that measures load temperature in one or more locations, depending on the size of the unit. Portable data-loggers that can be downloaded onto a computer may be used instead of a fixed device. Records should be checked daily. Internal air temperature distribution should be mapped on installation in the empty and full state and annually thereafter under conditions of normal use. Products should not be stored in areas shown by temperature mapping to present a risk (e.g. in the airflow from the refrigeration unit). Condensate from chillers should not be collected inside the unit.

Temperature alarms should be fitted to large and walk-in units and those smaller units used to store products at risk from freezing.

Controlled room temperature storage

The simplest monitoring would be with a max/min thermometer placed at a strategic location and read, recorded and reset at least weekly, more frequently during periods of exceptionally hot or cold weather. With the exception of very small stores, temperatures should be recorded at low and high levels. Continuous temperature recording is recommended for large warehouses. Self-contained storage areas within warehouses, (e.g. CD store, flammables store) should be included in temperature monitoring programmes.

All warehouses should be temperature mapped to determine the temperature distribution under extremes of external temperature. Mapping should be repeated every two to three years and after any significant modification to the premises, stock layout, or heating system. Medicines should not be stored in areas shown by temperature mapping or other consideration to be unsuitable, e.g. at high level in poorly insulated stores, or next to heaters.

Transportation

Cold-chain goods

The route and time of transportation, the local seasonal temperatures and the nature of the load should all be considered when arranging cold-chain distribution. For small volumes of cold-chain goods insulated containers may be used, in which case it is vital that products damaged by freezing are prevented from coming into direct contact with ice packs at sub-zero temperatures.

Larger volumes of cold-chain goods should be shipped in refrigerated transport, particularly if transit times may be prolonged. Temperatures within loads of products at risk from freezing should be strictly controlled and monitored with recording probes or individual temperature monitoring devices, giving consideration to the temperature gradient within the load. The temperature records for each consignment should be reviewed and there should be a procedure for implementing corrective action in the case of adverse events.

Distributors should ensure that consignments of cold-chain goods are clearly labeled with the required storage/transport conditions Receivers should satisfy themselves that the goods have been transported under appropriate conditions and should place them in appropriate storage facilities as soon as possible after receipt.

Other goods

Consideration should be given to the possible extremes of temperature inside uninsulated, unventilated delivery vehicles and precautions should be taken to protect all products from heat challenge. This includes representatives' samples kept in car boots and goods distributed using postal services.

Systems Checks and Calibration

Any systems whose performance is critical to preserving the product should be tested and demonstrated to achieve what is intended. Measuring and recording devices that are used in critical areas (e.g. temperature monitoring of storage and transport facilities for cold-chain goods at risk from freezing) should be calibrated at least annually against a traceable reference device. Records should include pre- and post-calibration readings and details of any adjustments made or corrections to be applied. Alarms should be checked for correct functioning at the designated set temperatures.

References

(1) Taylor J, Recommendations on the control and monitoring of storage and transportation temperatures of medicinal products. *The Pharmaceutical Journal*, 28 July 2001, Volume 267, pages 128-131.

(2) *MAIL* 131 May/June 2002.

Mutual Recognition Agreements on Good Manufacturing Practice (GMP) and manufacturing authorisation

The European Community has Mutual Recognition Agreements (MRAs) with several third countries with which it has substantial trade. The pharmaceutical or GMP sectors of these MRAs provide benefit to exporters and importers of medicinal products in the EU trading with these countries.

The basis for an MRA concerning medicinal products is equivalence of the principles and guidelines of GMP, the inspection systems and, in most cases, the arrangements for authorising manufacturers between both parties*. An MRA only becomes operational after a mutual agreement of equivalence.

The benefits of an MRA when in operation include:

- authority for an importer to accept a manufacturer's batch certification of compliance with GMP, the relevant marketing authorisation and certificate of analysis. The Qualified Person (QP) of the importer in the EU may certify an imported batch on the basis of such a certificate in place of full testing within the EU, in accordance with Article 51.2 of Directive 2001/83/EC. Importers and exporters who wish to benefit from a MRA should use this certificate. The format of the certificate is shown below.

- normal acceptance between competent authorities of inspection reports and certification of authorisation and GMP compliance of a manufacturer*;

MRAs that include a medicinal products sector have been negotiated between the EC and the following countries:

- Australia

- Canada

- Japan

- New Zealand

- Switzerland

- United States of America

At the time of writing these MRAs are in various stages of transition and may not be in full operation. The operational status and scope of individual MRAs at any given time may be checked on the Commission's website or with the MCA.

Agreements with similar benefits may be made under the Protocol on European Conformity Assessment and Acceptance of industrial products (PECA) between the EC and countries seeking accession to the Community. PECAs that include a medicinal products sector at the time of writing are in operation with the Czech Republic and Hungary. The operational status and scope of individual PECAs at any given time may be checked on the Commission's website or with the MCA.

---

* The MRA between EC and USA is limited to recognition of inspection reports.

Content of the fabricator's/manufacturer's batch certificate for drug/medicinal products exported to countries under the scope of a Mutual Recognition Agreement (MRA)

[Letterhead of exporting manufacturer]

1 **Name of product.**

Proprietary, brand or trade name in the importing country.

2 **Importing country.**

3 **Marketing authorisation number.**

The marketing authorisation number of the product in the importing country should be provided.

4 **Strength/potency.**

Identity (name) and amount per unit dose required for all active ingredients/constituents.

5 **Dosage form (pharmaceutical form).**

6 **Package size (contents of container) and type (e.g. vials, bottles, blisters).**

7 **Lot/batch number.**

As related to the product.

8 **Date of fabrication/manufacture.**

In accordance with national (local) requirements.

9 **Expiry date.**

10 **Name and address of fabricator(s)/manufacturer(s) – manufacturing site(s).**

All sites involved in the manufacture including packaging and Quality Control of the batch should be listed with name and address. The name and address must correspond to the information provided on the manufacturing authorisation/establishment licence.

11 Number of Manufacturing Authorisation/Licence or Certificate of GMP Compliance of a manufacturer/ fabricator.

The number should be given for each site listed under item 10.

12 Results of analysis.

Should include the authorised specifications, all results obtained and refer to the methods used (may refer to a separate certificate of analysis which must be dated, signed and attached).

13 Comments/remarks.

Any additional information that can be of value to the importer and/or inspector verifying the compliance of the batch certificate (e.g. specific storage or transportation conditions).

14 Certification statement.

This statement should cover the fabrication/manufacturing, including packaging and Quality Control. The following text should be used: 'I hereby certify that the above information is authentic and accurate. This batch of product has been fabricated/manufactured, including packaging and Quality Control at the above mentioned site(s) in full compliance with the GMP requirements of the local Regulatory Authority and with the specifications in the marketing authorisation of the importing country. The batch processing, packaging and analysis records were reviewed and found to be in compliance with GMP'.

15 Name and position/title of person authorising the batch release.

Including its company/site name and address, if more than one company is mentioned under item 10.

16 Signature of person authorising the batch release.

17 Date of signature.

Directive 2001/83/EC of the European Parliament and of the Council of 6 November 2001 on the Community code relating to medicinal products for human use.

Editor's note

Title VII is reproduced below. Reference should be made to the complete Directive for other Titles including the preamble, definitions and the general and final provisions.

Title VII: Wholesale distribution of medicinal products

Article 76

Without prejudice to Article 6, Member States shall take all appropriate action to ensure that only medicinal products in respect of which a marketing authorisation has been granted in accordance with Community law are distributed on their territory.

Article 77

1   Member States shall take all appropriate measures to ensure that the wholesale distribution of medicinal products is subject to the possession of an authorisation to engage in activity as a wholesaler in medicinal products, stating the place for which it is valid.

2   Where persons authorised or entitled to supply medicinal products to the public may also, under national law, engage in wholesale business, such persons shall be subject to the authorisation provided for in paragraph 1.

3   Possession of a manufacturing authorisation shall include authorisation to distribute by wholesale the medicinal products covered by that authorisation. Possession of an authorisation to engage in activity as a wholesaler in medicinal products shall not give dispensation from the obligation to possess a manufacturing authorisation and to comply with the conditions set out in that respect, even where the manufacturing or import business is secondary.

4   At the request of the Commission or any Member State, Member States shall supply all appropriate information concerning the individual authorisations which they have granted under paragraph 1.

5   Checks on the persons authorised to engage in the activity of wholesaler in medicinal products and the inspection of their premises, shall be carried out under the responsibility of the Member State which granted the authorisation.

6   The Member State which granted the authorisation referred to in paragraph 1 shall suspend or revoke that authorisation if the conditions of authorisation cease to be met. It shall forthwith inform the other Member States and the Commission thereof.

7   Should a Member State consider that, in respect of a person holding an authorisation granted by another Member State under the terms of paragraph 1, the conditions of authorisation are not, or are no longer met, it shall forthwith inform the Commission and the other Member State involved. The latter shall take the measures necessary and shall inform the Commission and the first Member State of the decisions taken and the reasons for those decisions.

Article 78

Member States shall ensure that the time taken for the procedure for examining the application for the distribution authorisation does not exceed 90 days from the day on which the competent authority of the Member State concerned receives the application.

The competent authority may, if need be, require the applicant to supply all necessary information concerning the conditions of authorisation. Where the authority exercises this option, the period laid down in the first paragraph shall be suspended until the requisite additional data have been supplied.

Article 79

In order to obtain the distribution authorisation, applicants must fulfil the following minimum requirements:

(a) they must have suitable and adequate premises, installations and equipment, so as to ensure proper conservation and distribution of the medicinal products;

(b) they must have staff, and in particular, a qualified person designated as responsible, meeting the conditions provided for by the legislation of the Member State concerned;

(c) they must undertake to fulfil the obligations incumbent on them under the terms of Article 80.

Article 80

Holders of the distribution authorisation must fulfil the following minimum requirements:

(a) they must make the premises, installations and equipment referred to in Article 79(a) accessible at all times to the persons responsible for inspecting them;

(b) they must obtain their supplies of medicinal products only from persons who are themselves in possession of the distribution authorisation or who are exempt from obtaining such authorisation under the terms of Article 77(3);

(c) they must supply medicinal products only to persons who are themselves in possession of the distribution authorisation or who are authorised or entitled to supply medicinal products to the public in the Member State concerned;

(d) they must have an emergency plan which ensures effective implementation of any recall from the market ordered by the competent authorities or carried out in cooperation with the manufacturer or marketing authorisation holder for the medicinal product concerned;

(e) they must keep records either in the form of purchase/sales invoices, or on computer, or in any other form, giving for any transaction in medicinal products received or dispatched at least the following information:

- date;

- name of the medicinal product;

- quantity received or supplied;

- name and address of the supplier or consignee, as appropriate;

(f) they must keep the records referred to under (e) available to the competent authorities, for inspection purposes, for a period of five years;

(g)   they must comply with the principles and guidelines of good distribution practice for medicinal products as laid down in Article 84.

Article 81

With regard to the supply of medicinal products to pharmacists and persons authorised or entitled to supply medicinal products to the public, Member States shall not impose upon the holder of a distribution authorisation which has been granted by another Member State, any obligation, in particular public service obligations, more stringent than those they impose on persons whom they have themselves authorised to engage in equivalent activities.

The said obligations should, moreover, be justified, in keeping with the Treaty, on grounds of public health protection and be proportionate in relation to the objective of such protection.

Article 82

For all supplies of medicinal products to a person authorised or entitled to supply medicinal products to the public in the Member State concerned, the authorised wholesaler must enclose a document that makes it possible to ascertain:

*   the date;
*   the name and pharmaceutical form of the medicinal product;
*   the quantity supplied;
*   the name and address of the supplier and consignor.

Member States shall take all appropriate measures to ensure that persons authorised or entitled to supply medicinal products to the public are able to provide information that makes it possible to trace the distribution path of every medicinal product.

Article 83

The provisions of this Title shall not prevent the application of more stringent requirements laid down by Member States in respect of the wholesale distribution of:

*   narcotic or psychotropic substances within their territory;
*   medicinal products derived from blood;
*   immunological medicinal products;
*   radiopharmaceuticals.

Article 84

The Commission shall publish guidelines on good distribution practice. To this end, it shall consult the Committee for Proprietary Medicinal Products (CPMP) and the Pharmaceutical Committee established by Council Decision Article 75/320/EEC (22).

Article 85

The provisions of this Title shall apply to homoeopathic medicinal products, with the exception of those referred to in Article 14(1).

Guidelines on Good Distribution Practice (GDP) of medicinal products for human use (94/C 63/03)

(Text with EEA relevance)

Introduction

These guidelines have been prepared in accordance with Article 10 of Council Directive 92/25/EEC of 31 March 1992 on the wholesale distribution of medicinal products for human use[1]. They do not cover commercial relationships between parties involved in distribution of medicinal products nor questions of safety at work.

Principle

The Community pharmaceutical industry operates at a high level of quality assurance, achieving its pharmaceutical quality objectives by observing Good Manufacturing Practice (GMP) to manufacture medicinal products which must then be authorised for marketing. This policy ensures that products released for distribution are of the appropriate quality.

This level of quality should be maintained throughout the distribution network so that authorised medicinal products are distributed to retail pharmacists and other persons entitled to sell medicinal products to the general public without any alteration of their properties. The concept of quality management in the pharmaceutical industry is described in Chapter I of the *Community Guide to Good Manufacturing Practice* for medicinal products and should be considered when relevant for the distribution of medicinal products. The general concepts of quality management and quality systems are described in the CEN standards (series 29 000).

In addition, to maintain the quality of the products and the quality of the service offered by wholesalers, Directive 92/25/EEC provides that wholesalers must comply with the principles and guidelines of good distribution practice published by the Commission of the European Communities.

The quality system operated by distributors (wholesalers) of medicinal products should ensure that medicinal products that they distribute are authorised in accordance with Community legislation, that storage conditions are observed at all times, including during transportation, that contamination from or of other products is avoided, that an adequate turnover of the stored medicinal products takes place and that products are stored in appropriately safe and secure areas. In addition to this, the quality system should ensure that the right products are delivered to the right addressee within a satisfactory time period. A tracing system should enable any faulty product to be found and there should be an effective recall procedure.

Personnel

1   A management representative should be appointed in each distribution point, who should have defined authority and responsibility for ensuring that a quality system is implemented and maintained. He should fulfil his responsibilities personally. This person should be appropriately qualified: although a degree in pharmacy is desirable, the qualification requirements may be established by the Member State on whose territory the wholesaler is located.

2   Key personnel involved in the warehousing of medicinal products should have the appropriate ability and experience to guarantee that the products or materials are properly stored and handled.

3   Personnel should be trained in relation to the duties assigned to them and the training sessions recorded.

Documentation

4.   All documentation should be made available on request of competent authorities.

Orders

5.   Orders from wholesalers should be addressed only to persons authorised to supply medicinal products as wholesalers in accordance with Article 3 of Directive 92/25/EEC or holders of a manufacturing or importing authorisation granted in accordance with Article 16 of Directive 75/319/EEC[2] .

Procedures

6.   Written procedures should describe the different operations which may affect the quality of the products or of the distribution activity: receipt and checking of deliveries, storage, cleaning and maintenance of the premises (including pest control), recording of the storage

conditions, security of stocks on site and of consignments in transit, withdrawal from saleable stock, records, including records of clients orders, returned products, recall plans, etc. These procedures should be approved, signed and dated by the person responsible for the quality system.

Records

7   Records should be made at the time each operation is taken and in such a way that all significant activities or events are traceable. Records should be clear and readily available. They should be retained for a period of five years at least.

8   Records should be kept of each purchase and sale, showing the date of purchase or supply, name of the medicinal product and quantity received or supplied and name and address of the supplier or consignee. For transactions between manufacturers and wholesalers and between wholesalers (i.e. to the exclusion of deliveries to persons entitled to supply medicinal products to the public), records should ensure the traceability of the origin and destination of products, for example by use of batch numbers, so that all the suppliers of, or those supplied with, a medicinal product can be identified.

Premises and equipment

9   Premises and equipment should be suitable and adequate to ensure proper conservation and distribution of medicinal products. Monitoring devices should be calibrated.

Receipt

10   Receiving bays should protect deliveries from bad weather during unloading. The reception area should be separate from the storage area. Deliveries should be examined at receipt in order to check that containers are not damaged and that the consignment corresponds to the order.

11   Medicinal products subject to specific storage measures (e.g. narcotics, products requiring a specific storage temperature) should be immediately identified and stored in accordance with written instructions and with relevant legislative provisions.

Storage

12   Medicinal products should normally be stored apart from other goods and under the conditions specified by the manufacturer in order to avoid any deterioration by light, moisture or temperature. Temperature should be monitored and recorded periodically. Records of temperature should be reviewed regularly.

13   When specific temperature storage conditions are required, storage areas should be equipped with temperature recorders or other devices that will indicate when the specific temperature range has not been maintained. Control should be adequate to maintain all parts of the relevant storage area within the specified temperature range.

14   The storage facilities should be clean and free from litter, dust and pests. Adequate precautions should be taken against spillage or breakage, attack by micro-organisms and cross contamination.

15   There should be a system to ensure stock rotation ('first in first out') with regular and frequent checks that the system is operating correctly. Products beyond their expiry date or shelf-life should be separated from usable stock and neither sold nor supplied.

16   Medicinal products with broken seals, damaged packaging, or suspected of possible contamination should be withdrawn from saleable stock, and if not immediately destroyed, they should be kept in a clearly separated area so that they cannot be sold in error or contaminate other goods.

Deliveries to customers

17   Deliveries should be made only to other authorised wholesalers or to persons authorised to supply medicinal products to the public in the Member State concerned.

18   For all supplies to a person authorised or entitled to supply medicinal products to the public, a document must be enclosed, making it possible to ascertain the date, the name and pharmaceutical form of the medicinal product, the quantity supplied, the name and address of the supplier and addressee.

19   In case of emergency, wholesalers should be in a position to supply immediately the medicinal products that they regularly supply to the persons entitled to supply the products to the public.

20   Medicinal products should be transported in such a way that:

a)   their identification is not lost;

b)   they do not contaminate, and are not contaminated by, other products or materials;

c)   adequate precautions are taken against spillage, breakage or theft;

d)   they are secure and not subjected to unacceptable degrees of heat, cold, light, moisture or other adverse influence, nor to attack by micro-organisms or pests.

21   Medicinal products requiring controlled temperature storage should also be transported by appropriately specialised means.

Returns

Returns of non-defective medicinal products

22   Non-defective medicinal products which have been returned should be kept apart from saleable stock to prevent redistribution until a decision has been reached regarding their disposal.

23   Products which have left the care of the wholesaler, should only be returned to saleable stock if:

     a)   the goods are in their original unopened containers and in good condition;

     b)   it is known that the goods have been stored and handled under proper conditions;

     c)   the remaining shelf life period is acceptable;

     d)   they have been examined and assessed by a person authorised to do so. This assessment should take into account the nature of the product, any special storage conditions it requires, and the time elapsed since it was issued. Special attention should be given to products requiring special storage conditions. As necessary, advice should be sought from the holder of the marketing authorisation or the Qualified Person (QP) of the manufacturer of the product.

24   Records of returns should be kept. The Responsible Person should formally release goods to be returned to stock. Products returned to saleable stock should be placed such that the 'first in first out' system operates effectively.

Emergency plan and recalls

25   An emergency plan for urgent recalls and a non-urgent recall procedure should be described in writing. A person should be designated as responsible for execution and co-ordination of recalls.

26   Any recall operation should be recorded at the time it is carried out and records should be made available to the competent authorities of the Member States on whose territory the products were distributed.

27   In order to ensure the efficacy of the emergency plan, the system of recording of deliveries should enable all destinees of a medicinal product to be immediately identified and contacted. In case of recall, wholesalers may decide to inform all their customers of the recall or only those having received the batch to be recalled.

28   The same system should apply without any difference to deliveries in the Member States having granted the authorisation for wholesaling and in other Member States.

29   In case of batch recall, all customers (other wholesalers, retail or hospital pharmacists and persons entitled to sell medicinal products to the public) to whom the batch was distributed should be informed with the appropriate degree of urgency. This includes customers in other Member States than the Member State having granted the wholesaling authorisation.

30   The recall message approved by the holder of the marketing authorisation, and, when appropriate, by the competent authorities, should indicate whether the recall should be carried out also at retail level. The message should request that the recalled products be removed immediately from the saleable stock and stored separately in a secure area until they are sent back according to the instructions of the holder of the marketing authorisation.

Counterfeit medicinal products

31   Counterfeit medicinal products found in the distribution network should be kept apart from other medicinal products to avoid any confusion. They should be clearly labelled as not for sale and competent authorities and the holder of marketing authorisation of the original product should be informed immediately.

Special provisions concerning products classified as not for sale

32   Any return, rejection, and recall operation and receipt of counterfeit products should be recorded at the time it is carried out and records should be made available to the competent authorities. In each case, a formal decision should be taken on the disposal of these products and the decision should be documented and recorded. The person responsible for the quality system of the wholesaler and, where relevant, the holder of the marketing authorisation should be involved in the decision making process.

Self inspections

33   Self inspections should be conducted (and recorded) in order to monitor the implementation of and compliance with this guideline.

Provision of information to Member States in relation to wholesale activities

34   Wholesalers wishing to distribute or distributing medicinal products in Member State(s) other than the Member State in which the authorisation was granted should make available on request to the

competent authorities of the other Member State(s) any information in relation to the authorisation granted in the Member State of origin, namely the nature of the wholesaling activity, the address of sites of storage and distribution point(s) and, if appropriate, the area covered. Where appropriate, the competent authorities of this (these) other Member State(s) will inform the wholesaler of any public service obligation imposed on wholesalers operating on their territory.

---

(1) OJ No L 113, 30.4.1992, p. 1.

(2) OJ No L 147, 9.6.1975, p. 13.

Part III

Inspection and Enforcement Division of the Medicines Control Agency

CHAPTER 9

INTRODUCTION TO THE INSPECTION AND ENFORCEMENT DIVISION

Aim

The aim of the Inspection and Enforcement Division of the Medicines Control Agency (MCA) is to ensure that the safety and efficacy of medicines is safeguarded by compliance with good practices of research, manufacture and distribution. This is achieved primarily by a system of licensing, inspection and investigation of suspected criminal activity. In addition the Division samples and tests medicines, handles reports of suspected quality defects, classifies 'borderline' products and performs inspections on an advisory basis of a number of activities where future regulation is proposed.

Organisation

The Division operates within four Groups, namely:

Inspections Group, which incorporates the UK Good Laboratory Practice Monitoring Authority and conducts inspections for compliance with Good Clinical Practice (GCP), Good Distribution Practice (GDP), Good Laboratory Practice (GLP) and Good Manufacturing Practice (GMP);

Laboratories and Licensing Group, which operates the licensing system for manufacturers, importers and wholesale dealers, issues Export Certificates (including the Certificate of a Pharmaceutical Product complying with the WHO scheme), considers notifications of intention to import unlicensed products, operates the Medicines Testing Scheme and the Defective Medicines Reporting Centre for receiving reports of suspected quality defects in medicinal products and informing health professionals of recalls, and manages the MCA's medicines testing laboratory;

Policy, Borderline, Intelligence and Standards Group, which provides advice internally and externally on the development and implementation of legislation and guidance relating to the Division's responsibilities, determines whether or not a product close to the 'borderline' is a medicinal product and is responsible for administering the Division's internal quality system. The Group also provides an Intelligence resource for the Agency;

Criminal Investigation Group, which investigates suspected breaches of the criminal law relating to medicinal products for human use and prepares appropriate cases for prosecution.

The Division manages the *British Pharmacopoeia* on behalf of the Department of Health.

The Division acts on behalf of the Veterinary Medicines Directorate of the Department for the Environment, Food and Rural Affairs (DEFRA) for licensing and inspecting manufacturers and wholesale distributors of veterinary medicinal products other than immunological products.

The Division represents the United Kingdom on European Union Working Parties of GCP, GLP and GMP Inspectors. It conducts GCP and GMP inspections in connection with Community marketing authorisations on behalf of the European Agency for the Evaluation of Medicines (EMEA) in the UK and worldwide.

The majority of the Division's operations are included in the scope of the MCA's certification to the International Standard on Quality Management Systems ISO 9000 and are externally assessed accordingly.

Advice

The MCA publishes a series of Guidance Notes relating to its statutory functions. Those of particular interest to manufacturers and wholesale dealers include:

GN 5   Manufacturer's Licences

GN 6   Wholesale Dealer's Licences

GN 8   Borderline Products

GN 9   Qualified Persons for authorised manufacturers
(being revised 2002)

GN 14 Supply of unlicensed relevant medicinal products 'Specials'

These Guidance Notes and a list of others available may be obtained on the MCA's website or from the MCA's Enquiry Point (page ii).

The Division is also able to provide specific advice and guidance on regulatory issues within its areas of expertise, though it is not its function to act as a consultancy. See Chapter 10 for information on the Division's advisory inspections.

Contacts

Contact may be made by e-mail to known individuals (the MCA publishes contact names in its subscription newsletter *MAIL* and on its website) or by telephone or telefax to the MCA's Enquiry Point (see page ii), naming the relevant Group if known.

Information on contacting the Defective Medicines Reporting Centre in urgent cases is given on page 341.

CHAPTER 10

VOLUNTARY INSPECTION SCHEMES FOR ACTIVE PHARMACEUTICAL INGREDIENTS, INVESTIGATIONAL MEDICINAL PRODUCTS AND CLINICAL TRIALS

General

The MCA Inspections Group offers advisory inspections on request of facilities and procedures that are likely in the future to become subject to statutory inspection under proposed legislation. This may be of great help for those preparing to meet the likely requirements and has also been found useful when an overseas customer or regulatory authority asks a company for a statement of compliance or audit. Such a statement for specific facilities or processes can be provided, if appropriate, for example after any non-compliances noted during the inspection have been satisfactorily resolved.

Prior to an inspection, the company may be asked to provide relevant documentation such as a site master file, trial protocol or quality manual as appropriate to facilitate the inspector's preparation.

Specific Inspections

Clinical Trials and Investigational Medicinal Products

Directive 2001/20/EC, when implemented, will require investigational medicinal products used in clinical trials on humans to be manufactured in compliance with GMP. Manufacturers will be required to be licensed and will be subject to inspection. The Inspectorate conducts voluntary inspections of manufacturers against the EC Guide to GMP and in particular its Annex 13.

Directive 2001/20/EC will also require clinical trials of medicinal products in humans to be conducted in compliance with Good Clinical Practice (GCP). The principles and guidelines of GCP will be proposed and adopted by the Commission. Sites concerned in any clinical trial including the trial site(s), laboratories used for analysis in the trial and the sponsor's premises will be subject to inspection. The Inspectorate is now offering sponsors, investigators, clinical research organisations and laboratories voluntary inspections against the ICH guide to GCP, on which the EC GCP will be based.

It is planned to introduce UK Regulations to make compliance with the Directive a statutory requirement by May 2004.

Active Pharmaceutical Ingredients (API)

Proposed amendments to Directive 2001/83/EC will, if and when implemented, require that active ingredients to be used in medicines are manufactured in compliance with GMP and manufacturers will be subject to inspection. Voluntary inspections are performed against the EC Guide to GMP Annex 18, identical to the ICH Q7A guidelines on GMP for APIs.

Requesting a voluntary inspection

A fee is charged to cover the cost of a voluntary inspection. If you wish to request a voluntary inspection or to discuss future requirements please contact the Inspections Group of the MCA.

CHAPTER 11

DEFECTIVE MEDICINES REPORT CENTRE

Manufacturers and importers are obliged to report to the Licensing Authority any quality defect in a medicinal product which could result in a recall or abnormal restriction on supply. Other users and distributors of medicinal products are encouraged to do this. The Medicines Control Agency's Inspection and Enforcement Division operates a Defective Medicines Report Centre (DMRC) to receive reports on products for human use and to co-ordinate the necessary assessment and action. (The Veterinary Medicines Directorate operates a comparable system in relation to veterinary medicinal products and the Medical Devices Agency a system dealing with medical devices.)

Telephone numbers
Office Hours (09.00 – 17.00)   020-7273 0574
Silent Hours   020-7210 3000
Fax (manned in office hours only) 020-7273 0676

Address
Defective Medicines Report Centre
Medicines Control Agency
18th floor, Market Towers
1 Nine Elms Lane
London   SW8 5NQ

Aim

To minimise the hazard to patients arising from the distribution of defective medicinal products for human use by providing an emergency assessment and communications system between the supplier (manufacturer and distributors), the regulatory authorities and the users.

Scope

Defective medicinal product for human use:

One whose quality does not conform to the requirements of its marketing authorisation or in some other way is not of the quality intended.

The DMRC does not deal with:

(a)	Adverse drug reactions	(Refer to ADR Section of MCA Post Licensing Division)	Dial 100 and ask for 'CSM Freephone' or telephone **020 7273 0400**
(b)	Defective medical devices	(Refer to Medical Devices Agency)	Telephone: **020 7972 8100**
(c)	Defective veterinary medicinal products	(Refer to Veterinary Medicines Directorate of DEFRA)	Telephone: **01932 336911**

Details to be reported

The report of a suspected defective product should contain, as far as possible:

Product name, manufacturer, supplier, batch/lot number, MA or PL number, dosage form, strength, container type/size, expiry date, name and position of person reporting and where contact(s) for further information can be made, and a summary of the suspected defect.

When the report is made by the licence holder, the following additional information is likely to be required at the same time as the report is made or soon after:

Site of manufacture, date when first distributed, distribution pattern, any remaining stock (including any returns).

Action by DMRC

The defect report is assessed professionally and the necessary action is discussed and agreed with the responsible licence holder. Any necessary recall or quarantining of products is the responsibility of the licence holder. In some cases, where the defect presents a significant hazard to health, it may be necessary for the MCA to issue a 'Drug Alert' letter to UK Health Authorities and a 'Rapid Alert' letter to EC and overseas authorities as appropriate, notifying a 'caution in use', quarantine or recall by the manufacturer of the defective batch. Appropriate advisory classification of urgency is included in the Drug Alert letter as follows:

Class 1   **Medicines Recall; Action Now,** including out of hours. Defects which are potentially life-threatening or could cause serious risk to health.

Class 2   **Medicines Recall;** Action within 48 hours. Defects which could cause illness or mistreatment but are not Class 1.

Class 3   **Medicines Recall;** Action within five days. Defects which may not pose a significant hazard to health but where a recall has been initiated for other reasons but are not Class 2.

Class 4   **Medicines Defect Information;** Caution in use. No threat to patients or serious defect likely to impair product use or efficacy.